D0421520

DAILY LIFE IN

THE
ROMAN CITY

The Greenwood Press "Daily Life Through History" Series

DAILY LIFE IN

THE ROMAN CITY

ROME, POMPEII, AND OSTIA

GREGORY S. ALDRETE

The Greenwood Press "Daily Life Through History" Series

GREENWOOD PRESS
Westport, Connecticut • London

Library of Congress Cataloging-in-Publication Data

Aldrete, Gregory S.
   Daily life in the Roman city : Rome, Pompeii, and Ostia / Gregory S. Aldrete.
      p. cm. — (The Greenwood Press "Daily life through history" series, ISSN
1080–4749)
   Includes bibliographical references and index.
   ISBN 0–313–33174–X (alk. paper)
   1. Rome—Social life and customs. 2. Pompeii (Extinct city)—Social life and
customs. 3. Ostia (Extinct city)—Social life and customs. 4. City and town life—
Rome. I. Title. II. Series.
DG78.A53 2004
937'.6—dc22   2004020943

British Library Cataloguing in Publication Data is available.

Library of Congress Catalog Card Number: 2004020943
ISBN: 0–313–33174–X
ISSN: 1080–4749

First published in 2004

Greenwood Press, 88 Post Road West, Westport, CT 06881
An imprint of Greenwood Publishing Group, Inc.
www.greenwood.com

Printed in the United States of America

The paper used in this book complies with the
Permanent Paper Standard issued by the National
Information Standards Organization (Z39.48–1984).

10   9   8   7   6   5   4   3   2   1

To Alicia

Contents

Acknowledgments

First, I would like to thank the many students in the various courses on Roman history and on the city of Rome that I have taught over the years for their curiosity and questions that have helped to shape the content of this book. The efficiency of Kevin Ohe and Mike Hermann at Greenwood Press made the publishing process a smooth one. I am grateful to my colleague in the history department at UW–Green Bay, Joyce Salisbury, for her role in getting this project started and for serving as an inspiring role model and a generous mentor. Also contributing to this book are the many enthusiastic conversations about ancient Rome and archaeology that I have had with David West Reynolds, which have done much to deepen my understanding of the ancient world. Finally, my deepest thanks and appreciation are due to my wife, Alicia, who not only accompanied me on many happy expeditions exploring the ancient sites of Rome, Ostia, and Pompeii, but also made invaluable contributions to this project at every stage from research to writing to editing.

Chronology

218–201	Second Punic War. Rome suffers several disastrous defeats at hands of Carthaginian general Hannibal. Under generalship of Scipio Africanus, Rome eventually defeats Carthage
c. 180	Emporium area of Rome developed
179	First stone bridge built at Rome
146	Rome destroys Carthage and Corinth. Rome's conquest of Greece completed
91–88	Social War of Rome against allies. Pompeii refounded as a Roman colony
73–71	Slave uprising led by Spartacus
67	Pompey suppresses pirates
63	Consulship of Cicero. Conspiracy of Catiline
60	Pompey, Caesar, and Crassus form First Triumvirate
59–50	Julius Caesar fights Gallic Wars
55	Pompey's Theater, the first Roman stone theater, built
54	Crassus killed at Carrhae
49	Julius Caesar crosses the Rubicon River and marches on Rome, thereby initiating civil war with Pompey
48	Battle of Pharsalus, where Pompey is defeated by Caesar
44	Assassination of Julius Caesar after he makes himself dictator for life
43	Octavian, Mark Antony, and Lepidus form Second Triumvirate
31	Octavian (the future emperor Augustus) defeats Mark Antony and Cleopatra at Battle of Actium and becomes sole ruler of Rome
27	Beginning of Roman Empire. Octavian reorganizes Roman state
27 BC—AD 14	Reign of Augustus, the first emperor. Augustus and his general Agrippa rebuild much of the city of Rome
14–37	Reign of Tiberius. Christ crucified c. AD 30
37–41	Reign of Caligula

41–54	Reign of Claudius. Construction of new harbor at Ostia
54–68	Reign of Nero. Great Fire of Rome in 64
69	Year of Four Emperors. Civil war
70	Vespasian establishes Flavian Dynasty of emperors, who rule until AD 96
79	Pompeii and Herculaneum buried by eruption of Mount Vesuvius
80	Flavian Amphitheater (Colosseum) completed
98–117	Reign of Trajan. Trajan's Forum, Trajan's Markets, and Trajan's Column built. Harbor of Portus constructed
117–138	Reign of Hadrian. Pantheon rebuilt in present form
180	Death of Marcus Aurelius, last of the "Five Good Emperors" of the second century AD. His son Commodus becomes emperor
180–284	Time of political instability. Rapid turnover of Roman emperors
211–217	Reign of Caracalla. Extension of Roman citizenship. Building of Baths of Caracalla
279	Aurelian Wall built
284–305	Reign of Diocletian. Military and economic reforms restore empire
312–337	Reign of Constantine, the first Christian emperor. Eastern capital established at Constantinople
395	Christianity made official state religion of the Roman Empire
410	Rome sacked by Visigoths under leadership of Alaric
476	Romulus Augustulus, last Roman emperor of the Western Empire, deposed by barbarians. Eastern (Byzantine) Empire continues
518–527	Reign of Justinian, in the Eastern (Byzantine) Empire. *Digest of Roman Law* assembled
1453	Constantinople conquered by Ottoman Turks, end of Eastern (Byzantine) Roman Empire

1

Introduction: Roman Cities

ANCIENT ROMAN CITIES

Roman civilization was an intensely urban culture. Wherever the Romans went, they established new towns, which became focal points of Roman administrative control and centers from which Roman culture was disseminated. In addition, Roman cities demonstrated a remarkable uniformity of architectural design and cultural focus all across the empire. Whether a Roman walked into a Roman city in the wild fens of Britain or in the cultured, ancient setting of Egypt, he or she could expect to find almost exactly the same set of urban structures and spaces: a forum, public baths, a local senate house, a theater, some colonnaded temples, and perhaps even an aqueduct. The model for all these cities was, of course, the heart of the Roman Empire—the great capital city of Rome itself, whose architectural wonders were imitated by all lesser Roman cities. For Roman travelers, there must have been a comfortable familiarity to this uniformity—an assurance that came from knowing that no matter how exotic the locale, how unintelligible the local language, or how strange the indigenous culture, in every province there were cities that resembled miniature Romes.

The Roman world is special not only because of the uniformity of its urban culture, but also because the model for that culture, the city of Rome itself, was by far the largest city to have existed up until quite recently. At its height (the first century BC to the second century AD), Rome's population achieved the staggering size of around one million inhabitants; several other cities, such as Alexandria in Egypt, boasted populations measuring in the hundreds of thousands.

Cities such as these were the great urban centers of the ancient world, but it was the network of smaller cities that gave cohesion and identity to Roman civilization. The Roman Empire, while conventionally filled in on maps as a solid mass of red or blue, might more accurately be portrayed as a series of dots denoting cities, with blank countryside in between. It was mostly in the cities that Roman culture could be found; it was there that people spoke Latin and where one would encounter Roman magistrates, buildings, and law. Out in the countryside, many provincials had their own ancestral languages, customs, and leaders. Thus, in reality the Roman Empire consisted of a system of nodelike cities embodying Roman culture connected to one another by a web of roads, leaving the interstitial spaces largely untouched.

As the Roman Empire spread, Roman cities were established in all conquered territories. Many new towns in Italy and in the provinces were founded by granting land to Roman soldiers upon their retirement from the army. Others grew up around or began as Roman army camps. Often these incorporated the gridlike arrangement of streets standard to military camps. The Romans developed a hierarchy of status for cities, just as there was for people. At the top were cities that received the designation of *colonia,* or colonies. Originally these were what the name suggests: colonies of Roman citizens or retired veterans. By the time of the empire, the term *colonia* became simply a designation of status: all the inhabitants of colonies would have Roman citizenship, and the city itself would enjoy a certain degree of autonomy from the local governor. Next were *municipia.* While *municipia* were not as prestigious as *colonia,* most inhabitants of *municipia* still possessed Roman citizenship. The remaining ordinary cities were called *civitates.*

Roman cities featured a number of distinctive architectural features. Chief among these was a general-purpose open space in the center of town known as the forum, around which usually clustered important government buildings and temples. Most Roman towns of any size or pretension also constructed baths, gymnasiums, a theater, an amphitheater, and perhaps a circus. Local aristocrats in the provinces who wished to rise in status would sometimes pay for the construction of such cultural centers in their hometowns. Whether in Spain or Gaul, North Africa or Judea, Roman cities tended to look similar because they all constructed the same types of buildings, which unmistakably identified them as Roman cities.

It is important to note, however, that the average inhabitant of the ancient Roman world did not actually live in a city. While around 90 percent of the people were farmers who lived their entire lives in a rural, agricultural setting, only the tiny remainder who lived in cities defined and shaped Roman civilization and history. Simply put, civilization itself was very much an urban phenomenon. Government, philosophy, religion, law, art, architecture, trade, literature, and even history itself were all generated in cities. Therefore, while a very small number of people in the ancient world actually lived in cities, a disproportionately large amount of the events and ideas that we tend to study and remember today happened and were produced in an urban environment.

Something about cities seems to generate new ideas and spur innovation. Law codes may have developed from the need to find a way for people to live in large, densely packed groups without descending into chaos. Great art and literature frequently flourished as the result of patronage by rulers who wished to glorify their capitals and commemorate their deeds. Cities and civilization are inseparable, and the history of one is really the history of the other.

GOALS AND STRUCTURE OF BOOK

The goal of this book is to provide an in-depth study of life in the Roman city and especially in the capital city of Rome itself. It is intended not just to provide a description of the physical buildings of the city, but also to explain how the city functioned, who lived there, and what the inhabitants' lives were like. It is a portrait of the city as an organism and of all its constituent parts. This book is not intended to offer a comprehensive survey of Roman history but rather to investigate what day-to-day life was like for those who lived in a Roman city. Therefore, the focus is on the typical inhabitant rather than on the exceptional one. Famous men like Julius Caesar may occasionally appear—and did in fact play key roles, but wherever possible, the emphasis will be on the lives of the thousands of more obscure, but also more representative, urban dwellers. It is hoped that this book will serve as a useful reference work for students, as a possible textbook for a course on Roman civilization, and as an accessible source of information for general readers interested in aspects of life in ancient Rome.

The study of ancient Roman cities is of more than just historical interest. The influence of Rome and its culture is still present nearly everywhere one looks today, and we in the modern world are still affected in a surprising number of ways by the culture of the ancient Romans. These influences include such basic areas as the language with which we communicate (a large percentage of words in English derive from Latin), the laws by which we organize our society (the majority of the world's legal systems are based on Roman law), and even how we tell time (our calendar is almost identical to the one developed by the Romans). Rome is arguably the most influential city in Western history. For nearly half a millennium, Rome dominated the Western world, and even when the empire fell and Rome lost its political dominance, it continued to be the seat of the Catholic Church, which itself occupied a central place in the next 1,000 years of history. It is really only during the last 400 years that Rome has ceased to be a center of power, but for 1,500 of the last 2,000 years of Western history, Rome has played a pivotal role. The many popular aphorisms associated with Rome, such as "All roads lead to Rome," "When in Rome do as the Romans," and "Rome, the Eternal City," reflect the cultural, religious, and historical significance of the city.

Even the individual buildings that made up the city have had long-reaching influence. The Flavian Amphitheater (popularly known as the Colosseum) is the direct ancestor of the modern sports arena, and the Pantheon, with its colonnaded facade and triangular pediment fronting a large dome, is the direct architectural inspiration for nearly every seat of government in the United States ranging from the Capitol building in Washington, D.C., to nearly every state capitol building. Even the more humble yet all-important engineering infrastructures of modern cities can trace their origins to Roman sewers, aqueducts, roads, and bridges.

Finally, Rome was the first megacity and as such is the precursor and model for all great cities today. Ancient Rome's population of one million people was probably not equaled for 1,500 years until Paris and London attained a similar size in the nineteenth century. Ancient Rome also embodied all the good and bad clichés of a big city. Two stereotypes of urban life dominate both ancient and modern perceptions. On the one hand, cities are seen as the focal point of opportunity, wealth, culture, and luxury, consisting of magnificent public works and ceremonial buildings. On the other hand, the city is also viewed as a place that is corrupt, decadent, crowded, and dangerous, with rampant poverty, crime, and disease. Since ancient Rome encompassed all of these stereotypes, both positive and negative, it is the prototype for the modern city; therefore, by studying it, we can hopefully also gain insights into cities today and the problems that are faced whenever large numbers of people live in a densely packed urban setting.

This book begins with a brief survey of Roman history to provide an overall context and then narrows its focus to present the geographical setting and chronological development of the city of Rome itself. Subsequent chapters describe the infrastructure of the city, the system of government, the groups that made up the urban population, housing conditions, the dangers and the pleasures of life in Rome, the famous (or infamous) entertainments that were staged for its populace, and the roles of religion, the economy, and emperors. While the majority of the book concentrates on Rome and on urban life in the Roman Empire generally, additional chapters offer portraits of two specific smaller cities: Ostia and Pompeii. These cities shared the characteristic of being among the best preserved of all Roman cities, but they also offer contrasting images of Roman urbanism. Ostia was a gritty, industrial port town, whereas Pompeii, located on the scenic Bay of Naples, was dominated by the wealthy. A conclusion compares the different experiences of urban Roman life presented by these three cities, and a number of appendixes offer guides to different aspects of Roman culture and bring the story of Rome up to the present.

Where ancient authors are directly quoted in the text, the author and common title of the quoted work are provided in parentheses. Nearly all of these sources are available in multiple modern translations; the bibliography of primary sources lists some of the more important ones. Two abbreviations appearing in the text refer to several multivolume collections of Roman inscriptions (in Latin): *CIL (Corpus Inscriptionum Latinarum)* and *ILS (Inscriptiones Latinae Selectae)*. A bibliography of secondary sources, organized by chapter, offers suggestions for further reading. The secondary-source bibliography has been restricted to English-language publications, although much important scholarship on the Roman world is only available in Italian, German, and French.

2

History of Ancient Rome

BRIEF SURVEY OF ROMAN HISTORY

Roman history falls into three distinct periods designated by the form of government in use during each era: the monarchy, the republic, and the empire. In Roman tradition, the city of Rome was founded in 753 BC by Romulus and Remus, twin offspring of the god Mars. Romulus promptly murdered his brother to become the first king of Rome. According to legend, Rome had a sequence of seven kings, and during this period many of the religious and cultural institutions of Rome were established. For most of the monarchy (753–509 BC), Rome was simply one of hundreds of small city-states in Italy, often under the control of more powerful neighbors such as the Etruscans. The last kings of Rome, in fact, seem to have been Etruscans, but in 509 BC there was a revolution; the last Etruscan king, Tarquin the Proud, was expelled from Rome; and the Roman Republic (509–31 BC) was established.

Over the next several hundred years, Rome began a gradual process of military expansion into the rest of Italy. This was a time of nearly constant warfare, and while the Romans were not superior to their enemies in either technology or tactics, they did practice a unique policy in their treatment of conquered cities. Rather than destroying them and enslaving the populace, the Romans granted full, or more commonly, partial citizenship or allied status to the captured peoples and demanded in return only that they contribute troops to the Roman army. This gave Rome enormous manpower reserves to draw upon, and many future wars would be won through a combination of determination and manpower. Over this same period, the Roman constitution developed, consisting of a system of annually elected magistrates, a legal code, and a kind of balance of powers among different organs of the state. The top position in government was held by two magistrates known as *consuls,* and former magistrates became members of the senate, whose deliberations carried great influence.

By the middle of the third century BC, Roman consolidation of Italy was largely complete and Rome soon became embroiled, whether by accident or design, in a series of wars with overseas enemies. The most significant of these were the Punic Wars, fought against another young, expanding empire in the western Mediterranean: the North African city of Carthage. In the Second Punic War (218–201 BC), Rome was brought to the verge of defeat by the brilliant Carthaginian general, Hannibal, who with his army successfully crossed the supposedly impassable Alps and inflicted three crushing defeats on the Romans in battles in which over 100,000 Romans were killed. Most of the Italians stayed loyal to Rome, however, and drawing on their manpower reserves, the Romans outlasted Hannibal and eventually won the war.

After passing through the crucible of the Second Punic War, Rome's armies were highly professionalized and over the next couple hundred years conquered nearly the entire Mediterranean basin, including the rich, highly cultured world of the Greek East. No longer did Rome share citizenship so freely; instead, these overseas areas were organized as tax-paying provinces. Rome's very overseas success, however, began to create internal tensions as individual generals amassed too much power and prestige, poor Romans lost their farms and fell into debt, the old Italian allies and half-citizens became resentful, and a government system developed to rule a city was strained by having to manage an empire.

These tensions exploded during the Late Republic (133–31 BC), when a sequence of bloody civil wars wracked the Roman world and a succession of ever-more-daring strong men made bids to dominate the state. This process culminated in the civil war between Julius Caesar and Pompey the Great, and after his victory Caesar established himself as dictator for life. His kinglike behavior soon led to his assassination by the senate on the ides of March, 44 BC, and his death touched off a final round of civil wars that ultimately were won by Caesar's adopted son, Octavian, in 31 BC.

Octavian, who was remarkably adept at what would today be considered image making and political propaganda, established himself as the dominant figure in Rome. Now called Augustus, he became the first emperor and ushered in the final era of ancient Roman history, the empire. Despite occasional eccentric or insane emperors such as Nero, the Roman Empire enjoyed relative stability and prosperity for the next 200 years.

In the third century AD, barbarian invasions, economic turmoil, and political instability led to a time of crisis, and complete collapse was only narrowly averted. In AD 312, Constantine became the first emperor to convert to Christianity, and soon after, the empire permanently split into eastern and western halves. The western half staggered along for another century or so but eventually fragmented into numerous barbarian kingdoms. The Eastern (Byzantine) Roman Empire, with its capital at Constantinople, continued to exist for many centuries, finally falling to the Ottoman Turks in 1453.

THE FOUNDATION OF ROME

Despite the importance that the Romans attached to the foundation of their city, it is difficult to determine what the true story was, since no contemporary account survives, and the later ones are heavily weighted with propagandistic purposes. Archaeological evidence can tell us that the site of Rome was inhabited from at least 1000 BC, from which time graves exist. The archaeological evidence also suggests that, starting from around 700 BC, the population increased very rapidly and the first signs of major urban structures in stone began to appear.

The Romans themselves told many (sometimes conflicting) stories about their origins, but over time, several figures came to dominate these accounts. The first of these centered on a man named Aeneas, a Trojan who escaped the destruction of his city by the Greeks at the end of the Trojan War, which supposedly happened around 1200 BC. He and his companions eventually landed in Italy and founded the city of Lavinium, and his son, Iulus, founded the city of Alba Longa. Iulus, incidentally, was identified as the founder of the Julian family of Rome, from which were descended such famous figures as Julius Caesar. Thus Aeneas became the founder of the Roman people.

The second important foundation story told how the city of Rome itself began and focused on the twins, Romulus and Remus. One of the descendants of Iulus became king by usurping the throne from his brother. He then forced his brother's daughter to become a Vestal Virgin to ensure that she would have no children who might seek revenge against him.

Eventually, however, the Vestal Virgin became pregnant, but she claimed that she had been raped by the god of war, Mars. She gave birth to twins, Romulus and Remus. Afraid to kill the babies directly, the king had them put in a basket and thrown into the Tiber River to drown. The basket washed ashore on the riverbank, and the babies were found by a wolf, which nursed them and, together with a helpful woodpecker, looked after them. (The wolf and woodpecker are animals associated with the god Mars.) Ultimately, the boys were found by a shepherd who raised them as his own. They grew up into strong young men who did various noble deeds such as suppressing bandits. Eventually, the shepherd revealed the secret of their birth, and they overthrew the king of Alba Longa.

They then decided to found a new city at the spot where the wolf had rescued them. Almost immediately, they got into an argument over who

Figure 2.1 Bronze statue of the wolf that, according to legend, nurtured Romulus and Remus when they were abandoned as babies.

should be the king of the new city since they were twins and did not know which one was older. In the end, they could not agree and decided to let the gods choose the king. To do this, each brother went to the top of one of the hills and looked for a sign, Romulus standing on the Palatine hill and Remus on the Capitoline. Remus received the first sign when 6 vultures flew overhead, but shortly afterward, 12 vultures flew over Romulus.

This left the brothers still arguing, each one claiming the gods had picked him—Remus saying he had the first omen and Romulus saying he had the better omen. In the end, they could not settle their differences and, growing angry, Romulus solved the problem by murdering his brother. Thus, the new city would be called Rome after Romulus, and Romulus was its first king. The traditional date for the founding of Rome is recorded as April 21, 753 BC.

Since the earliest version of the Romulus and Remus story dates from 200 BC, it represents later mythologizing and thus, from a historical standpoint, is highly untrustworthy. All these legends, however, contain some important themes, which are revealing in terms of the way the Romans viewed themselves. The focus of the stories is always the city of Rome. The Aeneas legend provides links to Greek civilization and culture and places Rome in a larger context. The Romulus story is an unusual foundation legend because it depicts a rape and a murder as the pivotal events that begin Roman history. It also introduces the theme of powerful men fighting each other to see who will control Rome, an idea that will recur many times throughout Roman history.

TOPOGRAPHY OF THE CITY: RIVERS, HILLS, VALLEYS, AND PLAINS

Rome is located about halfway down the Italian peninsula. The Apennine mountain chain runs like a spine up and down the Italian peninsula, and Rome is on the east side of this line. Rome is on the banks of the Tiber River about 22 km (15 miles) inland as the crow flies.

There are a number of reasons why this place was well suited to be the location of a major city, most of which have to do with the Tiber River itself. It is true that most large cities, particularly in the ancient world, grew up alongside rivers. Rivers provide irrigation for growing food, a source of water for drinking, a means of transportation to connect the city and its inhabitants to the wider world, and can serve as a ready-made sewage system for disposal of waste.

The Tiber (Tiberis in Latin, Tevere in Italian) is central Italy's longest river, flowing 409 km from where it starts in the Apennines to where it enters the Mediterranean Sea. At the site of Rome, the river makes a broad, C-shaped bend, and just below this bend is Tiber Island. The point below the island, sheltered by its presence, is the first natural crossing point over the Tiber when moving inland from the coast and as such almost inevitably became the site of a settlement. Making this spot even more attractive is the fact that this crossing was located along the Via Salaria (Salt Road), so named because the marshes near the mouth of the Tiber were a source of salt, an important early trade commodity. Thus the river crossing below Tiber Island was a natural communication node of great importance.

A second feature of the river up to this key point is that it was navigable by vessels up to small-ship size, which meant that Rome would have good access to the sea and to maritime trade and communication without actually having to be on the coast. One problem with the proximity of the river, however, is that the Tiber is prone to flooding, especially in the winter and spring.

The next important geographic feature that made the site of Rome an attractive one for settlement was that a number of hills were located close to the river crossing. One often hears that Rome has seven hills, whereas there are actually more. Hills are another highly desirable feature when selecting where to build a city since they provide natural defensive sites on which to build fortresses for protection and offer locations from which surrounding territory can be observed. High ground can also sometimes offer health benefits to those who live there. The three most important hills in Rome are the ones closest to the Tiber: the Capitoline, the Palatine, and the Aventine.

The Capitoline is the smallest of the hills but is probably the most important. The sides of this hill were fairly steep, and thus it constituted a natural fortress. There are two crests on the hill, with a low saddle

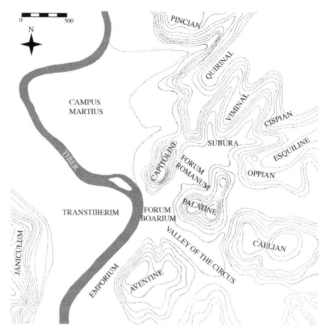

Figure 2.2 Map of the main topographical features of Rome. The original site of Rome was a mixture of small hills and swampy depressions. (Adapted by the author and David West Reynolds, Phaeton Group, Scientific Graphic Services Division, from map of Rome in *The Urban Image of Augustan Rome* by Diane Favro, 1996, with the permission of Cambridge University Press.)

between them. At the southwest end are some sharp cliffs overlooking the river, a point known as the Tarpeian Rock. Traditionally, criminals sentenced to death were flung to their doom from the Tarpeian Rock.

The Capitoline got its name from the Latin word for head (*caput*) because, when digging the foundation for an early temple, the workers supposedly uncovered a perfectly preserved human head. This was seen as a good omen, interpreted as meaning that this spot would become the head of the world. The temple built there became known as the temple of Jupiter Capitolinus, after the king of the gods, Jupiter, and the omen of the head. Throughout its history, this hill always functioned as the focal point of some of the most important religious rituals. The largest and most impressive temple in Rome was built here. At the northeast corner was a place called the *auguraculum*, where a special group of priests known as *augurs* determined the will of the gods by observing the flight of birds.

The Palatine is the central hill of Rome, around which the others cluster. It is also important because it directly overlooks the crucial Tiber River crossing; therefore, an outpost on the hill could control traffic across this point. The Palatine has a large, flat top of about 25 acres and seems to have been the location of the earliest dwellings as well as being another easily defensible outcrop.

Archaeologists have found the remains of a series of primitive oval huts on this hill. These were crude structures consisting of wooden posts stuck in the ground, with the spaces between filled in with wattle and daub and covered by simple thatched roofs. These huts may be evidence of some of the earliest settlers in the area. The Romans themselves said that the earliest inhabited site was the Palatine, and they preserved through the centuries one of these primitive huts, which they claimed had been the house of Romulus himself. Due to its central position, the Palatine provided easy access to both the crossing and the Roman Forum, which became the political center of the city; therefore, the Palatine became the most desirable place to live. During the republic, aristocratic homes clustered here, and later during the empire, the emperors selected this as the site for their palaces, which eventually expanded until they filled the entire top of the hill.

The Aventine is the southernmost hill that still had good proximity to the political centers and the eventual locations of the main commercial centers. It was a popular residential hill that early in Roman history was specifically granted to those of plebeian status, though this distinction seems to have dissipated by the empire.

These three hills close to the Tiber are enclosed by an arc of additional hills farther inland. Starting from the north, these hills are the Quirinal, Viminal, Esquiline, and Caelian. The Quirinal is a long ridge about two kilometers in length, which seems to have gotten its name from a shrine to the local deity Quirinus. When the inhabitants of Rome merged with the nearby Sabine people, this was supposedly the place where the Sabines lived. The Viminal is another ridge paralleling the Quirinal to the south and was probably the least important of the various hills of Rome. The Esquiline, a large bluff with various ridges extending out from it, was originally the site of a number of cemeteries, which were eventually displaced when the city's boundaries were expanded. The two main spurs sticking out from the Esquiline toward the river are sometimes considered hills in their own right, the Cispian hill and the Oppian hill. Finally, the Caelian is a long, narrow ridge curving to the south of the Esquiline. These are the traditional seven hills of Rome, but there are several others in the city that played important roles.

The Pincian hill runs north-south as a line of high ground that walls off the open end of the great bend in the Tiber River. The low-lying flatlands between the Pincian and the Tiber bend were known as the Campus Martius.

On the other side of the Tiber is a line of hills known as the Janiculum. In a fashion similar to the Pincian, it forms a wall across the open end of the reverse bend of the Tiber. The Janiculum is actually the highest hill in Rome in terms of altitude and today provides a scenic panorama of the city. In antiquity, the Janiculum was a key observation post from which to spot approaching enemies.

In between the various hills of Rome were a number of small, low-lying valleys, several of which would become important centers of the city. Of these, probably the most significant is the Forum Romanum, nestled in the depression between the Capitoline, the Palatine, and the Quirinal. This was the first marketplace of the city, and the original natural site would have been very swampy, with several streams running through it. Nevertheless, this was where most of the main streets converged.

Another such crossroads was the open space below and between the Palatine and the Aventine on the bank of the Tiber. This area, known as the Forum Boarium, was where the ferry that went across the river landed. Rome's first bridge was built here, spanning the ferry passage. The name of this transportation hub literally means "the cattle market." However, it would have been an unsuitable place to gather cows, and the name is probably derived from a famous early bronze statue of a bull that was erected there.

The Valley of the Circus Maximus is a long, narrow depression that begins between the Aventine and the Palatine and continues inland for several kilometers. A stream originally flowed through the bottom of this valley and emptied into the Tiber. The valley where the Colosseum would be built was a low-lying depression at the end of the Cispian and Oppian hills that was originally the site of a marshy lake.

A key aspect of all these valleys is how wet they were, and drains would have had to be constructed before they could be heavily built up. On the other hand, the areas were so wet because there were so many natural springs, and the presence of these sources of drinking water was another factor that made this an advantageous place to build a city.

Most of the central parts of the city were eventually located in and around this series of valleys, but just outside this central zone were several large, flat fields, which also served important purposes for the ancient city of Rome.

The most important of these by far was the Campus Martius. This large area, about two kilometers across by two kilometers wide, was enclosed by the bend of the Tiber on three sides and the Pincian hill on the other. Its name means "the field of Mars" (the Roman god of war). According to legend, this land had once belonged to the king Tarquinius Superbus, and when he was expelled from Rome, the land was dedicated to Mars. The field was used early on as public pasturage, and a low-lying spot in the center was known as the Palus Caprae, or literally, the "goat swamp." The entire Campus Martius was essentially a floodplain and, whenever the Tiber rose, was one of the first areas inundated. The Romans used this field for a wide variety of festivals and athletic events and, most importantly, as a place of assembly for the citizens. Roman citizens gathered here, grouped according to their centuries (units of 100), either as components in the Roman army prior to going to war or in order to vote. Some early temples were also located in the Campus Martius.

Another important area was the Transtiberim (Trastevere in Italian). Both in Latin and Italian, this name means "across the Tiber" and refers to the triangular, flat area between the Janiculum and the river. Most of the city of Rome always clustered on the left bank, but there was also a small enclave on the right bank in the Transtiberim region.

One final term that refers to a man-made feature rather than to a natural one is the *pomerium*. This was the sacred boundary of the city, and in a solemn religious ceremony, a bull and a cow were used to plow a furrow in the earth, which demarcated the boundary of the city and held great religious significance. Romulus himself was credited with creating the first *pomerium*, but as the city grew over time, it was repeatedly enlarged until, by the second century AD, it included all seven hills, the Campus Martius, and the Transtiberim. This boundary was marked with inscribed stones called *cippi*.

The natural setting and geographical features of the location of Rome are a bit unusual in that a variety of hills, valleys, and flatlands are interspersed along a river within a fairly small area. This landscape would play a central role in the course of the city's development.

CITY DEVELOPMENT IN THE MONARCHICAL PERIOD

The contribution of the kings of Rome to the city's development lay in two main areas—making the site more habitable and establishing the earliest versions of various important institutions and buildings. The first challenge was to transform the swampy areas between the hills, which were natural crossroads, into drier areas that could be used.

The first major construction project at Rome was to dig a drain from the Roman Forum area down to the Tiber. This first drainage ditch would eventually grow into the main Roman sewer, the Cloaca Maxima. This was difficult labor, and according to ancient accounts, the king had to force the people of Rome to work on it. In concert with the construction of this drain, the kings also raised the level of the Roman Forum by dumping dirt across the whole area. Having ensured that the Roman Forum was dry year-round, the kings then laid down the first paving of the forum around 600 BC.

The kings built the original temple to Jupiter on the Capitoline, that of Jupiter Capitolinus, and established many other cults and traditions, including several famous festivals. One, which was associated with the story of Romulus and Remus being raised by the wolf, was called the Lupercalia, literally meaning "the wolf festival." In this ritual, young, aristocratic men gathered in a cave on the slope of the Capitoline where the wolf had supposedly nursed the twins. A goat was sacrificed and blood and milk were smeared on the foreheads of the young men. The hide of the goat was then cut into long strips, and the young men took these and ran naked through the streets of the city. Women who wished to become pregnant gathered to watch them run by, and the men would whip the women with the goatskin strips since this was believed to increase fertility. The traditional date of the Lupercalia was February 15. When Christianity became dominant centuries later, the feast day of St. Valentine was set near this date in an effort to eradicate the earlier pagan holiday, although the earlier connection with fertility survived, transmuted into the current association of the day with romance.

Another important early festival was the October horse festival. This included chariot races, and one horse from the winning team was sacrificed. People from different regions of the city then fought over the head of the horse, and whichever group won got to nail it up and display it in their part of town. This festival reveals that even early on, the different neighborhoods of the city were taking on distinctive identities.

Another festival that showed the development of different regions of the city involved representatives from 27 local shrines scattered throughout the city who would construct straw effigies. These 27 straw men were taken to a bridge and thrown into the Tiber in what seems to have been a parody of human sacrifice. Finally, the kings divided the city into four regions.

REPUBLICAN ERA DEVELOPMENTS

With the establishment of the Roman Republic, there was obviously a desire to supersede or at least match the kings' actions. One example is the establishment of a new temple to Jupiter on the Capitoline, which would eventually supplant the earlier cult of Jupiter Capitolinus. This new temple to Jupiter was called the Temple of Jupiter Optimus Maximus (Jupiter the Best and the Greatest). A second important cult institutionalized during the republic was that of the Vestal Virgins, whose house was constructed adjacent to the Roman Forum. These six virgin priestesses were charged with maintaining the sacred fire of the city. At this point, the Romans were still imitating Etruscan styles of religious architecture. Also, by the sixth century BC, many houses of aristocrats were clustered on the Palatine hill.

Perhaps the most pivotal event in the development of the early republican city happened in 390 BC, when a large force of Gauls invaded from the north and sacked the city of Rome. Most of the Romans fled to other cities nearby, but some took refuge on the Capitoline hill and held out for some time against the Gallic attacks. Having failed to capture the Capitoline by frontal attacks, the Gauls decided to try a sneak attack at night. The Romans had not set proper guards, and the Gauls succeeded in climbing up the hill, but, as luck would have it, the point at which they climbed up was where the sacred geese of Juno, the queen of the gods, were kept. The geese began honking, and this roused the Romans, who were able to repel the Gauls and drive them off the hill. Thus, at least according to legend, the Romans were saved by the sacred birds. Eventually the Gauls were bribed to leave, but this experience caused the Romans to construct a circuit of walls enclosing the seven hills (but not the Campus Martius). This wall, which became known as the Servian Wall, was the first comprehensive set of defensive walls for the city. The area enclosed within this wall comprised about 400 hectares.

At the end of the fourth century BC, the censor of Rome, Appius Claudius Caecus, constructed several important works of infrastructure that served as precursors for many more that followed. Appius paved the main north-south road, which connected Rome with southern Italy. This was the first paved road in Italy, and the Romans would eventually become very famous for their network of finely made roads. This road, named in his honor, was known as the Via Appia. It was so well made that it remained in use for hundreds of years, and even today, stretches of the Roman paving can be walked upon more than 2,000 years later. The same man was responsible for another important first by constructing the earliest aqueduct, bringing water to the city in 312 BC. This was also named after him: the Aqua Appia.

The city grew steadily, and another burst of activity took place around 180 BC, focusing on the Emporium district, which was the area where ships unloaded. This commercial region stretched from the Forum Boarium south along the bank of the Tiber to below the Aventine hill. In 179 BC, the first stone bridge was built, connecting the Transtiberim with the Forum Boarium. Also around this time, the docks along the Tiber were improved, and south of the Aventine, the Porticus Aemilia was built, which was a long, covered colonnade that served as a general-purpose, commercial clearinghouse.

Some highlights of the middle to Late Republic included the development of buildings related to politics in the area of the Roman Forum. Among these were a new senate house, a platform from which speakers could address crowds of citizens in the forum, and an office to house important public records.

Just as the politics of the Late Republic were dominated by the important generals and politicians, the same men were responsible for initiating the main building activities of this period. The general Pompey the Great wished to promote himself by constructing buildings for the benefit of the city's inhabitants but faced the problem that the main part of the city was largely filled up by this time. His solution was to turn to the still-empty Campus Martius. In the southern part of the Campus Martius, he erected a huge complex, including the first permanent stone theater for the entertainment of the people as well as public gardens and parks surrounding it. Julius Caesar, the rival of Pompey, had ambitious plans to rebuild the city, but his assassination took place before these could be put into effect; it would remain for Caesar's adopted son, Augustus, to take up where he had left off.

IMPERIAL ROME

Perhaps more than any single person up to this time, the first emperor, Augustus, was responsible for changing the city of Rome. One of his famous quotations is "I found the city made of brick and left it made of marble," and there is a good deal of truth to this statement.

Figure 2.3 Head of the first emperor, Augustus, who transformed Rome "from a city of bricks to one of marble."

Augustus began by reorganizing the city and dividing it into 14 districts, which would be known as the 14 Augustan regions. He repaired all the buildings that had fallen into neglect during the civil wars and rebuilt no fewer than 82 temples. He also had a number of buildings reconstructed using marble facing rather than the earlier brick or concrete, which gave a new, more-impressive appearance to the city. He (or his assistants) extensively overhauled the infrastructure, including the streets, aqueducts, and sewers.

His work did not end with these renovations, for once they were complete, he undertook the construction of many new buildings and monuments as well. Among these were two high-profile temples. Julius Caesar's body had been cremated in the Roman Forum during a riot, and on this spot, Augustus built a new temple to the deified Julius Caesar. Augustus also swore to take revenge on the people who had killed his adoptive father, Caesar, and once he had succeeded, he showed his gratitude to the gods by building a gigantic new temple dedicated to Mars Ultor (Mars the Avenger), enclosed within the equally spectacular Forum of Augustus.

Augustus then built even more structures that were intended as works of propaganda praising himself and his virtues. Some of the most famous of these were the Ara Pacis (altar of peace) and the *horologium.* The latter was an enormous sundial in the Campus Martius 150 meters wide by 80 meters deep. The gnomon, or spike, of the sundial was an obelisk brought from Egypt. It was constructed so that on Augustus's birthday, the shadow cast by the obelisk pointed directly at the Ara Pacis.

The emperors after Augustus continued to add to the city. Most notable among these developments was the gradual expansion of the emperor's palace on the Palatine until it took up the entire top of the hill. The emperor Claudius also constructed an enormous new harbor, Portus, near the mouth of the Tiber.

An important event in the city's life took place in AD 64 during the reign of Nero, when a fire broke out and spread until it affected the entire city. This fire raged for a week and destroyed 10 of the 14 regions. When Nero rebuilt the city, he instituted wider streets and also took advantage of this disaster to build for himself a fantastic new palace called the Domus Aurea (Golden House), which included an octagonal dining room, a mile-long colonnade, and a 33-meter-tall naked statue of Nero himself.

After the depredations of Nero, the next family of emperors, the Flavians, wished to show that they were returning the city to the people. Therefore, they razed much of the Golden House and, where it used to stand, built in its place the Flavian Amphitheater, today known as the Colosseum.

Several emperors of the second century AD were active builders in Rome. Especially notable among these was Trajan, who built a new forum north of the old Roman Forum. In or around Trajan's Forum were also

Figure 2.4 Map of the main structures and buildings of Rome. (Adapted by the author and David West Reynolds, Phaeton Group, Scientific Graphic Services Division, from map of Rome in *The Urban Image of Augustan Rome* by Diane Favro, 1996, with the permission of Cambridge University Press.)
1. Mausoleum of Hadrian; 2. Mausoleum of Augustus; 3. Sundial of Augustus; 4. Altar of Peace (Ara Pacis); 5. Stadium of Domitian; 6. Baths of Nero; 7. Pantheon; 8. Temple of Hadrian; 9. Odeon of Domitian; 10. Baths of Agrippa; 11. Saepta Julia; 12. Theater of Pompey; 13. Portico of Pompey; 14. Sacred Area of Largo Argentina; 15. Porticus Minucia; 16. Diribitorium; 17. Theater of Balbus; 18. Porticus Octaviae; 19. Theater of Marcellus; 20. Temple of Jupiter Optimus Maximus; 21. Forum of Trajan; 22. Forum of Augustus; 23. Curia (Senate House); 24. Basilica Aemilia; 25. Rostra (Speakers' Platform); 26. Temple of Concord; 27. Temple of Saturn; 28. Roman Forum; 29. Basilica Julia; 30. House of the Vestals; 31. Basilica of Maxentius; 32. Palace of Tiberius; 33. Imperial Palace (Domitianic); 34. Temple of Venus and Rome; 35. Flavian Amphitheater (Colosseum); 36. Ludus Magnus; 37. Baths of Titus; 38. Baths of Trajan; 39. Baths of Constantine; 40. Baths of Diocletian; 41. Temple of Claudius; 42. Circus Maximus; 43. Baths of Sura; 44. Baths of Decius; 45. Baths of Caracalla; 46. Horrea Galbana; 47. Porticus Aemilia; 48. Via Ostiensis; 49. Via Appia; 50. Via Salaria; 51. Via Flaminia; 52. Pons Aelius; 53. Pons Neronianus; 54. Pons Agrippae; 55. Pons Fabricius; 56. Pons Cestius; 57. Pons Aemilius; 58. Pons Sublicius; 59. Servian Wall; 60. Monte Testaccio

the famous column and the Markets of Trajan, which were a multistory precursor to the modern shopping mall. Other emperors continued to develop the Campus Martius.

Construction trailed off somewhat in the late empire, as Rome had to contend with threats such as the barbarians. Nevertheless, a number of these later emperors still managed to build a series of truly gigantic public bath complexes, such as the Baths of Caracalla. In AD 279, in response to fears of invasion, a new wall system was constructed called the Aurelian Wall, which enclosed all of the 14 regions, including the Campus Martius and the Transtiberim.

In the fourth century AD, the first Christian emperor, Constantine, focused most of his attention on his new capital city of Constantinople in the East, but at Rome he did build a famous arch and a basilica—a type of building that would become the basis for all later Christian churches.

POPULATION OF ROME

One of the most contentious debates about the city of Rome concerns its most basic characteristic: its size. All scholars seem to agree that ancient Rome was big, at least twice the size of any other city at the time. They also tend to agree that it was the largest city before the modern era, meaning up until the last 200 years or so. But beyond these basic order-of-magnitude estimates, there is no agreement on just what the actual population was. Reasonable estimates offered by various scholars range from a couple hundred thousand to several million. There may have been some non-Western cities with comparable populations, but the available data for these is unreliable. Ancient Rome was, at any rate, clearly the largest Western city until recently.

Nowhere does an ancient source give us an actual population figure for the city at its height. Instead, what we have are several separate bits of data from which scholars have attempted to extrapolate or estimate the population. Three key pieces of hard data have to do with the number of people who received monthly handouts of free grain from the government, a set of statistics that give total numbers of dwellings in the city, and estimates that are based on the area of the city.

One ancient source states that in 5 BC, 320,000 inhabitants of the city received the free monthly grain dole. To be eligible for this dole, you had to be three things: an adult, a male, and a citizen. If there were this many adult, free males, one can perhaps double this number to account for women, add the same number again for children, and then add an estimate for the number of slaves. Such a calculation would yield a population estimate well in excess of one million people. There are many problems with such a calculation, however. Did all citizens who were eligible collect the dole? How accurate were the lists? Also, as with cities in many eras, ancient Rome seems to have had a population that included large numbers of young males who left their family farms seeking fame, fortune, or simply adventure in the big city. At this time in Roman history, there may well have been large numbers of veterans swelling the numbers of urban dwellers as well. All these factors indicate that the number of women and possibly of children may have been much less than the number of men, suggesting a lower overall population number. Estimating the number of slaves also involves considerable guesswork; therefore, population estimates that begin extrapolating from the 320,000 grain dole recipients can reasonably vary quite widely.

A second piece of information that might shed light on the number of inhabitants is a document called the *Regionary Catalog*, dating to the fourth century AD, which lists the total number of different types of residential buildings that existed in the city at this time. According to the *Regionary Catalog*, Rome at this point had 1,782 *domus* (private homes) and 43,580 apartment buildings. Using these two bits of information, one can create an estimate of what the population of the city might have been. Obviously, much depends on one's assumptions about how many people on average lived in a house and in an apartment building. If one assumes 100 residents in a typical apartment building, then one will arrive at a huge estimate for Rome's population, but if one chooses a small number, the result will be dramatically different.

A final strategy for estimating Rome's population rests upon the fact that it is known fairly precisely how large the occupied area of the ancient city was. The Aurelian Wall enclosed approximately 1,370 hectares. Using this piece of information, it should be possible to estimate the density of inhabitants per acre and thereby calculate the total population. A complicating factor for this type of calculation is taking into account what percentage of the area within the walls was used by nonresidential purposes such as streets, open spaces, gardens, and public buildings. The density of large modern cities can perhaps be used as a partial guide to estimating density figures for ancient Rome.

An enormous amount of ink has been spilled by scholars using these various methods and arguing with one another over whose estimates are most accurate. The grain dole approach tends to yield very high numbers, while the density method suggests a lower range, with the *Regionary Catalog* data spanning both extremes. In the end, most estimates for Rome's population seem to cluster around one million at its height (first century BC through second century AD). The debates and uncertainty surrounding such a basic statistic as the size of ancient Rome illustrate how difficult it is to study ancient cities when so much data is lacking.

The estimate of around one million inhabitants, if reasonably accurate, makes Rome unique because no other Western city seems to have reached this size for nearly 2,000 years—not until Paris and London achieved this population in the nineteenth century. The famous cities of the Italian Renaissance rarely reached 100,000 inhabitants. Rome's enormous population also makes it a particularly relevant and interesting object of study for us today because the ancient Romans had to struggle with certain types of urban problems, such as crowding and sanitation, that no other people have had to contend with until recently. Therefore, Rome is the original prototype for all great modern cities, and by studying how the Romans faced these problems, we can perhaps gain some insights into how to handle them today.

3

Infrastructure of Ancient Rome

REPUBLICAN AQUEDUCTS

One of the most fundamental requirements for any town or city is an adequate supply of water. Providing this basic human need must be one of the principal concerns of urban planners, and water must be managed in two ways. First, water must be brought to the city in sufficient quantity and of sufficient purity to be drunk by the populace. In addition to water for drinking, a city consumes substantial amounts of water for several other basic functions, including cooking and cleaning. Second, and equally as important as bringing water to the city, are arrangements made for removing unwanted water, either because there is too much of it and there is a risk of flooding or because the water is contaminated by human use and poses a health hazard.

By any standards, ancient or modern, Rome was extraordinarily well supplied with the means both to bring water to the city and to take it away. By the early fourth century AD, Rome was being supplied by over a dozen aqueducts, which collectively were capable of bringing more than a million cubic meters of fresh water to the city every day. This bounty was distributed to the populace through a complex network of pipes and tanks that delivered the water to nearly 1,500 public fountains and pools and almost 900 public and private baths. This system was overseen by a high-ranking state official who supervised a large staff of specialists, including engineers, and the system was maintained by 700 well-trained slaves organized into several divisions.

Much of our knowledge of the Roman water supply system comes from a book called *De Aquis Urbis Romae (About the Waters of the City of Rome)*, which was written by Sextus Julius Frontinus around AD 98. Frontinus was a career administrator who moved through a succession of important posts in the Roman government, including praetor, consul, and governor of Britain. In AD 97, he was appointed the *curator aquarum,* which was the top official charged with overseeing the water supply of the city, and in connection with this office he wrote his book, which he hoped would prove useful to subsequent *curatores.*

The opening line of Frontinus's work succinctly sets the stage for the story of Rome's aqueducts: "For 441 years from the foundation of the city, the Romans were content with the use of the water which they took from the Tiber river, wells, and springs" (1.4). As a number of Roman writers noted, among them the famous orator Cicero, the site of Rome was naturally blessed with copious springs providing fresh water. At least 20 such springs lay within the ultimate walls of the city.

While these springs together with the Tiber provided adequate water for several hundred years, in 312 BC, the energetic censor Appius Claudius Caecus undertook construction of the first aqueduct to bring water from outside the city's borders. This first aqueduct, named the Aqua Appia after its builder, took its water from some springs about 25 kilometers outside the city. It had a capacity of approximately 75,000 cubic meters of water per day, which was delivered to the area around the Aventine hill. Contrary to the modern stereotype of Roman aqueducts as a series of tall, stone arches, this first aqueduct was located mostly underground. Later aqueducts would include some sections carried on impressive aboveground arches, but even in the fully developed system, the overall percentage of aqueducts that were on such arches was less than 10 percent.

The next aqueduct, built in 272 BC and called the Anio Vetus, was 64 kilometers long. It was constructed out of booty obtained from the Roman military victory over King Pyrrhus of Epirus and, like the Appia, was mostly an underground conduit. It had a capacity of around 180,000 cubic meters per day and, as its name suggests, drew its water from the Anio River. The Anio River valley was located to the east of Rome, and of the eventual 11 major aqueducts, no fewer than 9 of them would draw their water from this region, either from the Anio itself or from springs in the hills around it. The underground channels were pierced by openings at standard intervals, which provided both ventilation and access for workers to carry out repairs and to clean out mineral deposits that constricted the flow.

The third aqueduct, the Aqua Marcia, was constructed in 144 BC by Quintus Marcius Rex, after whom it was named. While the first two aqueducts were built by censors, Marcius was an urban praetor who was given a special commission by the Roman senate to undertake the work. It had a

Figure 3.1 Remains of the Aqua Marcia outside Rome. The majority of most Roman aqueducts were underground, but some portions were carried on above ground arcades such as these.

capacity of 194,000 cubic meters per day. This aqueduct would achieve fame for four reasons. First, it supposedly provided the best drinking water. Ancient sources praise its purity and coolness, and its source was springs located in the upper Anio River valley. The emperor Nero had a villa near these springs, and he caused a scandal among the people of Rome when they learned that he had desecrated the purity of these waters by bathing in them. Second, it was the longest of all the aqueducts, stretching some 91 kilometers. Third, it was notable for the enormous amount of money necessary for its construction—180 million sesterces (the annual wage of a Roman legionary was 900 sesterces). The fourth notable aspect of the Aqua Marcia was that it was the first aqueduct to incorporate a long section that was elevated upon arches. The final stretch of the aqueduct before it entered the city was carried on such elevated arches, forming an impressive sight, and even today the remains of this stretch can be seen by passengers on the main train line heading south to Naples.

The fourth and final republican aqueduct was the Aqua Tepula, built in 125 BC by the censors. It was heavily rebuilt later, so exact statistics are uncertain, but it seems to have been about 17 kilometers long, carrying 18,000 cubic meters of water per day. Its name, unlike those of the earlier aqueducts, is not derived from its builder but rather is a description of the water itself. The Tepula's springs, which were located in the Alban hills, yielded unusually warm water, around 16 degrees Celsius.

IMPERIAL AQUEDUCTS

As with so many other aspects of the city, Augustus was responsible for dramatic renovations and innovations to the city's water supply. Most of these actions were not undertaken by Augustus personally but rather were the work of Augustus's friend, assistant, and general, Marcus Vipsanius Agrippa. After the devastation and confusion produced by decades of civil war during the Late Republic, the city's infrastructure had fallen into serious disrepair, and in 33 BC, Agrippa assumed the office of urban aedile and began an aggressive program to repair and modernize the city's essential services. Among the areas that Agrippa turned his attention to was the water supply. He repaired and rebuilt the existing aqueducts as well as constructing new ones.

One of these new ones was the Aqua Julia, which ran for nearly 22 kilometers and could carry around 31,000 cubic meters of water per day. To save on new construction costs, most of the course of the Aqua Julia, as well as the Aqua Tepula, was built on top of the already existing Aqua Marcia, creating a triple-decker aqueduct. Along sections of the aqueduct near Rome, where there is a break in the arcade, the three channels of these aqueducts can clearly be seen, one on top of the other. However, the arches of the Marcia were not designed to support this additional weight, causing problems with portions of the aqueduct cracking or settling. Later Romans repeatedly had to add extra supports to the Marcia to bear this weight.

Agrippa erected a number of buildings in the Campus Martius, including a public bath complex, and in order to provide an adequate supply of water to this newly developed region of the city, he constructed the Aqua Virgo. There are various explanations for how the aqueduct got this unusual name, but the one recounted by Frontinus says that it was a young girl (*virgo* in Latin) who showed the Roman engineers the location of the springs that were its source. The Virgo, 20 kilometers in length, is notable because it was one of the few not to come from the Anio Valley to the east; instead, it drew its water and entered the city from the north. This aqueduct also had perhaps the longest lifetime in terms of continual operation, being used as a source of water up to the modern era. It carried about 104,000 cubic meters of water per day.

The third and final Augustan-era aqueduct was the Aqua Alsietina, which also drew its water from the north, in this case from Lake Alsietinus, and it served the Transtiberim region. This aqueduct had poor-quality water for drinking but was constructed specifically to provide water for *naumachia*, "aquatic spectacles," which Augustus staged to entertain the populace on the western bank of the Tiber. It was 33 kilometers long and had a capacity of 16,000 cubic meters of water per day. In addition to building aqueducts, Agrippa rebuilt and added to the distribution network within the city, including the construction of 700 basins, 500 public fountains, and 130 distribution reservoirs. These practical structures were adorned with 300 bronze or marble statues and 400 marble pillars.

As significant as the Augustan-era additions to the physical infrastructure were, the accompanying reorganization of the administrative structure was no less important. To continue the kind of supervisory role played by Agrippa, Augustus set up the permanent office of *curator aquarum* to be responsible for overseeing the water supply, with the charge that he ensure "that the water may flow to the reservoirs and public fountains without interruption day and night" (Frontinus, *De Aquis Urbis Romae* 103). Originally this office consisted of a board of men but was later reduced to a single *curator*. The headquarters of the *curator* would eventually be established at the Porticus Minucia, the location of the grain supply administration. The *curator* was assisted by a full staff, including surveyors, scribes, and engineers.

Agrippa organized a gang of 240 of his own slaves who were trained in maintaining and repairing the aqueduct system, and he bequeathed this group to the state so that they became a permanent feature of the office. Later, this group was augmented by an additional unit of 460 slaves established by the emperor Claudius. The office of *curator aquarum* appears to have been a fairly prestigious post, entrusted only to experienced administrators, as exemplified by the career of Frontinus, who had already held most of the higher posts in the Roman administration prior to being appointed *curator aquarum*.

Augustus and his agents certainly were responsible for fundamentally reorganizing and improving the entire water system. Once when a crowd of people was complaining about the high price of wine, he lost his temper and rebuked them, saying, "My son-in-law Agrippa by building several aqueducts has ensured that no one has to go thirsty" (Suetonius, *Life of Augustus* 42).

Later emperors continued to add new aqueducts to the city. The most important additions were made by the emperor Claudius, who built the Aqua Claudia and the Aqua Anio Novus. Water from both of these came from the Anio Valley, and both were also among the largest of the aqueducts, with the Claudia having a capacity of 191,000 cubic meters per day and the Anio Novus 197,000. They were among the longest aqueducts, the Claudia being 67 kilometers in length and the Anio Novus 87 kilometers. Of the 11 main aqueducts, the final two were the Aqua Traiana built by the emperor Trajan in AD 109 (58 kilometers) and the Aqua Alexandrina built by the emperor Severus Alexander in AD 226 (22 kilometers).

Aqueducts require constant maintenance to patch leaks and to remove mineral deposits, which can otherwise block the channels. While it is clear that some of the aqueducts remained in use long after the fall of the

Figure 3.2 Portrait of Marcus Vipsanius Agrippa, Augustus's friend and general who expanded and rebuilt Rome's sewers and aqueducts.

Roman Empire, it is difficult to accurately trace the fortunes of any individual aqueduct. During the war with the barbarian king Vitigis in AD 537, the aqueducts were severed in an attempt to cut off the city's water supply. However, there seem to have been subsequent repairs, and in the 770s, at least four, including the Claudia, Virgo, and Traiana, were still in service.

HOW THE WATER SYSTEM FUNCTIONED

One of the interesting characteristics of the Roman water-supply system that differentiates it from modern water systems is that the Roman one was a continual-flow system. The water passed through the pipes and into and out of the fountains and basins constantly, whether people were using them or not. Overall, there were few valves to turn the flow of water on and off. The entire system operated by gravity. There was minimal to no use of pumps, so the elevation of the water was vitally important. The entire course of the aqueduct had to be carefully graded so that the water flowed fast enough to prevent stagnant pools or backflow, but not so fast that it became difficult to deal with. The average gradient in the Roman aqueduct system seems to have been about a three-meter drop in elevation per kilometer of distance.

The velocity of the water in the pipes would have been around 1 to 1.5 meters per second, although in some spots it might have flowed as quickly as 4 meters per second. At these typical rates, it might have taken about a day for water to travel from the farthest source to the city. Channels through which the water flowed were made from a variety of materials,

Figure 3.3 Cross-section of aqueduct showing the covered channel through which the water flowed.

including stone lined with hydraulic cement and pipes made of clay or lead.

At strategic points along the aqueducts, the water would enter large tanks or reservoirs. These served to stop the flow of water so that sediment or debris could be separated out. Water usually passed through a succession of these settling tanks so that by the time it reached consumers, it would hopefully have been fairly free of contaminants. In the city, the water was distributed to various storage towers called *castella*. From the *castella*, water was directed to the various access points, such as fountains, baths, or basins.

Only a tiny fraction of Romans had running water in their dwellings, but fountains or basins were located at nearly every street intersection. These probably served as focal points of neighborhood social interaction where people gathered to draw water and exchange gossip. Naturally, if you lived many stories up in a building, the daily routine of hauling water to your dwelling could have been quite arduous. Wealthy Romans would likely have had slaves whose job was to carry jars of water to their homes. One profession in Rome was the *aquarius*, the neighborhood water deliveryman who would bring water to your door for a fee. The satiric poet Juvenal mentions the *aquarius* as a stereotypical figure with whom sexually frustrated women would find relief (Juvenal, *Satires* 6.332).

Approximately one-third of the aqueduct water was consumed outside the city boundaries for purposes such as irrigation. Roughly another third went to the public fountains, baths, and basins. Of the remainder, a substantial part was used by the emperor, including the supply for the imperial baths. Water was a form of benefaction that the state supplied to the citizens. There was no fee for drawing water from the fountains, and even many of the great bath buildings were free or had only token admissions.

One of the greatest challenges faced by those charged with maintaining the system was the problem of private individuals illegally tapping into an aqueduct. People would bore holes into the aqueduct and then attach their own pipes to bring water to their dwellings or businesses. This was such a problem that the *curatores* had to have their staffs constantly patrolling all the exposed sections of aqueduct, and they were continually removing such illegal taps and fixing the holes they made. Frontinus identifies illegal tapping as a serious problem that could divert up to half the capacity of an aqueduct. He indignantly reports that he had found "fields, shops, apartments, and even brothels illegally hooked up to the system with private water taps" (Frontinus, *De Aquis Urbis Romae* 76).

One of the greatest problems in assessing the Roman water-supply system from a modern perspective is that so much of our statistical evidence comes from Frontinus. While he supplies a great deal of numerical data, there is enormous scholarly debate about how these numbers should be interpreted. Much of this uncertainty stems from the fact that Frontinus expresses the volume of the aqueducts in terms of units called *quinariae*.

This is a measurement expressing the size of a cross section of pipe and as such does not take into account factors, such as the velocity of the water, that are essential to knowing the volume of water being transported. This has led to endless academic arguments about how to translate his figures, resulting in estimates of the total volume of water supplied to the city that range from 300,000 cubic meters per day to well over 1 million cubic meters per day.

The Romans built aqueducts not only for the capital city, but all over the empire as well, and these provincial aqueducts feature some of the most impressive architecture. The Pont du Gard in southern France is an astonishing engineering feat consisting of a multilevel arcade 50 meters high built to carry an aqueduct across a gorge. The town of Segovia in Spain has a lengthy section of well-preserved and imposing aqueduct, and the city of Vienne in Gaul was served by no fewer than 11 aqueducts, although they are considerably smaller than Rome's.

Overall, the Roman water-supply system was a truly impressive achievement and one that the ancients themselves marveled at. Frontinus asked, "How could you compare such an array of indispensable structures carrying so much water with the idle pyramids or the useless although famous works of the Greeks?" (Frontinus, *De Aquis Urbis Romae* 16). Pliny the Elder wrote, "If we take into careful account the plentiful supply of water to public buildings, baths, pools, canals, homes, gardens, and villas near the city; if we contemplate the distances traveled by the water before it arrives, the raising of arches, the tunneling through mountains, and the construction of level courses across deep valleys, we will have to concede that nothing more remarkable has ever existed in all the world" (Pliny the Elder, *Natural History* 36.24.123).

ROMAN SEWERS

The second consideration in urban planning regarding water is providing a mechanism to get rid of unwanted water. In the most simple case, this entails constructing a drainage system sufficient to carry away or divert rainwater. In cities such as Rome that are situated on a river prone to flooding, provision for dealing with floodwaters can also be a factor. Finally, there is the problem of disposing of water that has become contaminated, especially that which has been mingled with excrement. In modern cities, the drainage system and the sewage system are separate networks, but in ancient Rome, as in most cities until quite recently, the two were combined.

The earliest Roman drainage system was clearly built to deal with the problem of excessive water rather than as a way to get rid of sewage. The site of Rome, with its many springs, its proximity to the Tiber, and its many low-lying valleys situated between hills, meant that the low-lying areas had an excess of water and, at least during parts of the year, seem to have taken on the character of swamps or marshes. A number of literary sources emphasize the swampy nature of early Rome; the situation was so bad that a regular ferry apparently operated among the main hills during the wet season. These marshy areas included some of the most geographically significant crossroads, such as the Forum Boarium and the Forum Romanum; therefore, the development of the city depended on rendering these areas drier and more habitable on a year-round basis. The earliest public work known at Rome was intended to accomplish exactly this purpose.

Rome's first drain would become its most famous—the Cloaca Maxima, "the great sewer." The earliest version of this drain was constructed by the kings and ran through the Roman Forum, crossed the Velabrum between the Capitoline and Palatine hills, and then emptied into the Tiber. Its original form seems to have been an open ditch, and as late as the third century BC, there was still a danger of pedestrians in the forum falling into it. The kings had to employ compulsory labor in the construction of this drain and, according to legend, the work was so arduous that some laborers committed suicide rather than continue to be forced to work on it. Later reconstructions of the Cloaca Maxima eventually transformed it into a completely underground conduit, and numerous other drainage sewers built by a succession of administrators, including Cato, were added to serve the other sections of the city.

In their fully developed form, these sewers were impressive engineering achievements made of concrete or even high-quality stone. The capac-

Figure 3.4 Outlet of the Cloaca Maxima into the Tiber River.

ity of the sewers was also astonishing. Portions of the Cloaca Maxima were more than four meters tall and three meters wide, leading Pliny the Elder to claim that one could drive a fully loaded wagon of hay through Rome's sewers (Pliny the Elder, *Natural History* 36.108). The Cloaca Maxima in its final form covered a distance of 900 meters in a straight line from its origin to the Tiber, but due to its many twists and turns, its actual course was 1,600 meters in length. This drain remained in use until modern times, and even today its outlet is readily visible, embedded in the modern embankments. A certain type of fish that lived in the Tiber and fed off refuse from the *Cloaca Maxima* was a particularly prized delicacy that could fetch a high price for the lucky fisherman who managed to catch one.

As with the aqueducts, Agrippa was a key figure in the development of the sewers. As part of his aedileship in 33 BC, he had the sewer system cleaned and rebuilt much of it. According to several sources, his zeal for ensuring a proper job of renovation was so great that he himself conducted a personal tour of the sewers, traveling through them by boat. Over time, more sewers were added that drained other parts of the city until, by the empire, there was an extensive network of underground sewers beneath the city's streets.

This system played an essential role in keeping the low-lying areas of the city dry and would also have helped to expedite the drying-out process after a flood. A secondary function was to carry away waste, particularly the estimated 100,000 pounds of excrement produced daily by the inhabitants of the city. The majority of sewage that found its way into the system did not come directly from latrines; only a tiny handful of houses had toilets linked directly to the sewers, and there were very few public latrines. Most waste was dumped in the streets, and from there might find its way into the sewers. The overflow from the fountains served a vital role in cleaning the city by washing some of this filth into the drains, a point recognized by Frontinus.

This arrangement seems disturbing from a modern perspective, but there were very practical reasons why one would not want a direct link from one's dwelling to the sewer.

Since there were neither water nor traps in Roman toilets, a connection with the sewer would have served as an entry point into one's home for all the unpleasant smells and gases building up in the sewers. In addition to the obvious olfactory distress this would have caused, these gases could even prove deadly, since the buildup of methane can actually cause explosions (as has been attested for similar sewer systems, such as that of Victorian Britain). Those who had to venture into the sewers to clean them faced the real possibility of choking to death, and this task seems to have been given, at least on some occasions, to criminals. A further danger was posed when the Tiber flooded, which would inevitably have caused the flow of the sewers to reverse, resulting in their contents being disgorged up into the city from any access points, including private homes linked to the sewers. Finally, a direct connection to the sewer would have been a point of ingress for unwanted vermin. While rats would have been the most common of such unwelcome visitors, there are accounts of more exotic intruders as well. According to the writer Aelian, the house of a fish merchant was invaded each night by an opportunistic octopus, which forged its way up out of the sewer and raided the house's stock of preserved fish (Aelian, *On Animals* 13.6).

Ancient authors expressed great awe at Rome's sewer system, even counting it as one of the greatest wonders of the city (Dionysius of Halicarnassus, *Roman Antiquities* 3.67.5; Pliny the Elder, *Natural History* 36.104–8). Their admiration is summed up by the rhetorical question of Cassiodorus: "What other city can compare with Rome in her heights, when her depths are so incomparable?" (Cassiodorus, *Variae* 3.30.1–2).

ROADS

While many Roman cities that originated as military camps were laid out with a logical grid system of streets meeting at right angles, the capital city had no such convenient organization. Its streets are a confusing jumble that reflects the organic and unplanned growth of the city. The famous roads connecting Rome with other parts of Italy and the empire were termed *via.* Of streets within the city limits, most were termed either a *vicus* if its course was more or less flat or a *clivus* if it went up or down a hill. A small number of particularly important or old streets that lay within the city possessed the *via* designation.

Due to the premium placed on space in the crowded city, Rome's streets were generally quite narrow by modern standards and were overhung by balconies projecting from the close-set buildings. There do seem to have been repeated attempts by the government, however, to ensure certain minimum widths. The ancient law code of the Twelve Tables dictated that a *via* had to be at least 8 Roman feet wide on straight sections and 16 feet wide around curves (Varro, *On the Latin Language* 7.15). When Nero rebuilt the city after the Great Fire of AD 64, he widened the major thoroughfares considerably. While this step had the utilitarian purpose of serving as a firebreak in future conflagrations, it drew criticism from the people, who complained that the streets were unbearably hot because they no longer lay within the shade of nearby buildings.

Early in Roman history, the urban roadways must have been simple dirt tracks. Eventually, this was probably replaced in key areas with gravel paving, and by 238 BC, there is evidence of stone paving. Livy reports that the censors of 174 BC were responsible for covering streets all around the city with stone paving, and from this point on, urban streets probably followed this model (Livy, *History of Rome* 41.27.5–8). The most elaborate of these streets were crowned in the center so that water flowed down

Figure 3.5 A section of urban Roman road showing paving stones, raised sidewalks, stepping stones, and ruts carved by wagon wheels.

toward the sides and into gutters, which led to openings to the sewers. They also sometimes had raised sidewalks and, at key intersections, stepping-stones that could have been employed by pedestrians crossing even a partially flooded street. Such architecturally sophisticated urban roadways can still be seen in a number of well-preserved Roman towns, such as Pompeii.

The most famous street in the city was the Sacra Via, or the "Sacred Way," which ran from the Capitoline hill through the Roman Forum. A number of important religious and civic rituals included a procession along its course, and, since it lay at the heart of the city, it was the scene of many notable events. Other main thoroughfares ran along the valleys between the various hills. The Via Lata ran across the central Campus Martius, connecting the center of the city with the Via Flaminia, the main road heading north.

Maintenance of the city streets fell under the general jurisdiction of the urban aedile, although Roman legal texts suggest that property owners were at least in theory supposed to look after the section of street that abutted their property. One text states that "each person is to keep the public street outside his own house in repair and clean out the open gutters.... They are not to throw excrement, dead animals, or skins into the street" (*Digest of Roman Law* 43.11.1.1). The ultimate responsibility for ensuring that the streets were properly maintained lay with the *aediles,* as evidenced by an incident when the emperor Caligula thought the streets were too filthy and therefore had his soldiers fill the unfortunate urban aedile's toga with mud taken from the streets as punishment for neglecting his duties.

Since the size of many of the city's thoroughfares was established before the city's population swelled, crowding in the city streets must have been quite severe. In addition to foot traffic, pedestrians would have had to contend with animals such as horses and cattle and wagons transporting food and other goods. To ameliorate these traffic problems, it was decreed that wagons transporting materials could only enter the city at night. While this may have alleviated crowding, it would also have made sleep more difficult for the city's inhabitants as the night air would have been filled with the braying of animals, the shouts of the drovers, and the creaking of the wagons. The poet Juvenal offers a vivid portrait of the dangerously crowded conditions that the unfortunate pedestrians in Rome's streets would have had to deal with: "Even though we might try to hurry, the surging crowd blocks our progress, and the dense mob crushes against us from behind. In the press, one man shoves me with his elbow, another sticks me with a pole, a third smacks a board over my head, and yet another cracks his wine jar up against my forehead. My legs become encrusted with stinking mud, from all sides big feet trample on me, and a passing soldier grinds my toes under the hobnails of his boots" (Juvenal, *Satires* 3.244–48). The already congested condition of Rome's streets became even worse during festivals and spectacles, when curious throngs from the surrounding areas flocked to the city to witness these events. When Julius Caesar staged three days of spectacular entertainments, people poured into the city, with many pitching tents in the streets themselves. The resultant crowding was so severe that large numbers of people were crushed to death, including even two senators.

The truly impressive Roman roads were the thousands of miles of roadway that linked Rome with the rest of the empire. This road system was made up of the best-built roads up until very recently. Roman roads were carefully constructed with foundations that went down one and a half meters and were graded to drain water off of them. The roads were also paved, and the Romans were proud of making their roads go straight even when this meant constructing long bridges over deep valleys or tunneling through solid rock mountains.

The first major Roman road was the Via Appia, which was begun in 213 BC by the man who gave his name to the road, Appius Claudius. It connected Rome with Brundisium at the heel of Italy, which was a departure point for ships sailing to the east. By the end of the second century BC, additional roads such as the Via Flaminia and the Via Aurelia had been constructed running up and down the length of Italy and joining the cities of the peninsula by a web of well-built roads. As the Roman Empire expanded outside of Italy, the Romans doggedly extended their network of carefully built roadways into the provinces. Legions stationed around the Mediterranean spent much of their time constructing roads, and a typical Roman soldier spent far more time digging than fighting. These soldiers left records of their construction work with thousands of stone mile markers that proudly recorded the name of the military unit that built a particular section of road.

These roads served many purposes. They helped the Romans keep control of their empire by enabling troops to be rushed to trouble spots. They encouraged and facilitated long-distance trade and bolstered the economy. They sped up communication among the different regions of the empire, a function that was aided by an imperial messenger service. Finally, they served as a powerful symbolic marker that a territory was indisputably Roman. Like an animal marking its territory, Rome used the presence of roads as an unmistakable signal that an area belonged to the Roman Empire.

However, travel along these roads was fraught with dangers. Bandits were very common, and anyone venturing outside of large cities was literally risking his life. Roman literature is full of examples of people who simply disappeared, who set out on a journey and were never heard from again. Presumably they fell victim to bandits along the road. Rich Romans traveled with bodyguards and armed slaves, but even such protection was not proof against bandits. One senior magistrate and his entire party vanished only a few miles from Rome. The Bible even provides good evidence of the ubiquity of bandit attacks. The parable of the good Samaritan centers around a man who had been beaten and robbed. He was journeying during the daytime along the road from Jerusalem to Jericho, a distance of about 24 kilometers, along what was perhaps the most heavily traveled road in the province (Luke 10:25–37). A common phrase on tombstones is *interfectus a latronibus*, "killed by bandits." In a list of the duties of a Roman governor, the first thing mentioned was to suppress bandits.

BRIDGES

By the fourth century AD, Rome boasted at least seven well-made stone bridges within the city limits that connected the right and left banks of the Tiber. The Romans were excellent practical engineers, and many of their bridges remained in active use long after the fall of the Roman Empire.

The Roman word for bridge is *pons,* and the oldest and most famous bridge in Rome was the Pons Sublicius, which linked the Forum Boarium with the Transtiberim just below Tiber Island. This was roughly the site of the old ferry crossing that served the early trade route of the Via Salaria and thus was a logical site for Rome's first permanent bridge. This bridge had religious connections, as evidenced by the title of the chief priest of Rome, the Pontifex Maximus. (It is from this title that the modern term *pope* is derived, and even today, the official title of the pope is the Pontifex Maximus.) A unique quality of the Pons Sublicius was that it was constructed out of wood without the use of any metal, apparently due to religious requirements. The bridge was repeatedly destroyed by violent floods but continued to be rebuilt using only wood for several hundred years.

The first stone bridge in Rome, the Pons Aemilius, was built in 179 BC, also just below Tiber Island, close to the site of the Pons Sublicius. This bridge remained standing for over 1,500 years until the sixteenth century, when a section was carried away by a flood. Two other bridges of note connected Tiber Island to the east and west banks. The Pons Cestius linked the island with the Transtiberim and the Pons Fabricius joined the island to the left bank. Both of these seem to have been in place by the Late Republic. The Pons Fabricius is today known as the Ponte Quattro Capi and is essentially the original Roman bridge with some modern accretions to its superstructure; as such, it is the best-preserved Roman bridge in the city.

WALLS

The first architectural defenses of Rome were constructed by the legendary founder of the city, Romulus, who fortified the Palatine hill. These works probably consisted of nothing more elaborate than a simple wooden palisade augmenting the steep natural walls of the hill itself. Both the Palatine and the Capitoline hills would have served as natural fortresses for the inhabitants of the city.

The oldest known comprehensive circuit of walls was attributed to the sixth king of Rome, Servius Tullius, and thus were known as the Servian Walls. Servius Tullius had divided the city into four regions, and his walls were said to surround these four regions. The Servian circuit of walls enclosed the central portion of the city near the Tiber, including the Capitoline, Palatine, and Aventine hills, and also extended inland, encompassing the spurs of the Quirinal, Viminal, Esquiline, and Caelian hills. It did not include the Campus Martius or the Transtiberim, and the eastern edge cut rather awkwardly across the middle of the parallel lines of hills on that side of the city. While Servius Tullius may have erected some sort of fortifications, the walls that bear his name are actually believed to have been constructed several centuries later, in the fourth century BC, as a response to the Gallic sack of Rome in 390 BC.

Standard Roman fortifications consisted of an embankment of earth known as an *agger* with a ditch in front of it known as a *fossa*. This was the defense put around Roman legionary camps on the march, and a similar structure may have been built around Rome at an early stage. The stone walls of Servius ran for 11 kilometers and at sections were 10 meters high and 4 meters thick. They were composed of rectangular blocks of cut stone that are consistently 2 Roman feet high (0.6 meters), although the length of the blocks varied. The blocks seem to have been laid atop one another dry, without the use of mortar. The Servian Walls are known to have been rebuilt and augmented on a number of occasions, most notably at times when the city was in peril due to warfare in Italy—for example, in 217 BC during the Second Punic War and in 87 BC during the Social War. These later rebuildings introduced some modifications, including the addition of mountings on the walls for *ballistae* (a form of catapult).

Although by the early first century AD, the built-up part of the city extended considerably beyond the old Servian Walls, a new circuit of walls to encompass the whole city was not constructed for several centuries. This clearly reflects the security that the Romans felt that no enemy threatened the heart of the empire and illustrates the dominance and stability of Rome during this period, so they felt it unnecessary to bother fortifying their capital city.

This situation changed dramatically in the third century AD, when barbarian incursions grew more serious and the empire was racked by civil wars that often saw rival Roman armies fighting for control of the capital. These events prompted the emperor Aurelian to construct a new, larger circuit of walls in the 270s AD. These walls, known as the Muri Aureliani, were 19 kilometers long and included the Campus Martius and a section of the Transtiberim, as well as stretching farther to the south and east than the Servian Walls. The walls were 6.5 meters high and 4 meters thick, with towers placed every 100 Roman feet. They had a concrete core with brick facing. The towers were equipped with emplacements for two *ballistae* on swivels as well as numerous loopholes for archers. The gateways were heavily fortified with towers as well, with the main entrances flanked by large, semicircular towers.

The Aurelian Walls show evidence of having been constructed in haste. For example, they make considerable use of existing structures, which are incorporated into the circuit of the walls, including the walls of the camp of the Praetorian Guard, houses, and even stretches of aqueducts. It has been estimated that nearly one-sixth of the walls is actually composed of preexisting structures. These walls also were rebuilt and augmented on numerous occasions. Some of the most important of these additions were made by the emperor Maxentius in AD 311 in preparation for his fight with Constantine. He may have doubled the height of sections of the wall, adding additional stories to the watchtowers. Other rebuildings included those undertaken by the emperors Honorius and Theodoric, and Pope Leo incorporated the Vatican within the circuit of walls.

The walls continued to be maintained and rebuilt throughout the Middle Ages, and the Renaissance popes likewise put effort into refurbishing these fortifications so that they could continue to protect Rome for centuries after the Roman Empire. Today, considerable stretches of the Aurelian Wall are still visible and quite well preserved, particularly around a number of the gates, among them the Porta Metrovia, the Porta Appia, and the Porta Aurelia on the Janiculum hill.

4

Government of Ancient Rome

CITIZENSHIP

One of the most important distinctions in Roman society was that between citizens and noncitizens. The number of citizens was always a small minority of the total populace. In the early empire, when there were perhaps 50 million people living in the entire Roman Empire, it is estimated that there were only about 6 million citizens. To be a citizen, you had to be an adult, free male. Thus, by definition, women, children, and slaves were excluded from citizenship. In addition, you had to have passed the census, which identified your age, geographical origin, family, wealth, and moral virtue. For hundreds of years, the Romans were reluctant to extend citizenship to even the thoroughly Romanized inhabitants of Italy until they were forced to by the Social Wars in the Late Republic. Once Rome acquired overseas provinces, it often remained reluctant to grant citizenship on a large scale to provincials. A major change came in AD 212, when the emperor Caracalla declared that all adult, male, free inhabitants of the empire would now be citizens.

Early in Roman history, one of the main duties of a citizen was to fight in the army. Later, once Rome's army had been professionalized, the main duty of citizens was to vote. Being a citizen gave you protection under the law, and in theory, all citizens were treated equally by the law. One of the rights of a citizen was that he could not be punished without some form of trial, and this trial had to be held at Rome. For example, when Christians were being persecuted, if they were citizens, they had to be sent to Rome; if not, the local magistrate could deal with them.

One of the most potent phrases in Roman society was *Civis Romanus sum,* meaning, "I am a Roman citizen," because declaring this instantly gave you certain protections and rights. This phrase entered Roman legend when a corrupt governor, Verres, seized a Roman citizen and, ignoring the man's repeated protestations of *Civis Romanus sum,* illegally ordered that he be beaten and tortured.

Roman citizens were formally divided into two groups, the patricians and the plebeians. This distinction went back to the earliest days of Rome, when the society was dominated by a small number of wealthy landowning families who collectively became known as the patricians, literally, "the fathers." This dominance became institutionalized in laws that stated that only patricians were eligible to hold high political office. The monopoly was maintained by further laws dictating that patricians could only marry members of other patrician families. All nonpatricians—the vast majority—were labeled as plebeians. These distinctions resulted in considerable social unrest, culminating in a struggle known as the Conflict of the Orders. As a result of these struggles, the privileges of patricians were eroded and eventually eliminated, although being a member of a patrician family continued to convey a certain status throughout Roman history. From 445 BC on, patricians and plebeians were allowed to legally intermarry.

Another way in which Roman citizens were divided up was by wealth. Every so often, the state appointed a special magistrate called a censor, who reviewed the wealth and moral worthiness of all citizens. If your total wealth was more than 400,000 sesterces, then you were granted equestrian status. *Equites* wore a special gold ring and togas with a narrow purple stripe. Many equestrians seem to have operated successful commercial enterprises, and during the empire, a number of important government posts were allotted to equestrians.

One final, significant component of Roman social structure, although not delineated by a formal set of rules or laws, nevertheless played an important part in daily life. This was the patronage system, which developed as a way to link together Romans of varying status. Powerful men would serve as patrons to a group of their social or economic inferiors, who were known as the man's clients. Patrons provided financial or legal help and protection to their clients. In return, the clients performed actions that enhanced the prestige or reputation of their patrons. For example, clients were expected to support their patron with their votes during an election or, if their patron were giving a public speech, to attend and to applaud enthusiastically. In a ritual known as the *salutatio,* clients gathered at the house of their patron in the morning to receive his greetings (and perhaps also some food or money).

THE MAGISTRATES

The governmental institutions of the Roman Republic evolved over several hundred years and persisted into the period of the empire, even after the emperors had effectively reestablished one-man rule. The core of the government centered around a series of magistracies. All of these magistracies shared a number of characteristics: officeholders obtained their positions by election, served one-year terms, and had to meet minimum age requirements for each office. Also, each office was collegial, meaning that more than one person held the same title at the same time. Ambitious aristocrats aspired to be elected to each of these offices in turn, and the entire sequence of offices became known as the *cursus honorem*, "the course of honor."

The lowest magistracy was the quaestorship. Under the fully developed system, quaestors were supposed to be 30 years old and were in charge of a range of financial affairs. Originally, only 2 quaestors were elected each year, but over time, as there was need for more and more officials, the number grew to 20. Different quaestors had varying specific duties, with some, for example, in charge of monitoring taxation, others overseeing financial matters in a province, and others controlling government finances.

The next magistracy was the aedileship. Aediles had to be 36 years old, and four were elected each year. The aediles were responsible for a number of urban affairs, including maintaining and repairing urban infrastructure, monitoring markets to ensure fair trade and enforce uniform standards of weights and measures, and staging public festivals.

Above the aediles were the praetors, who had to be 39 years old. As with the quaestors, the number of praetors gradually increased over time from one to as many as eight. Praetors mainly served judicial functions, overseeing law courts and running the judiciary system.

The most prestigious post of all was the consulship. Consuls had to be 42 years old, and only two were elected each year. They acted as the chief executives of the state and, at least during most of the republic, served as the generals of Rome's armies as well.

In extreme emergencies when the state itself was threatened, the Romans might appoint a dictator, who held almost absolute power. However, they were very uncomfortable with the idea of one man monopolizing power, so this office was only to be invoked in dire circumstances and a dictator could hold this post for no longer than six months.

One other important elected office was the tribuneship. The number of tribunes varied, but they were charged with protecting the interests of the plebeians. To do this, they had a number of unusual powers. A tribune could propose legislation, and he himself enjoyed a special status of immunity intended to protect him. The tribunes' most potent prerogative, however, was the tribunician veto, which gave them the right to declare laws invalid, to revoke actions of other officials, and to overturn legal decisions. This powerful privilege was rarely used but was intended, by its very existence, to serve as a curb upon the worst excesses of patrician power.

Each of the main magistrates was appointed a number of assistants, or lictors, whose job was to enforce their orders. The number of lictors granted to each magistrate varied, with the highest office, consul, having the most and the junior magistrates having fewer. As a symbol of the magistrates' power, each lictor carried a fasces, an axe surrounded by a bundle of rods tied together with a purple ribbon. In theory, the magistrate could order lictors to dispense punishment by beating offenders with the rods or cutting off their heads with the axe.

The Roman senate, composed of roughly 300 members, was not an elected body and possessed no legislative powers; rather, its function was mainly advisory. Membership in the senate was obtained by having held one of the higher magistracies, so the senate was composed of ex-magistrates. Membership was for life. Because the senate consisted of Rome's political and financial elite, its advice on matters both domestic and foreign was usually taken seriously.

THE VOTING ASSEMBLIES

The body of Roman citizens was divided up into three separate voting assemblies, which elected different officials. Patricians were simultaneously members of two of these assemblies, and plebeians were members of all three.

The first was called the *comitia centuriata*. This assembly gathered together to elect consuls, praetors, and censors. It also presided over trials for treason and, before the Punic Wars, voted on most legislation; after the wars, another assembly became responsible for legislation. Citizens were divided up into 193 groups called centuries, and which century you were placed in was based upon your net worth as determined by the census. In the actual election, each century had one vote. Thus there were 193 total votes. To determine how the century would cast its vote, the members of each century voted among themselves; whatever the majority of the members decided was how the century's vote was cast. The system was similar to the American electoral college system in which all the electoral votes of a certain state are given to just one candidate.

The process at first glance seems democratic, but it really was not because citizens were not evenly divided among centuries. The very small number of wealthy Romans controlled the majority of the centuries. In essence, the vote of a rich man was weighted much more than the vote of a poor one. Not everyone voted at the same time; instead, voting started with the richest centuries, who would cast their votes, and then moved downward. As soon as a majority (97 votes) was reached, the election was over. Therefore, poor voters were often deprived of the opportunity to cast their ballots.

The next assembly was called the *comitia tributa*. In this case, instead of being divided up by wealth, all citizens were divided up by geography into 35 tribes. There were 4 urban tribes and 31 rural ones. The *comitia tributa* elected aediles and quaestors and voted on most legislation. The system was similar to that of the *comitia centuriata* in which each tribe voted among themselves and then the entire tribe cast a single vote. In this election, there were 35 total votes, and whoever got a majority of 18 won. Once again, even though it looks democratic, the system favors the rich, though in a more subtle way. Elections were held at Rome, and one had to be physically present to cast a vote. There were no absentee ballots, and everyone voted in one place. Thus if you wanted to vote, you had to travel to Rome, which required time and money—things only the rich had. The poor people who lived in Rome could and did certainly vote, but since they were all grouped into the four urban tribes, they only had 4 out of 35 votes.

The final important assembly was the *concilia plebis*. It was organized in the same way as the *comitia tributa* with 35 tribes and voted in the same way. The only difference was that all patricians were excluded, and its main function was to elect tribunes.

THE ROMAN FORUM: BUILDINGS AND MONUMENTS

The Roman Forum (Forum Romanum in Latin) is a rectangular open space roughly 150 meters long and 75 meters wide, with its long axis running from the Capitoline hill in a southeasterly direction toward the valley of the Colosseum. This space is the heart of the city and was the focal point for Roman political and legal activity; it was the scene of meetings of the senate, political assemblies, and famous trials. Many of the most important religious shrines and temples were also located in the forum or nearby, and important religious sacrifices and rituals took place in it. Early in the city's history, the Roman Forum was a commercial center and remained a hub of financial transactions and money lending. Finally, it was the stage for many impressive urban spectacles, such as funerals, gladiatorial combats, and public feasts. By Late Antiquity, it had become crammed with honorific statues, shrines, arches, columns, and other monuments commemorating Roman heroes and conquests. Even when its political and legal functions declined during the empire, it always remained the symbolic center of the city and of the empire.

The Roman Forum changed dramatically from the early to the middle to the Late Republic and throughout the first couple of centuries of the empire, but over this entire span of nearly 1,000 years, there was a set of core buildings and shrines that remained constant and helped to define this space.

The southeast border of the Roman Forum was delineated by the Regia, a small structure of great antiquity. It was consecrated as a *templum* and, as its name suggests, was associated with the kings, although it was probably not the house of the kings. During the republic, it was associated with the chief priest, the Pontifex Maximus. It was rebuilt many times but always had an unusual tapering, rectangular outline (with the broad end

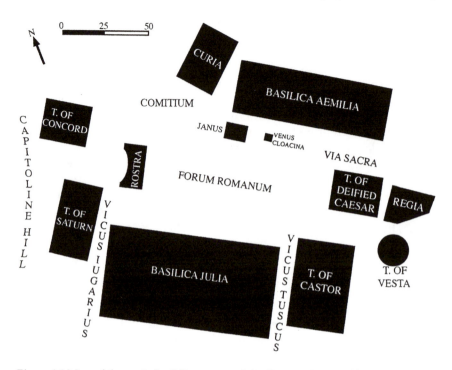

Figure 4.1 Map of the main buildings around the Roman Forum. (Gregory S. Aldrete, Phaeton Group, Scientific Graphic Services Division.)

facing the Roman Forum) defined by the streets that passed on either side of the building. On the other side of one of these streets at the very southeast corner of the forum was the circular Temple of Vesta, housing the sacred flame of the city that was tended by the Vestal Virgins.

Turning the corner, one approaches the southwest side of the Roman Forum, which is defined by two temples, one at each end. At the southern end was the Temple of Castor near the place where the gods Castor and Pollux were supposedly seen watering their horses following a battle in 496 BC. This was one of the frequent meeting places of the senate during the republic. At the northern end of this side was the imposing Temple of Saturn, which housed the state treasury. The northwest side of the Roman Forum backed up against the Capitoline hill, and in the center of this side, the Temple of Concord was located on the slopes of the hill.

The northern corner of the Roman Forum was the seat of structures associated with Roman government. Chief among these was the Curia, or the Roman senate house. It was rebuilt a number of times in slightly different locations but always at this corner of the forum. The Curia, the ordinary meeting venue for the Roman senate, was rectangular in shape (25 by 18 meters) with a high roof. It consisted of a single, large room with bronze doors facing the Forum at one end and a low dais at the opposite end

Figure 4.2 General view of the Roman Forum as seen from the Capitoline hill.

where presumably the presiding magistrate would have sat. Running down the two long sides of the building were three broad, raised steps upon which the senators' chairs would have been placed, leaving a large central open space. Different versions of the building had decorations of various sorts, including paintings of Roman military successes and a statue of Victory. The floor and walls were adorned with decorative marble in geometric patterns. The front of the building had a porch with Ionic columns and stairs leading down to the forum. The building that survives today is a reconstruction by the emperor Diocletian of Augustus' Curia. Its current preservation is due to the fact that it was consecrated as a Christian church in the seventh century AD, although efforts have been made today to restore it to its original appearance. The Roman orator Cicero refers to the Curia as "the shrine of holiness, of majesty, of intellect, of public policy, the head of the city, the sanctuary of our allies, the haven of all races, the dwelling place accorded to a single order by the whole people" (Cicero, *Pro Milone* 90). The northeast side of the Roman Forum featured two religious sites, the shrines of Janus and of Venus Cloacina (Venus of the sewers).

This set of eight buildings and shrines scattered around the different sides of the Roman Forum comprised some of the constants that helped to define this space and that survived the various reconstructions. The long sides of the Roman Forum were given definition early on by rows of shops. Those along the south side were sometimes referred to as the Tabernae Veterae, or "old shops," and those along the north side as the

Figure 4.3 The Curia, the usual meeting place of the Roman senate.

Tabernae Novae, the "new shops." The old shops seem to have been largely taken over by bankers and moneylenders, and, at least early in the republic, the new shops housed a number of butchers. Over time, these merchants were gradually displaced, and the north and south sides of the forum were given a more impressive, monumental shape by the construction of the Basilica Aemilia along the north side and, later, the Basilica Julia along the south side. A basilica is a type of Roman building consisting of a series of covered colonnades with a central nave. They were employed as a kind of general-purpose structure that could house merchants or magistrates or simply serve as public gathering spaces. In their final form, these were enormous, multistory buildings made of fine marble. The final Basilica Julia was over 100 meters long and 60 meters wide.

The corner of the Roman Forum with the Curia was the location of several other political structures. One of these was a *templum* called the Comitium, which was a site of public assembly and in particular the place

Figure 4.4 The northwest side of the Roman Forum, with remains of the Rostra in the foreground and the Capitoline hill in the background. The eight columns to the left are all that remains of the Temple of Saturn.

where the Comitia Curiata, one of the citizen assemblies that voted on laws, met. By the midrepublic, the Comitium seems to have consisted of a kind of circular depression with tiers of seats where the assembly gathered and voted. The side facing the Roman Forum featured a curved, raised platform from which speakers could either address the assembly in the Comitium or else turn around and speak to larger crowds in the Roman Forum itself.

Between the various judicial magistrates and public assemblies, there was a need for multiple platforms from which speakers could address crowds, and after the naval victory at Antium in 338 BC, a speaker's platform was erected in the Roman Forum and decorated with the rams of enemy ships captured in the battle. Because of this, the platform was called the Rostra, which was the term for the beaks or rams of ships. *Rostra* subsequently became a generic name for various other speaker's platforms that were similarly adorned with ships' rams. A public assembly of Roman citizens, known as a *contio*, could be summoned by a magistrate or by a priest for such purposes as describing pending legislation and discussing important public issues or the proposals of prominent politicians. These platforms were the stages for many of the dramatic speeches of the Late Republic, such as those in which Cicero denounced Mark Antony. While for much of his life Cicero enjoyed considerable success stirring up crowds at *contiones* using his oratorical skills to address the people from the Rostra, this same platform was the scene of an ignominious end to Cic-

Figure 4.5 Reconstruction of the northwest side of the Roman Forum with the Rostra in the center and the temples of Vespasian and Saturn behind it. (From G. Gatteschi, *Restauri della Roma Imperiale*, 1924, p. 11.)

ero's career. After his death at Antony's instigation, Cicero's head and hands were chopped off and put on display on the *Rostra*.

By the early empire, the assemblies held in the Comitium had been transferred to larger venues and the area was paved over. Augustus constructed a new Rostra oriented squarely facing the Roman Forum along the northwestern side. This Rostra and the area around it became festooned with honorific statues, columns, and monuments. Among these was the Miliarium Aureum, the "golden milestone," from which distances were measured.

One interesting monument that has been uncovered in the area of the Comitium is the Lapis Niger—the "black stone." This is an irregularly shaped region of black paving slabs and a number of seemingly randomly placed monuments, including a U-shaped altar, a tufa cone, and a *cippus* with an inscription written in a very archaic form of Latin. The whole area seems to have been marked off to prevent people from treading upon it, and there is considerable debate over the translation of the inscription, which may be among the earliest Latin texts. Various legends are associated with this place of seemingly ill omen, including that it marks the place of either the death or burial of Romulus or perhaps one of his ancestors.

One suggested translation of this inscription begins, "Whoever defiles this spot, let him be forfeit to the spirits of the Underworld. Whoever contaminates it with refuse, let the king deprive him of property according to the law. Whomever the king finds passing along the road, let him order the herald to seize the reins of their draught animals and force them to detour. Whoever does not take the proper detour but traverses this spot, let him be sold at auction according to the law." Whatever the actual nature of this monument, it was plainly a taboo site that people were not supposed to cross over.

Over time, buildings began to encroach upon the open space of the Roman Forum. The most dramatic of these was the Temple of the Deified Caesar, which was built over the spot where his body was cremated by rioting mobs in 44 BC. This happened at the southeast end of the forum, so the temple was erected there, in front of the Regia, hiding it from view. The stairs of this temple were constructed to form another speakers' platform squarely facing the Augustan Rostra at the other end. This new one became known as the Imperial Rostra, and was a favorite spot from which emperors addressed the people.

In addition to the many political, economic, and religious activities that transpired in the Roman Forum, it was also a social center of the city and a kind of crossroads at which all classes of people mingled. Someone walking through the forum would see, in addition to aristocratic senators and magistrates, people of considerably lower status. Plainly, many individuals idled about among the cool colonnades simply people watching and vicariously being a part of the bustling scene. Some seem to have entertained themselves while loafing on the steps of the basilicas by playing various popular board and dicing games. Lacking formal boards, some people adopted the simple expedient of hacking a crude game board into the fine marble on which they were seated. A number of these carvings are still visible today in the ruins of the Basilica Julia.

A portrait of the various types of unsavory people that one might encounter in and around the Roman Forum is offered by a character in Plautus's play, *Curculio:* "Perjurers can be found near the Comitium, while liars and braggarts hang around the Temple of Venus Cloacina and wealthy married idlers can be found in the basilica. In the same spot can be found worn out prostitutes and their pimps. Near the fish market are members of eating clubs, while respectable, wealthy citizens stroll through the lower Forum. In the middle Forum, you can find flashy fellows near the sewer ditch. Around the *Lacus Curtius* are loud, insulting bravos who like to denounce others without justification but who are worthy of criticism themselves. Near the *tabernae veteres* are the money-lenders, and lurking behind the Temple of Castor are even more unsavory vendors. In the *Vicus Tuscus* are the male prostitutes who are willing to do anything. In the *Velabrum* are butchers, bakers, and fortune-tellers" (Plautus, *Curculio* 470–82).

5

The People of Ancient Rome

FAMILY STRUCTURE

The duties and obligations of citizens have already been discussed in the chapter on government, so this chapter will consider the lives of some other groups of people who lived in Rome and in particular how some of the marginalized members of Roman society lived.

Rome was a male-dominated society that accorded the male head of a family, the paterfamilias ("father of the family"), enormous respect and power. He wielded *pater potestas*, "paternal power," over all the members of his extended family, including adults, children, and slaves, and this power gave him nearly unlimited authority to control the lives of his family. In the most extreme example, a paterfamilias could even put to death his own children, and this was viewed as being within his proper rights. In addition, he arranged marriages for his children and could command them to divorce, he could sell members of his family into slavery, and he could order a newborn baby to be abandoned. Naturally, he exercised complete control over lesser familial matters as well. The father's role within the family was one of authority and decision making.

Women did not have equivalent legal status with men, but Roman mothers were still expected to be strong figures within the household, playing an important role in supervising the upbringing and education of children and maintaining the smooth daily running of the household. Above all, the Roman wife was expected to be self-effacing and to provide strong support for, but not any challenges to, the paterfamilias.

It is difficult to discern from the primary sources the emotional bonds that existed within Roman families. In the idealized portraits presented in literature, the mother and father appear as rather stern and remote figures, but sometimes glimpses emerge of warmer, more intimate relationships, as in a letter written by the orator Cicero in which he expresses deep grief over the death of a daughter (Cicero, *Letter to Atticus* 12.46).

WOMEN

Roman women in poor families often had to work hard, just like the men of the family. Thus, for most women, their day-to-day lives were not a whole lot different from men's, although they were accorded inferior legal status. Women did not possess Roman citizenship, could not vote in elections or run for political office, and were not permitted to take part in the speechmaking and debates that characterized the lively public life at Rome.

Upper-class girls were raised in the household, rarely venturing outside the house itself. The chief figure in their lives was their mother, who supervised whatever education they received. In terms of reading, writing, and literature, the education that these girls obtained varied enormously from house to house. There are a few famous examples of highly educated women, but excessive knowledge or intellectual ability in women was regarded with suspicion and disfavor. The main focus of a girl's education was to learn how to spin thread and weave clothing. Eventually she would be married to a man selected by her father, often for economic or political reasons.

Once married, she became subject to her husband, who gained all the powers over her that her father had once exercised. In legal terms, she was treated like her husband's daughter; her property became his, and he even had the right to kill her if given sufficient provocation, such as discovering her committing adultery. (A husband, by contrast, could freely cheat on his wife without fear of blame or reprisal.) It was a woman's responsibility to run her husband's household, which entailed supervising the slaves and overseeing the education of their young children. Spinning wool, weaving cloth, and sewing were seen as important skills for her to possess, regardless of whether her husband could afford to buy cloth or whether the slaves could make it. Even the emperor Augustus required that his wife and daughter spin, weave, and produce the clothes for his household. While other abilities and talents in a woman were praised on occasion, suspicion was sometimes aroused by women who were considered excessively intelligent or accomplished. It was believed that cleverness could lead to improper behavior. In early Rome, even a talent for singing and dancing was viewed as an incitement to vice.

Generally speaking, a woman was supposed to spend most of her time within the confines of the household. When upper-class women did venture out of the house—to visit the marketplace, the baths, temples, or

Figure 5.1 Upper-class Roman woman making the gesture of *pudicitia* (modesty).

women friends—they were often transported in curtained litters carried by slaves, both to avoid the filth in the streets and to stay concealed and unseen in public. Women were supposed to be modest and chaste. A Roman matron's clothing was intended to cover her completely, and statues frequently depict women making a gesture to indicate their *pudicitia*, or modesty. Fidelity to one's husband was crucial. The most famous story about a heroic woman is revealing: Lucretia wins a contest as best of wives because she is at home sewing late into the night rather than visiting and gossiping with friends, and when she is raped, she commits suicide because she has betrayed her husband, albeit against her will. Although her husband and father told her she was blameless, she felt disgraced and feared that her ruined reputation would sully her family's good name. Roman girls were instructed to view Lucretia as a role model and self-sacrifice as a virtue. Cornelia, the mother of the Gracchi, was also lauded as a heroic woman: she bore 12 children who all died before her but stifled her grief and endured her losses bravely. The republican ideal of womanhood called for frugality, industriousness, restraint, piety, self-effacement, obedience to one's husband, and the ability to control one's emotions and maintain a stoical demeanor. It was considered wrong for a woman to be avaricious, ambitious, ostentatious, or self-promoting.

However, there was a certain degree of divergence between the ideal behavior of wives and the reality. Women did commit adultery and divorce their husbands in order to marry others. Particularly during the empire, some women were able to obtain a degree of legal independence. A few who were married or related to powerful men were even able to have an impact on politics and government and exercise power, such as Mark Antony's wife, Fulvia. Women who dared to assume masculine roles were derided, as when Valerius Maximus describes a small number of women advocates as being unwomanly and monstrous (Valerius Maximus, *Memorable Deeds and Sayings* 8.3). Under the empire, many writers decried the growing decadence and immorality of contemporary society and praised the good old days of early Rome, when men and women had still been virtuous. Sumptuary laws were passed to regulate the clothing and jewelry of wealthy women. Satirists lampooned women for enhancing their appearance through excessive makeup, hair dyes, and wigs, all of which were seen as suggesting dishonesty and falseness of character. Augustus instituted laws meant to promote marriage and procreation, which he thought were on the decline. The supposed deterioration of women's virtue was considered an indicator that something was wrong with society as a whole.

Comparatively little is known about the lives of lower-class women who had to work outside the home in order to help support their families or themselves. They might have worked as vendors in the marketplace or learned a trade, such as cloth making or perfume manufacturing. The medical profession was one of the few open to women; there is record of a number of female doctors, although women more commonly served as midwives and as wet nurses in wealthy families.

While women could not act onstage in theatrical productions, they could perform in mimes and pantomimes, although this imparted a shady reputation. A bad reputation also plagued women who worked at *tabernae* (taverns) as tavern keepers, waitresses, barmaids, and cooks and who were considered to be practically on the level of prostitutes—another career open to poor women. Contact with the public sphere, in whatever capacity, seems to have compromised a woman's reputation.

MARRIAGE

Roman girls led sheltered lives and many may have hardly ventured outside their homes until their marriages. Boys were considered to be ready for marriage at the age of 14, but girls were thought to be ready for marriage at 12, and a woman who was not married by 20 was considered a deviant. The emperor Augustus formalized this sentiment by passing a law that heavily penalized any woman over the age of 20 and any man over the age of 25 who was not married.

The Romans allowed marriages between closer family members than we usually do today. It was permissible for first cousins to marry, and from the early empire on, uncles could even marry their nieces. Roman law did not recognize a marriage with a foreigner, a slave, or a freedman. Also, up until AD 217, soldiers were not allowed to marry. It was, of course, common for soldiers to form long-lasting relationships with women and for the two to live together and consider themselves a couple. However, their union was not formally recognized by law. The two great drawbacks to this arrangement were that the soldiers' partners were not subject to inheritance laws, and any children they had were considered illegitimate.

At least among the aristocracy, nearly all marriages were arranged by the parents. The paterfamilias would negotiate with his counterpart in the other family to arrange the marriage. Even if two people somehow met, fell in love, and wished to marry, it was still necessary to have the permission of the paterfamilias; lacking such permission, a marriage could not occur. There were only two ways to get married without the express permission of a paterfamilias. The first was if the paterfamilias were judged to be insane, and the second was if he had been captured in war and had been a prisoner for at least three years.

Marriages were not love matches but rather were seen as political tools and as a way to cement an alliance between two families or political factions. It was extremely common for politicians to marry, divorce, and remarry as their political allegiances shifted or to contract marriages among their children. The desire to use offspring as political pawns led to children being engaged at very young ages, sometimes even as babies. In an attempt to curb this practice, a law was passed stating that to be engaged, the two people had to be at least seven years old.

To symbolize the engagement, the man (or boy) placed an iron ring on the middle finger of the left hand of his fiancée. While conducting dissections of human bodies, Roman doctors believed that they had discovered a nerve that ran directly from this finger to the heart. To make a marriage legally binding was very simple. The only requirement was a public statement of intent. Marriage was viewed as a religious duty whose goal was to produce children to ensure that the family gods would continue to be worshiped.

There were two basic types of Roman marriages. During the republic, almost all were *manus* marriages. *Manus* means "hand" in Latin, and this marriage receives its name from the fact that the woman was regarded as a piece of property that passed from the hand of the father to the hand of the husband. In this type of marriage, the woman had no rights, and any property she had was under the control of her husband. She herself was considered the equivalent of a daughter to her husband, and he had all the powers of life and death that a father holds over a daughter. There were two further subcategories of the *manus* marriage. The first was called *coemptio*. In this type of marriage, the groom symbolically gave money to the bride's father and "bought" her. The second was called *usus*. In this type, the man and woman simply began to live together, and on the day after they had lived together continuously for one year, the woman passed into the control of her husband in a *manus* marriage. Some women who did not wish to lose their independence made sure that each year they spent three consecutive nights away from their husband, and because of this they never came under his control.

The second basic type of marriage was very rare in the republic but became quite common under the empire. It was known as a free marriage, and in it the woman retained all her own property and was not under the control of her husband. If they separated, she could take anything she owned with her.

Just like today, there were many rituals associated with the marriage ceremony. First, the bride dedicated her childhood toys to the household gods, symbolizing that she was making the transition from child to woman. While still a child, she usually would have worn her hair in a ponytail, but on her wedding day, her hair was parted into six strands, which were then tied together on top of her head in a complex fashion, forming a cone shape. It was the tradition that her hair be parted using a bent iron spearhead, and the best spearhead of all was one that had been used to kill a gladiator. Gladiators were sometimes seen as symbols of virility, so perhaps this custom was viewed as a way to ensure a fertile union. The bride then donned a veil of transparent fabric that was bright orange or red, which matched her shoes. Her tunic was white, and she placed a wreath of marjoram on her head.

Before a gathering of friends and relatives, various sacrifices were performed, and the woman declared to her husband, "I am now of your family," at which point their hands were joined. This ceremony was followed by a feast at which the new bride and groom sat side by side in two chairs over which a single sheepskin was stretched. At the feast, it was customary for the guests to shout *Feliciter!*, which means "happiness" or "good luck." Toward the end of the evening, the bride was placed in the arms of her mother and the groom came and tore her out of her mother's grasp.

All this occurred at the bride's house. The bride, groom, and guests then marched to the bride's new home, the home of her husband. As they went through the streets in a torch-lit procession, the guests threw nuts and shouted *Talassio*, a traditional Roman wedding acclamation; they also often sang obscene songs. When they reached the groom's house, the couple threw one of the torches, a special one known as the wedding torch, into the crowd of guests; whoever caught it was supposed to enjoy long life. The bride then rubbed oil and fat on the doorposts, and her new husband picked her up and carried her over the threshold. Once inside, she symbolically touched fire and water, indicating that she was now the guardian of the hearth. In the entry hall was placed a miniature marriage bed intended for the spirits of the bride and groom, and after the fire and water ceremony, the new couple went off to their marriage bed.

None of this elaborate ceremony was necessary to make a marriage legal. It was the statement of intent that actually made a marriage legal, but performing some or all of these rituals was common practice.

Usually the wife's family had to provide some kind of dowry, which among very rich families could easily amount to one million sesterces, equivalent to the minimum wealth qualification for a senator. Whatever the sum, dowries were usually paid in three annual installments.

The main duty of the wife was to produce children, and because many were married before they were physically mature, not surprisingly, many young wives died from complications in childbirth. One of the main sources of information on Roman women is their tombstones. Many of these record the sad stories of girls who were married at 12 or 13, gave birth five or six times, and died in childbirth before they reached the age of 20. These tombstones are also the best guide to what Roman men considered the ideal qualities of a wife. Some of the most common positive adjectives and phrases used by husbands to describe their deceased wives include chaste, obedient, friendly, old-fashioned, frugal, content to stay at home, pious, dressed simply, good at spinning thread, and good at weaving cloth.

Conversely, one way that men were praised on their tombstones was to say that they had treated their wife kindly, with the implication that such kindness was not necessary and was unusual. In a *manus* marriage, the husband could beat his wife with impunity and was expected to do so if she misbehaved. In one famous instance, a man beat his wife to death because she took a drink of wine; all his friends and family approved since her action was seen as a clear sign of immorality. During the republic, regardless of the type of marriage, a husband could kill his wife if she was caught committing adultery. Augustus put a stop to this but still allowed husbands to kill their wives if they were found in the house committing adultery with someone of lower status. A father could kill his daughter if he caught her committing adultery as long as he killed, or at least tried to kill, her lover at the same time.

Divorce was as easy as marriage. All a couple had to do was declare that they were getting divorced, and they were. Augustus passed another law declaring that if a woman was between the ages of 20 and 50 and got divorced, she had to marry again within six months; if her husband had died, she was granted a longer time for mourning but still had to get remarried within one year.

CHILDREN

When a child was born, it was placed on the floor in front of the father. If it was a male and he wanted to acknowledge it as his son, he picked it up. This action meant that he agreed to accept it as his own son and to raise it. If it was a girl, he did not pick it up; he just instructed one of the women, either his wife or a slave, to feed it. If, for whatever reason, he did not want it, he would leave it on the floor and the child would be taken outside and abandoned.

Romans thought that in order to produce strong children and soldiers, it was important not to be too nice to babies. Thus they were always bathed in cold water, and all throughout childhood they were forbidden to take warm baths for fear that it would make them soft. For the first several months of life, the baby was tightly wrapped in cloth so it could not move, with its arms and legs tied to sticks so they could not be bent. Eventually parents freed the right arm but not the left in an attempt to make sure the baby grew up right-handed since left-handedness was regarded as unlucky. The only time infants were released was for their cold bath, at which time the nurse would also knead the baby's head to try to form it into a pleasant round shape.

A Roman boy was known as a *puer,* and the symbol of his childhood was his clothing, the *toga praetexta,* a toga with a purple stripe along the edge. Roman boys were usually given a little leather bag filled with magical amulets called the *bulla,* which was worn at all times around his neck. The Romans believed that children were vulnerable to evil influences, and wearing this *bulla* was intended to protect the child while he passed through this vulnerable state. As a further effort to toughen them up, boys were forbidden to eat lying down, which was a mark of an adult. They were also not allowed to get much sleep since it was believed that too much sleep decreased intelligence and stunted growth. Until the age of six or seven, the child was raised in the family.

All children, both free and slave, grew up together and played together. This resulted in the common phenomenon that, when grown up, personal slaves would be loyal to and fond of their masters since they were, after all, old childhood playmates. Often a man would instruct his wife to breast-feed not only her own children but the slave children as well, with the idea that when the master and the slaves grew up, the slaves would be unusually loyal since they had all been raised on the same milk.

EDUCATION

Early in Roman history, and particularly before Rome's overseas conquests, formal education was conducted by the father, who taught his son whatever he thought was necessary. The stern patrician Cato, for example, personally taught his son to read, write, use weapons, and swim. In this period, a basic level of literacy and military training was the totality of education thought necessary. Education was primarily restricted to male children.

The great change in Roman education happened, as did so many other major changes, when Rome conquered Greece. Exposure to Greek literature and culture raised expectations of what an aristocrat should know. Thereafter they would be expected to know both Greek and Latin, to be familiar with the literature of both cultures, and to be able to give formal orations in public.

The hundreds of thousands of Greek citizens who were enslaved by Rome provided a ready source of teachers. From this time on, the structure of Roman education was such that the student, who was almost always male, passed through a series of teachers, and the highest goal toward which all their education aimed was to produce an eloquent speaker.

The first of these teachers was known as the *paedagogus*. This was a household slave to whom the young boy was entrusted. Ideally the *paedagogus* was an educated Greek slave who could give the boy his preliminary instruction in Latin and Greek. Technically, the main duty of the *paedagogus* was to look after and protect the child. Thus, whenever the boy went out in public, he was always accompanied by his *paedagogus*. Another of his duties was to restrain and discipline a mischievous child, usually either by twisting his ear or beating him with a cane. Depending on their relationship, Romans tended to look back on their *paedagogus* with either fondness or hatred. There are many instances of men who, once they became adults, freed their old tutors out of gratitude. The emperor Augustus is one example.

Around the age of six or seven, the student began to go to a more formal type of school. The new teacher was not a family member but rather was a man who made individual contracts with parents to instruct their children in reading, writing, and arithmetic. He was known as the *litterator.* Often, a boy would go through a series of these teachers so that he might learn basic reading, writing, and counting from one, more sophisticated knowledge of the same subject from a second, and then go to a third who would emphasize literature. A teacher of the more advanced levels was called a *grammaticus.*

On a typical school day, classes began at dawn, so the boy had to get up long before this, get dressed, eat a simple breakfast, and then, accompanied by his *paedagogus,* walk to wherever the school was being held. If the boy was very young, he might be carried on the shoulders of the slave.

There were no actual school buildings, so classes might be held anywhere. Sometimes a teacher would rent a shop or an apartment, or he might set up his school in a corner of the Roman Forum or in a colonnade. This would certainly have made for a distracting academic environment, since the teacher and students might have found themselves trying to hold classes surrounded by the bustle of people buying and selling or officials conducting state business and trials. The teacher sat on a thronelike chair, while his pupils sat on simple benches gathered around him. There were no chalkboards or paper; instead, students had small, wooden tablets with a shallow indentation filled with wax to write upon. Into this wax, they scratched out their lessons. The instrument they used to write with, a metal cylinder pointed at one end and flattened at the other, was called a *stilus.* For doing math, they might employ an abacus.

Since texts were extremely expensive and fragile, only the teacher would likely have any. Therefore, much of Roman education consisted of the teacher reading aloud from these texts and the students memorizing long passages by heart. The lack of visual aids could sometimes be overcome by imaginative teachers. One *grammaticus* who specialized in teaching the alphabet had a large troop of slaves, each of whom had a giant wooden copy of one of the letters of the alphabet strapped to his back.

Classes lasted from dawn until noon, but there were some holidays when the students got off from class. The main break was summer vacation, which usually started around early June and lasted until the middle of October. This was not a fixed schedule, however, and depended on the individual teacher; one particularly zealous *grammaticus* kept his students in class almost all the way through July.

The two main characteristics of this phase of schooling were endless amounts of memorization reinforced by brutal beatings whenever a student failed to perform properly. The teacher had a wide range of punishments available. The most common and simplest was to have the student hold out his hands or lay them flat on a piece of wood, and the teacher would then beat them with a cane made of reeds. For more egregious offenses, the teacher would beat the student's body with a whip consisting of multiple strips of leather. The ultimate punishment was the *catomus,* for which the student was stripped naked and stretched out across the backs of two other students, one of whom would grasp his legs and the other his arms. The unfortunate victim was then savagely flogged with a wooden stick by the teacher. In view of this, it is not surprising that many Romans' memories of school were not pleasant and that they often referred to their old teachers not by their names but instead by suggestive nicknames such as "The Whacker."

The last couple years of this instruction focused on literature, particularly on Homer, and Roman historical literature, including Virgil. This phase of education usually ended around the age of 13 or so.

There were no colleges or universities. The wealthiest, most ambitious, or most promising students went on to a third class of instructor known as the *rhetor.* The *rhetor* was a specialist in training students to be effective public speakers. Oratory, or the art of public speaking, was a central component of the career of anyone who wanted to be in the Roman government or army. Since everything about Roman life was public, the ability to get up in public and persuade others of your opinion was a highly prized talent.

The students began by composing and delivering short speeches about mythological topics. These were simply descriptive essays. In the next phase, they prepared comparisons. Some topics included comparing Homeric heroes such as Achilles and Odysseus, seafaring with agriculture, or town versus country life. The next step up in complexity was for the students to put themselves in the place of a famous mythological character and compose a speech he might have given in a certain situation. This exercise emphasized psychological insight and imagination. One popular topic was Achilles talking over the body of his dead friend Patroclus. The ultimate level of their training involved doing the same thing using real historical events, as this was felt to be the best preparation for the speeches they would actually have to give.

SLAVES

Today when we think of slavery, we tend to imagine the form of slavery practiced in the American South, but Roman slavery was a very different institution for a number of reasons. The first and by far the biggest difference is that Roman slavery was not racial slavery. There was absolutely no correlation between race and slavery. Slaves were any and all races, cultures, ages, and genders. A second major difference is that the line between slave and free person was not rigid. It was a permeable boundary through which large numbers of people passed in both directions. A great many slaves were eventually freed, and perhaps even greater numbers of free people became slaves.

The most common source of slaves in the Roman world was military conquest. Whenever a Roman army took the field, it was inevitably followed by a train of slave dealers. The soldiers caught people and sold them on the spot to the slave dealers, who in turn sent them to one of the great slave markets; for example, the markets of the strategically located island of Rhodes could process tens of thousands of slaves each day. The number of slaves generated by Rome's wars was truly astounding. Rome's destruction of Carthage in the Third Punic War glutted the slave markets with a quarter million new slaves at once. In the course of Julius Caesar's campaigns in Gaul, his legions sold over a million people into slavery. Other sources of slaves included children born of slaves and free people becoming slaves as the result of legal action, most commonly when they fell into debt and were unable to pay it off. Sometimes abandoned children were picked up by slave dealers and raised as slaves. Finally, desperate free people could actually voluntarily sell members of their family, or even themselves, into slavery.

An unskilled, adult male slave might sell for around 2,000 sesterces, but obviously skilled slaves could sell for considerably more. Slaves could be bought outright, which was most common, but some dealers ran rental businesses in which a slave could be rented for a certain period ranging from a few hours to an entire year.

Under law, slaves were regarded as property, just like any other object owned by their master. Thus, when a slave ran away, the actual crime he was committing in the Romans' eyes was theft because he had stolen himself from his master. Varro famously offered a classification of types of property one might find on a farm. To him, all objects used by the farmer were tools, of which there were three types: "dumb tools" were things like wagons or baskets; "semiarticulate tools" were animals, such as oxen; and, finally, there were the "articulate tools," slaves (Varro, *On Agriculture* 1.17.1).

The lifestyle of Roman slaves could vary enormously, and one significant distinction was between rural and urban slaves. Rural slaves were unskilled farm workers whose lives were often very harsh. They were frequently chained together or had their feet chained and spent their time doing heavy manual labor in the fields under the eyes of cruel overseers. At night, they were locked up in a jail-like enclosure known as an *ergastulum*. This type of slave was rarely freed by his master and had little to look forward to in life. Cato the Elder wrote down his advice for managing rural slaves, which included the callous suggestion that if a slave became too sick or too old to work, he should be sold so that the owner didn't have to waste any food on him (Cato the Elder, *On Agriculture* 2.7).

Urban slavery encompassed a much wider range of experiences. Some of these slaves, particularly family ones raised together with the master's children, were the confidantes and even friends of their masters and might receive educations, have their own families, and live nearly as well as the free members of the family. Many skilled professions, such as teacher, carpenter, doctor, and clerk, were often practiced by slaves who enjoyed, at least to some degree, the high standard of living and the respect due to one with their talents. The imperial bureaucracy included huge numbers of slaves as clerks and accountants, and public services such as aqueduct maintenance were conducted by slaves as well.

Many of these slaves cherished the hope that they might actually buy their freedom from their masters through an odd Roman institution known as the *peculium*. A *peculium* was a fund of money that the slave was allowed to save up, and once it reached his own value, he could give it to his master and literally buy his own way out of slavery. The *peculium* was viewed by the Romans as an incentive for slaves to work harder. Thus, a master might tell a slave who was a teacher that he could keep 5 percent of all the tuition money that he generated or a slave who worked as a salesman that he could keep 5 percent of the profits from the sales he generated. With this incentive, presumably the slave would work harder and generate more money for his master. Romans usually calculated that it would take a particularly industrious slave approximately seven years to build up his *peculium* to the level at which he could buy his freedom.

Many urban slaves were also freed outright by their masters. The act of freeing a slave was known as manumission. Manumission most commonly occurred either posthumously in a will or when a man became a paterfamilias and freed his childhood slave friends. So many Romans were freeing slaves in their wills that Augustus actually passed a law prohibiting anyone from freeing more than 100 slaves in a will. When a slave was freed, he was presented with a floppy, cone-shaped red hat that was known as the liberty cap, which he was supposed to wear to demonstrate his new status.

Because of the sheer number of slaves in Roman society, the Romans were extremely fearful—almost paranoid—that their slaves would turn against them. The most obvious example of this is a law stating that if a slave killed his master, then all the slaves owned by that person would be put to death. The harshness with which some Romans punished their children and each other for misbehavior was extended to their slaves, who might be whipped, beaten, and tortured for the slightest error.

Once, at a dinner party that Augustus attended, one of the slaves serving the meal dropped a glass and broke it. The master ordered that the slave be thrown into a pool of man-eating lampreys. Augustus intervened to save the slave, but this incident is representative of the sort of punishment meted out for even trivial offenses. Even normally humane slave owners might abuse their slaves in moments of anger, and again this illustrates how slaves were regarded as property more than as human beings. Augustus once had both legs broken of a slave who had annoyed him, and when another slave ate one of the emperor's fighting quails, Augustus had him nailed alive to the mast of a ship. Also, in a moment of annoyance, the culture-loving and enlightened emperor Hadrian stabbed one of his slaves in the eye with a *stilus.*

Urban slaves who misbehaved were threatened with being sent to the country to work on a farm. Slaves were often branded to mark them as such, and many times the branding was done on the face so that the slave could not hide the marks with clothing. Some masters outfitted their slaves with iron collars from which were hung tags inscribed with messages such as "If you find this slave, he has run away. Please return him to his owner at the following address." These were exactly the same as modern dog tags in both purpose and appearance. When slaves were summoned as witnesses in law cases, the only way their testimony was considered valid was if they had been tortured.

Despite such instances of cruelty, some masters treated their slaves with great kindness. Pliny the Younger, who owned 4,116 slaves, was very concerned about the health of his slaves and bragged that he did not place chains on his agricultural slaves. Once when a favorite slave contracted tuberculosis, Pliny sent him on a luxurious cruise up the Nile River in Egypt to recuperate.

Romans were always fearful that their slaves would band together against them. An indication of the depths of their fear can be seen in the fact that, despite their obsession with public pronouncements and indications of status, a proposal that all slaves should be made to wear some distinguishing item of clothing was rejected on the grounds that if slaves were able to recognize one another, they would realize how vast their numbers really were and be incited to rebellion.

During the republic, there were a number of times when groups of slaves rose in rebellion against their masters. The most famous of these slave revolts was led by Spartacus, a Thracian who had served as an auxiliary in the Roman army. Later falling into slavery, he was sent to the gladiator school at Capua. In 73 BC, he led his fellow gladiators in slaughtering their overseers and then pillaging the countryside. He collected a huge army of 90,000 slaves, barbarians, and discontented people and defeated three Roman armies and two consuls as he marched up Italy. His army successfully reached the Alps, at which point Spartacus urged his followers to disband and escape back to their homes in the north. His army had developed a taste for plundering, however, and refused, so Spartacus led them back down into Italy. Eventually he was cornered near the heel of Italy by three Roman armies. Spartacus negotiated with several pirate fleets to transport his army away, but at the last moment they deserted him, and Spartacus and most of his followers were killed in a battle. The 6,000 who were captured were crucified on the Appian Way, so for hundreds of miles along this main road there was a constant row of crucified slaves serving as a warning to any others who might revolt. Indeed, after this, there were no other major slave revolts.

During the Roman Empire, laws were gradually changed to ensure more humane treatment of slaves, and once Christianity became a dominant force, it also caused slaves to be endowed with more rights and receive better treatment. Roman slavery was a curious mixture of brutality and kindness, oppression and hope. The most famous stories are those of the lucky slaves who obtained their freedom and went on to experience success. At the time of his death, one ex-slave owned 7,200 oxen, had a net worth of 60 million sesterces, and himself owned 4,000 slaves. Such stories, though, represent the exception, and a more typical attitude can perhaps be summed up in the words of a slave in a Roman play by Plautus: "Being a slave, you have to suffer many injustices. It's a hard burden to bear" (Plautus, *Amphitryon* 174–5).

FREEDMEN

When a slave was manumitted by his master, he became known as a freedman, and due to the large number of urban slaves who received their freedom, they formed a significant portion of the population of Rome. If a slave was freed in a will, the public reading of the will was the official, legal way that the slave was freed. If a man wanted to free his slave while still alive, the master and the slave had to appear before the praetor and the master declare his intention to set his slave free. At this point, the praetor touched the slave with a rod, and this action was what legally freed the slave.

All free citizens were divided into two groups. The *ingenuus* group consisted of people who were born free and therefore had higher status. The other group, the *libertinus*, had formerly been slaves but had gained their freedom. A freedman received a liberty cap, which was the most obvious symbol of his new status.

Even though a freedman was technically a citizen, there were a number of restrictions and obligations placed upon him that in reality made him inferior to free-born citizens. A freedman was excluded from holding high office or becoming a senator. A freedwoman was not allowed to marry a senator. A freedman could never bring any legal charges against his former master. The main obligation placed upon him was that a freedman became the client of his former master. All clients were expected to honor, respect, and help their patrons, but the expectations were the greatest by far if your patron had been your former master. A freedman client was expected to treat his ex-master with *obsequium*, the respect that a child should show his or her father. Considering the power of the paterfamilias in Roman society, this was a heavy burden. Freedmen also owed their ex-master something called *operae*—literally, "days." A freedman was expected to donate a certain number of days' labor to his master every year for the rest of his life. The number of days varied, but it could be as much as a couple of weeks.

Freedmen who had gained special skills or training under their former master had to ensure that they did not compete for business with him. Thus, for example, if a doctor had freed one of his slaves and the slave desired to put the knowledge he had gained to use by setting up a medical practice himself, he was required either to move to a different city from that of his master or, if he stayed in the same city, to pay his master a portion of his income as compensation for any patients he might take away.

On the other side of the relationship, the ex-master in his role as patron was expected to help and assist his protégé. In addition, a master was not allowed to revoke his manumission unless the freedman acted ungratefully toward his former master. If a master could prove that a freedman had not treated him with the respect or gratitude that society deemed appropriate, the praetor could (and would) take away his freedom and make him a slave once again to his former master.

Freedmen had an interesting and awkward status in Roman society. People who were *ingenuus* looked down on freedmen and despised them as social inferiors. Since most slaves were captives of war and thus foreigners by birth, people who had been born citizens, and particularly those who were Italian, were extremely resentful that so many foreigners were being granted citizenship. This resentment could turn to hatred because freed-men sometimes became very wealthy. Since those slaves who were freed were those most likely to have acquired a professional talent or skill, once freed often they were able to amass considerable wealth. Many professionals in Rome were freedmen, as were most merchants and small-business owners. However, while they were often better off than the free-born poor, the majority of freedmen probably only attained modest means.

There were nevertheless a few rare cases of freedmen who became fantastically wealthy, and these few tended to capture the public's imagination, creating the misconception that these foreign-born ex-slaves were getting rich at the expense of "real" citizens. Such freedmen are an example of "status dissonance." Status dissonance occurs when an individual becomes powerful in some way that does not seem to correspond to his formal place in the social hierarchy. Thus with freedmen, the dissonance occurred because, although they were denied the right to hold office and belonged to a despised social class, they were able to acquire as much wealth as an equestrian or senator.

One of the most famous rags-to-riches stories of a freedman involved a man named Ctesippus. He was a slave who worked in a laundry as a fuller. This was a particularly demeaning job since the way Romans bleached clothes was to immerse them in human urine and then have slaves stomp on them. Ctesippus thus spent his days stomping around waist-deep in vats of urine. Eventually the laundry went out of business and all of its property was auctioned off. An old, rich widow who had attained independent status bought a candelabrum at the auction, and as a sort of bonus, the auctioneer threw in Ctesippus for free. He charmed his new mistress and became her lover. She freed him, and when she died a little bit later, she left him her entire fortune, which instantly made the ex-fuller one of the richest men in Rome.

Because of instances like this, a common way to refer to freedmen was to call them "the sons of fortune," a title implying both the degree to which their lives were ruled by chance and the wealth with which some of them unexpectedly ended up. This led to a popular stereotype of the freedman as a vulgar, boorish person lacking social graces but addicted to luxury and to ostentatious displays of his wealth. The most famous portrait of such a freedman is the character of Trimalchio in Petronius's novel, *The Satyricon.* Banned from both political and social life, many freedmen got their revenge after death by having enormous, elaborate tombs made to draw attention to themselves posthumously.

Another famous freedman was Cicero's personal slave, Tiro. Tiro had been Cicero's faithful companion throughout his life and had received an education equal to his master's. His official duty as a slave had been to be Cicero's personal secretary, and to keep up with his master's verbosity, Tiro invented a system of shorthand note taking, which others imitated. Even after he was freed, Tiro devoted himself to cataloging and publishing Cicero's writings. After Cicero's death, Tiro wrote a biography of his former master, which, interestingly, was not completely positive.

The Romans were famous for having a minimalist bureaucracy, and nowhere is this more apparent than in the fact that emperors were not provided with any official staff to assist them. Thus, despite having to personally rule over a gigantic empire and to make important political and economic decisions, emperors had to rely on their own servants to run the state. Therefore, the slaves and freedmen of the emperor became the most important officials in the government. The emperors' freedmen, in particular, became notorious for the powers they wielded, not the least of which was controlling who got access to the emperor. If someone wanted to petition the emperor or get an audience with him, the best strategy was to bribe one of the freedmen who acted as his secretaries. Because of this, some imperial freedmen amassed gigantic fortunes.

The most famous of these was a freedman named Narcissus, who was the personal secretary to the emperor Claudius. Taking full advantage of the opportunities presented by his position, Narcissus acquired a fortune of 400 million sesterces. This is the single largest fortune known from antiquity to have been possessed by someone other than a king or head of state. It is easy to see how individuals such as Narcissus and Ctesippus aroused the jealousy and hatred of free-born citizens, and despite their influence, freedmen were always regarded with suspicion and often hostility. Over time, however, many senators were the grandsons or great-grandsons of freedmen. Rome was unusual in the upward mobility that an admittedly small, yet influential, number of people was able to attain.

SOLDIERS

Throughout the republic, there was no regular contingent of soldiers stationed in the city of Rome. This changed when Augustus established the Praetorian Guard, who were intended to serve as bodyguards for the emperor. Originally this unit was composed of nine cohorts of 500 men each, drawn from men of Italian origin. The Praetorians enjoyed a number of perks denied to ordinary soldiers, including higher status, and they received double pay. Subsequent emperors, including Tiberius, expanded and refounded the guard. The number of soldiers in each cohort was doubled to 1,000, and the number of cohorts was raised, first to 12 and eventually to 16. Each cohort also had attached to it a squadron of cavalry, for a total of 1,200 additional troops.

Augustus also set up a group known as the Urban Cohorts, whose principal duty was to maintain order in the city. Originally there were three cohorts of 500 men each, although these too were soon doubled to 1,000. Many of the emperors also made use of a group of fiercely loyal personal bodyguards, usually numbering around 500, who were frequently drawn from frontier groups such as the Germans.

Figure 5.2 Sculptural relief of Roman legionaries showing typical arms and armor from the early empire.

When other paramilitary units, such as the fire-fighting *vigiles,* are included, we see that the total number of armed soldiers in the city of Rome steadily increased, from around 8,000 under Augustus at the beginning of the first century AD to 13,000–20,000 under Trajan at the beginning of the second century AD to 26,000–32,000 by the time of Septimius Severus at the beginning of the third century AD. While Rome is not often thought of as being a militarized city, the sheer number of troops stationed there during the empire would have made their presence in the streets of the city very visible. The ratio of soldiers to civilians in the city increased from around 1:125 under Augustus to perhaps as high as 1:25 by the third century AD, at which time the troops stationed in Rome numbered the equivalent of five or six legions.

Housing this many soldiers presented its own difficulties. Originally the troops seem to have been quartered at various locations scattered in and around the city, but the need for a more centralized, permanent billet soon became obvious. In AD 23, the emperor Tiberius constructed a fortress on the northeast edge of the city to house the Praetorian Guard and the Urban Cohorts in one place. This fortress, known as the Castra Praetoria, consisted of a rectangular circuit of walls 440 meters long by 380 meters wide covering just over 41 acres. The walls, made of concrete with brick facing, were 4.73 meters high, and there were gateways at the center of each of the four walls.

The interior of the camp was taken up mostly by barracks to house the soldiers as well as by the necessary attendant storerooms, armories, administrative buildings, and shrines. The camp was laid out using the sort of grid pattern standard for all Roman military installations, including even temporary legionary marching camps. Granaries were also located within the walls so that the guard was not dependent on the city for food supplies. One weakness was that the camp lacked an internal source of water, and this became an issue on at least one occasion when the camp was besieged.

The space enclosed by this fortress was not overly large for the number of men stationed there and, particularly after the number of praetorians was increased, would have been fairly crowded. More barrack space was probably obtained by adding extra stories to the existing buildings, forming the military equivalent of *insulae* (apartment buildings). Immediately in front of the camp in the direction of the city was a large, open space used as a parade ground and mustering area for the troops. This was known as the Campus Praetoriarum.

Eventually the Urban Cohorts were split off from the Praetorian Guard and given their own lodgings and camp in a different region of the city. The barbarian personal bodyguards of the emperor were often housed in the Transtiberim region, and the *vigiles,* the fire-fighting force, were strategically scattered throughout the city in seven stations.

The duties of the Praetorian Guard included accompanying the emperor wherever he went, and its protection was also extended to the other members of the imperial family. One cohort was always on duty on the Palatine hill in and around the imperial palace. The Praetorians were usually fully equipped with arms and armor, but occasionally, when a less obtrusive presence was desired, they would dress in togas—although with swords concealed beneath their garments. These troops must have played a significant role in the economy of the city, due in particular to their high salaries, and one can easily imagine that they contributed substantially to the prosperity of many bars, restaurants, and brothels. The scorpion frequently appears as a badge on the standards, helmets, and spears of Praetorians and is perhaps a reference to the guard's permanent establishment by Tiberius, since this was his zodiacal birth sign.

The Praetorian Guard's history as protector of the emperor is mixed since, on a number of occasions, emperors were assassinated by members of their own guard. They often played a role in the selection of the next emperor, most notably when their acclamations elevated Claudius to the throne in AD 41. After defeating Maxentius, the emperor Constantine abolished the Praetorian Guard as a permanent organization in the early fourth century AD, and the Praetorian camp was demolished at the same time.

6

Living and Dying in Ancient Rome

The inhabitants of the countryside lived in houses made of stone or mud brick, often with several generations of the family sharing rooms along with farm animals. Rich people in the city lived in a house called a *domus,* from which our word *domestic* is derived. The wealthy often also owned sumptuous country villas. The majority of people living in Rome, however, rented apartments.

A document known as the *Regionary Catalog* lists all the different buildings in ancient Rome and includes the number of houses and apartment buildings in the city. At the time the list was made in the fourth century AD, there were 1,797 buildings identified as a *domus,* but there were 46,602 apartment buildings. This difference is even more pronounced if you consider that each *domus* only contained one family, but an apartment building could shelter dozens of families.

DOMUS: PRIVATE HOMES

Roman houses in the city had few or no windows, and from the outside, a house would seem like a blank wall. The center of the house, and its focal point, was the atrium—a courtyard with a large opening in the ceiling to admit light. The entryway to the house, called the *vestibulum,* usually connected directly to the atrium. In the center of the atrium there was often a pool of water, the *impluvium.* Opening onto the atrium was a raised platform called the *tablinum,* which was where the paterfamilias would sit when receiving visitors of lower status. For example, when a

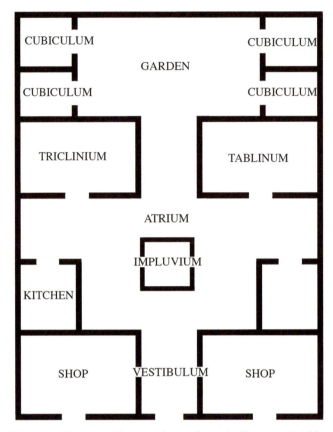

Figure 6.1 Diagram of a typical Roman *domus* (house). (Gregory S. Aldrete, Phaeton Group, Scientific Graphic Services Division.)

man's clients came every morning to pay their respects at the *salutatio,* the patron would greet them seated in the *tablinum.* The dining room, or *triclinium,* also usually opened onto the atrium. In the back of the house was a series of tiny rooms that served as bedrooms. Each of these was called a *cubiculum.* The quarters for slaves and women were also at the rear of the house. Some Roman houses also included a walled area at the back that was open to the sky and served as a garden. Roman houses were more or less the same range of sizes as modern houses, with the average house measuring around 184 square meters.

The most obvious and famous feature of these houses was the lavish decoration of the walls and floors. Much of the expense and effort that, in a modern home, might be spent on furniture and decorative objects, the Romans directed toward ornamenting the structure itself. In many rooms, all four walls were plastered over and then completely covered with elaborate wall paintings, while the floors were coated with intricate mosaics.

To a modern viewer, the palette of colors employed in Roman wall paintings might well appear strange, dominated as it was by large expanses of black, gold, and a distinctive, deep blood-red shade. Art historians have divided the types of wall paintings into four basic styles, a system that, while being somewhat reductionist and arbitrary, nonetheless gives a sense of chronological development. The earliest phase, known as First Style wall painting, features panels painted to look like marble blocks, along with three-dimensional molded cornices and other elements protruding from the wall in low relief. The Second Style is characterized by columns painted on the wall at regular intervals and, between them, increasingly complex illusionistic panels that attempt to give the impression of three-dimensionality and depth as if the viewer were looking through a series of windows. These scenes often consisted of fantastic cityscapes or architectural vistas of arches, tripods, gardens, and buildings. The Third Style employs large, plain rectangles of solid colors within which are painted smaller rectangular paintings, creating an effect reminiscent of a series of pictures hung on a wall. Mythological scenes and human figures were frequent subject matter for these pictures. The Fourth Style encompasses a variety of effects, such as painted architectural elements rendered in a spindly, attenuated style and small, delicately painted garlands, designs, and figures.

Floor mosaics were made by taking very small, cut pieces of colored stones and pressing them into wet mortar to create images ranging in complexity from simple black-and-white geometric patterns to astonishingly detailed color pictures. The subject matter of these mosaics was extremely diverse, with some of the most elaborate examples depicting historical scenes, mythological stories, wild beasts both exotic and mundane, and realistically rendered sea life.

By current standards, Roman houses would have appeared surprisingly empty. Much of the basic furniture was made of bronze. To sit on, Romans could choose from an assortment of bronze chairs, stools, and sofas with varying numbers of legs. Several types of low, bronze braziers testify to attempts to heat the cold house interiors in the winter. Marble was also employed for benches and tables, and some of the more elegant types featured elaborately carved legs and supports. In addition to furniture, smaller household objects would have included a full range of pots and pans, eating utensils, wood and wax tablets to write on, and the ubiquitous olive oil–burning clay lamps that brought light to dark interiors.

The *domus,* or aristocratic Roman house, was not so much the dwelling place of a nuclear family but rather of an extended household, including relatives, slaves, and servants. Roman homes do not seem to have had pronounced internal divisions among areas inhabited by men, women, and children or even between master and slave, and standards of privacy were probably less than what many modern people are accustomed to.

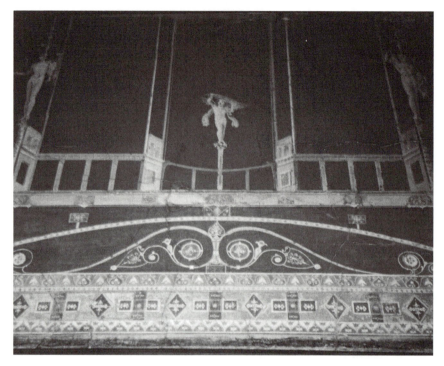

Figure 6.2 Roman wall painting with illusionistic painted architectural elements.

The rooms tended to serve multiple purposes as well. The atrium, for example, was a site where the male head of the household might receive clients, meet with peers, and conduct business, but it was also a space shared by his wife, and it served as a playground for his children. The Romans believed that a person's house reflected the owner's character and status, and the social function of the house included significant public as well as private uses. The patron-client system that bound together Romans of different ranks and statuses involved a number of social rituals that took place in the main rooms of the *domus* or in the street in front of it.

INSULAE: APARTMENT BUILDINGS

In Rome and other big cities, only a tiny percentage of urban Romans could afford their own homes. The rest lived in high-rise apartment buildings. The Romans called them *insulae*, or "islands," because of the way they often occupied entire city blocks. *Insulae* were located all over the city of Rome, and some of the larger ones might have had 10 or more stories. Because of the destruction caused by poorly built *insulae* collapsing, emperors set limits on the height of *insulae* several times. Usually these limits were around 60 or 70 Roman feet (20–25 meters), and the fact that

Figure 6.3 Reconstruction of a typical Roman *insulae* (apartment building) from Ostia. (Drawing by Alicia Aldrete, Phaeton Group, Scientific Graphic Services Division.)

the emperors felt the need to repeatedly pass such legislation suggests that these limits were routinely ignored. The poet Martial mentions one wretched *insulae* dweller who had to trudge up 200 stairs to reach his squalid apartment in the attic (Martial, *Epigrams* 7.20).

Insulae housed a wide variety of tenants of differing socioeconomic classes. The ground-floor apartments would have been rented to the wealthiest tenants, who did not want to have to climb up many flights of stairs to reach their dwellings. Often, the row of rooms opening onto the street was rented out as shops and small businesses. As you climbed up the levels of the *insulae,* the wealth of the tenants declined and the number of people per room increased. The least desirable rooms, located under the eaves of the roof, frequently leaked and were inhabited by vermin. A chamber pot served as a toilet, and despite legislation prohibiting such actions, full pots were routinely dumped out the window.

Romans living in such apartments would have had a much more rudimentary set of possessions than was owned by wealthy Romans in a *domus*. Their sum total of worldly goods may have been nothing more than some clothing, bedding, footwear, a lamp, cookware and utensils, and perhaps some crude furniture. The poet Juvenal lists the belongings that one unfortunate *insulae* dweller lost in a fire, which consisted only of

Figure 6.4 Reconstruction of the interior courtyard of a Roman *insulae* (apartment building). In this drawing, the lower stories are being used for commercial purposes to store and sell goods while the upper floors are being used as apartments. (From G. Gatteschi, *Restauri della Roma Imperiale*, 1924, p. 19.)

an undersized bed, a cupboard, an old storage chest, six cups, a flagon, and a statue (Juvenal, *Satires* 3.203–8).

Ancient sources record numerous instances of *insulae* collapsing, but Roman law did not offer tenants much protection. Juvenal describes the walls of a typical *insulae* as having gaping cracks, which the unscrupulous landlord attempted to conceal, and only the liberal use of wooden props prevented the whole edifice from immediately crumbling to the ground (Juvenal, *Satires* 3.193–96).

The owners of *insulae* included many famous Romans, and the orator Marcus Tullius Cicero was one such slumlord who owned several *insulae*, including one that collapsed because it was so poorly made. Cicero expressed no concern for the lives lost in the disaster and cheerfully noted that he would rebuild it and be able to charge higher rents for the new building (Cicero, *Letters to Atticus* 14.9, 14.11).

HEALTH AND MEDICINE

As with many other aspects of their culture and arts, the Romans got their ideas about medicine from the Greeks. The most influential of these sources was the philosopher Aristotle, who recorded the classic interpretation of how the body functioned that would be accepted and used for hundreds of years. He believed that all things were composed of four elements: earth, air, fire, and water. These produced in the human body four corresponding forces or fluids called humors: dry, moist, hot, and cold.

The equilibrium among these humors determined the health of the body. The ideal combination was one that favored hot and dry, and the worst was moist and cold. The Greeks believed that men were superior; hence, their bodies were considered hot and dry. Women, who were inferior, were consequently dominated by moist and cold humors. When a person's humors got out of balance, it caused disease. Thus, much of a doctor's practice was devoted to restoring the balance among the humors.

In early Roman society, the Romans seemed to have felt a disdain for physicians and relied on folk remedies for cures. For example, a cure for jaundice directed sufferers to concoct a mixture of ashes from a deer's antler and the blood of an ass diluted in wine (Pliny the Elder, *Natural History* 28.64). All things associated with the body got similar treatment. Sleepiness could be cured by taking calluses from a donkey, soaking them in vinegar, and thrusting them up your nostrils—a procedure that might well jar one awake (Pliny the Elder, *Natural History* 28.67).

The stereotypical traditional Roman was a man named Cato the Elder, who despised doctors. He wrote several books on how to run a farm so his advice became well known. His recommended cure for everything was cabbage. To Cato, cabbage was a miracle substance. Eating it could cure ulcers, headaches, tumors, arthritis, and heart disease. If you fried it, it cured insomnia, and if you dried it, crushed it into a powder, and inhaled it, it would cure respiratory ailments. If boiled, it cured ear problems (Cato the Elder, *On Agriculture* 157).

A common Roman belief was that many diseases of the body were caused by diseases of the soul. Problems with the mind caused problems with the body. They posited links between virtue and good health and between immorality and disease. One reason Cato thought there was no need for doctors is that they were unnecessary if you lived a virtuous life.

The only real need for doctors, therefore, was for problems clearly not caused by behavior. These included injuries such as trauma, broken bones, cuts, and wounds received in war. Since Rome was at war so often, the treatment of wounds caused by weapons was of particular concern.

In 219 BC, the Roman state brought a Greek doctor from Greece and set him up at Rome for the specific purpose of treating military injuries. This was the first known doctor at Rome, and the Romans even granted him citizenship. At first, he was popular, but he quickly got a bad reputation because he was very quick to resort to the knife to cure any ailment. Due to his fondness for amputation, he was given the nickname "The Executioner" (Pliny the Elder, *Natural History* 39.12).

Despite this bad experience, Greek doctors were soon coming to Rome in great numbers and setting up practices. Patients were mostly the wealthy, who were the only ones who could afford their fees, which one paid either per visit or per disease. The best doctors were always thought to come from the East, in particular from Greece and Egypt. No official certification process and no standardized training or schooling were required to become a physician. Anyone who wanted to could proclaim himself a doctor, and many quacks set up practices.

One of the most famous doctors was a man named Celsus. He wrote down a number of principles for treating patients, many of which sound quite modern. The core of his beliefs was that good health came from living a healthy lifestyle, including exercise, proper sleep, and a well-balanced diet.

Celsus was interested in the psychological aspects of medicine as well. He instructed doctors not to tell patients with a fatal prognosis the truth because it would depress them and cause them to give up. If a doctor had to tell bad news, he should break it to the patient gently. He thought that the outcome of a case depended equally on three factors: the patient, the doctor, and the disease itself. He also noted that the rich were the most trouble as patients because they constantly made demands and expected an instant cure.

Galen, born in AD 128 in the East, was the most famous and influential of all Roman doctors. He studied philosophy and then medicine under other doctors in several cities and for five years was the doctor of a gladiator school, which would have given him firsthand experience with trauma wounds. Finally he came to Rome, where he became the doctor to the imperial family and other aristocratic people.

Galen was very idealistic. He thought that the best physician was half doctor and half philosopher. He also wrote that a good doctor should despise money and that profit was incompatible with art. He criticized doctors who practiced medicine to get rich and instead thought of it as a philosophical art. In keeping with this philosophical bent, he was a follower of Aristotle's theory of the four humors, which he further elaborated upon. He believed the three most important organs were the liver, heart, and brain.

Galen thought that to understand how the body worked, one had to practice dissection, but because there were moral proscriptions against cutting up humans, he had to experiment on animals. He dissected many pigs and goats and once even an elephant. His animal of choice for dissection, however, was the ape, because he thought they were most like humans. He ran experiments such as feeding apes colored water and then cutting them open to see where it went. He criticized doctors who did not study anatomy for their ignorance.

Galen wrote several important texts recording the results of his experiments, including *On the Uses of the Parts of the Body* and *Bones for Beginners*. Physicians such as Galen still primarily prescribed treatments based on plants and potions. Actual surgery was not practiced much, except in the army.

Each Roman legion had one or more doctors, each of whom was called a *medicus* (the root of the words *medicine* and *medic*). For stab wounds that penetrated the abdomen and pierced the intestines, the result was almost always fatal due to the infection that would inevitably set in; for these, the *medicus* could do little. Thus, most of his practice consisted of stitching up shallow cuts, setting broken bones, and amputating severely injured limbs. There was no effective anesthesia, although sometimes Romans tried to use root of mandrake as a drug or plied their patients with alcohol.

One specialized job of military doctors was to remove arrows. The problem with arrows was that the head of the arrow was often barbed and thus could not be pulled out without ripping the flesh. There were two solutions to this dilemma. The *medicus* could push the arrow until it came out the other side. For injuries in areas of the body where this method was not practical, they developed a special instrument called the Scoop of Diocles. It consisted of a set of spoon-shaped cups on long handles. These were worked into the body until the cups were positioned around the barbs of the arrowhead, and then the arrow and scoops could be pulled out without tearing additional flesh.

Overall, Roman medicine was fairly primitive. They had no concept of bacterial or viral causes of diseases, there was not much surgery that could be performed, and doctors relied heavily on magical potions. Despite all this, they did fairly well at treating trauma, and the enlightened attitudes of men like Celsus and Galen helped to establish medicine as a valid, educated profession with ethical standards rather than merely a group of con artists.

BURIAL

Romans had enormous reverence for their ancestors, who were the focal point of family rituals. Naturally, the moment at which someone became an ancestor was when he or she died, so it is no surprise that death and burial were subjects of great concern to the Romans. Despite this reverence and concern, however, when a Roman died, the fate of his or her body was ultimately dependent on his or her economic status in life.

The very poorest Romans sometimes received no burial at all and were simply tossed into open pits called *puticuli* just outside the city walls. This name possibly derives from the verb *putescare*, meaning "to rot or decompose," or from the word *putor*, meaning "a terrible smell." These suggestively named pits contained a mixture of human and animal corpses, garbage, and excrement. Some of them were quite large, and one is estimated to contain 24,000 corpses. The Roman authorities were concerned that having these pits so close to Rome did not reflect well on the city, so they attempted to pass legislation aimed at forcing people to dump their corpses farther away from the city. All around Rome, there were stones inscribed with senate decrees ordaining that corpses and garbage be carried farther than the marker. These warnings do not seem to have done much good, however.

Anyone who could afford to joined a burial club. The usual entry fee was around 100 sesterces, a fair amount of money for a person of average means, and new members sometimes also had to provide a jar of good wine. In addition, one had to pay monthly dues, which appear to have been quite modest. In one club, for example, the monthly dues were only one and one-quarter sesterces. Interestingly, some of these clubs seem to have consisted of mixtures of slaves and free people. If a member of the club died, the others would pay for the funeral expenses. If someone committed suicide, however, he was considered to have forfeited his right to a funeral. Burial clubs had elaborate sets of formal rules governing precisely what the members had to do for each other. For example, there were different requirements if someone died within the city, outside the city limits but within 20 Roman miles, or at a distance of more than 20 miles from the city.

At times, a burial club would pool its money to buy a mausoleum where urns containing the ashes of cremated members could be kept. These were sometimes dug into the ground like caves. These structures were called columbaria. Some of these are quite large, with niches provided for up to 700 urns. One way for the club to earn money was to rent out some of the extra spaces to nonmembers. Very often, attached to the columbaria were dining facilities, where they would hold their feasts. In addition to burying any members who died, the other main activity of the club was to hold a series of feasts, usually about one every other month. Some of the dues were used to fund these feasts, and at each one, several members were responsible for providing a certain minimum amount of food. The purpose of these feasts is somewhat unclear. They seem to have been a combination of a way to pay honor to the dead and an excuse to have a good party.

Only the truly wealthy could afford to have individual tombs built for themselves. These tombs were constructed along the roads leading into Rome. Thus, to reach the city of the living, one had to first pass through the city of the dead. Tombs were frequently very elaborate and took many forms. Perhaps the most common type resembled miniature marble houses. Others were shaped like columns, towers, or cones.

One of the most famous tombs, which can still be seen today, belongs to Gaius Cestius. He had his tomb constructed in the form of a marble pyramid 20 meters high. The inscription on the tomb notes that it took 330 days to build it. Another man who seems to have taken pride in his profession as a bread baker had his tomb built to resemble a gigantic, marble bread oven, into which his body was placed.

Tombs often had pipes protruding out from the top of them. The idea behind these was that the family would come out from the city to have a picnic on the tomb and share the feast with the deceased by dropping food down the tube and pouring in wine.

It was traditional that rather than building one's own tomb, one's heir would construct it. To ensure that heirs built a suitably impressive structure, many wills contained detailed directions for the type of tomb the

Figure 6.5 Pyramid-shaped tomb of Gaius Cestius.

person wanted. It was often stipulated that the heir could not receive his inheritance until he had buried the person in the specified manner. No doubt many heirs resented having to expend such effort and money on these monuments, but as a small consolation, they would include their own name on the monument as well. On over a quarter of the monuments excavated, the name of the commemorator who built it is given more prominence than the name of the deceased.

Because standard Roman religious beliefs did not really include a well-developed notion of an afterlife, Romans seemed particularly concerned with leaving some enduring memory of themselves behind. Elaborate tombs were one way to do this. Demands placed on your descendants— that they celebrate a feast on your tomb for instance—were another. Some men tried to make sure that they were remembered by setting up funds of money, the interest from which was to be used for certain activities. One man left a fund of 250,000 sesterces, the interest from which was to be used to provide an annual feast for the people of his hometown.

Despite all the effort that went into leaving an enduring legacy, many of these measures were in vain. Tombs were often sold and their valuable marble reused. Poor people broke into mausoleums, threw out the corpses, and used them as dwellings. Christian churches plundered Roman cemeteries for building materials, and the reason why many Roman funerary inscriptions have survived up to the present is because they were built into the walls of churches. Even the Romans sometimes seem not to have shown much reverence for their own tombs. The public toilets in the town of Ostia, for instance, were constructed out of old tombstones.

A full-fledged burial ceremony for a wealthy Roman nobleman could be very complex. The deceased was dressed in fine clothing, and a wreath was placed on his head. A solemn parade from his house to the Roman Forum then took place. The man's family, friends, and clients all marched in it. The wax masks of his illustrious ancestors were placed on current family members, who also dressed up in clothing indicating the highest rank that that ancestor had attained. Thus, for example, if one of the ancestors had celebrated a triumph, the person wearing his mask would wear the clothes of a *triumphor*.

When they reached the Roman Forum, the people impersonating the ancestors sat on a row of ivory chairs placed on the Rostra. The corpse was also placed on the Rostra and propped upright. One of the sons or another close family member would deliver a eulogy in which he recounted the deeds of the deceased as well as of his ancestors. The procession then traveled outside the city boundaries, where the corpse was usually cremated. During the funeral procession, close female relatives were expected to scream, beat themselves, tear out their hair, scratch their cheeks until they bled, roll in the dirt, and pound their heads against the ground. The family also hired musicians and sometimes even professional mourners. The latter were people who made a living by screaming and wailing at funerals as if they were family members. Males were generally expected to be more restrained, although when a father was burying his son, he was expected to throw himself on the corpse and talk to it, asking why the deceased had abandoned him.

Certainly the most famous of all Roman funerals was that of Julius Caesar. Mark Antony supposedly gave a particularly moving speech on this occasion. The crowds at Caesar's funeral were so large that they could not see his body very well, so a large, wax copy was constructed. This figure, placed upright on a revolving platform, featured realistic depictions of the 23 stab wounds that he had suffered at the hands of Brutus and the assassins. The crowd was so moved by this sight and by Antony's words that they rioted and decided to cremate Caesar's corpse on the spot. They ripped apart whatever they could find to build the bonfire, including the benches of the senators, and in the ensuing chaos they burned down the senate house itself. Later, when Caesar had been deified as a god, the emperor Augustus built a temple dedicated to him on the spot in the Roman Forum where his body had been cremated.

FUNERARY INSCRIPTIONS

Funerary inscriptions offer a fascinating glimpse into the lives of ordinary Romans. Whereas most tombstones today include only a simple epitaph usually consisting of the name of the deceased and his or her years of birth and death, Romans sometimes commissioned highly personalized funerary inscriptions. If written by a relative, it might describe the deceased person's life, his or her personality, or even recall specific events in his or her life. If drafted by a person before his or her death, the text might feature bits of personal philosophy or a message that he or she wished to leave for posterity. Roman tombstones often included a wealth of other information as well, such as the person's profession, the cause of death, offices held, and lists of other family members. Collectively, these funerary inscriptions preserve data about the lives, achievements, and aspirations of ordinary Romans that otherwise would be lost to history.

Those people whose funerary inscriptions have survived span a broad spectrum of Roman society, from the most powerful aristocrats to humble artisans. Thus we can read the epitaph of a member of the illustrious Scipio family who had been elected to the highest offices in the government and had conducted successful military campaigns: "All will agree that Lucius Scipio was the very best of Romans. He served as aedile, consul, and censor. He captured Corsica and the city of Aleria. He built a temple to the goddess of Weather" (*CIL* 1.7), but we can also learn of simple craftsmen such as "Gaius Atilius, son of Gaius, cobbler of soldier's boots" (*ILS* 7545), merchants such as "Lucius Cluvius, freedman of Lucius, olive oil dealer from the Carinae district" (*ILS* 7491), or even slaves such as "Zeuthus, barber and slave of Aulus Plantius" (*ILS* 7414).

Some inscriptions succinctly summarize the entire life story of the deceased, which at times can be quite dramatic: "Gaius Julius Mygdonius, born a free man in Parthia, was captured in his youth and sold as a slave in Roman territory. Once I became a freedman and a Roman citizen, thanks to kind Fate, I saved up a nest egg for when I reached fifty. Ever since my youth I have been traveling toward old age, so now, O gravestone, receive me willingly. In your care I will be released from my worries" (*CIL* 11.137). In a few brief sentences, this man's colorful life, during which he passed from freedom, to slavery, to freedom, and to ultimate prosperity, is memorialized.

Some tombstones preserve the careers of public entertainers such as gladiators. One reads, "To the departed spirit of Marcus Antonius Niger, veteran gladiator of the Thracian style. He lived 38 years and fought 18 times. Flavia Diogenis paid for this monument to be made for her well-deserving husband" (*ILS* 5090). Another epitaph records a tragic story of a child who raced chariots but apparently died in a crash: "I, who rest here, was named Florus. I was a child charioteer who wanted to race swiftly, but was even more swiftly overtaken by death. Ianurius put up this monument to his dear adopted son" (*ILS* 5300). Another aspiring charioteer had his career cut short by disease, as described on his tombstone: "To the spirits of the departed. Here is Eutyches, charioteer, 22 years old. In this grave rest the bones of a novice charioteer, who nevertheless knew how to handle the reins. Glory in the circus was not granted to me. Disease burned away my body, and the doctors could not cure it. Please, traveler, sprinkle flowers on my grave. Perhaps you were a fan of mine when I lived" (Sherk, *Roman Empire* 168).

Funerary inscriptions reveal that many women worked, among them a number who were doctors: "Here lies Secunda, physician and slave of Livilla" (*ILS* 7803), and "To the departed spirit of Julia Saturnina, 45 years of age, wonderful wife, excellent physician, most blameless woman. Erected by her husband Cassius Philippus out of gratitude. She lies here and may the earth rest lightly upon her" (*ILS* 7802). Other interesting professions mentioned on women's tombstones include scribe: "To Hapate, short-hand writer of Greek. She lived 25 years. Pittosus erected this monument to his most affectionate wife" (*ILS* 7760); merchant: "Thymele, Marcella's dealer in silk" (*ILS* 7600); and actress: "Luria Privata, actress in mimes, lived 19 years. Bleptus made this monument" (*ILS* 5215).

The epitaphs of men also illustrate an enormous variety of jobs, from humble laborers such as "Publius Marcius Philodamus, construction worker, freedman of Publius" (*CIL* 9.1721) to those with more specialized jobs: "Here lie the bones of Quintus Tiburtinus Menolavus, freedman of Quintus, who made a living slaughtering animals for sacrifices" (*CIL* 1.2.1604). Some men plainly took great pride in their jobs, as in the case of a teacher whose epitaph states, "Having left the famous city of Bithynia Nikaia as a young man, I came to the land of the Italians, and in the sacred city of Rome I taught mathematics and geometry. This is the monument that I, Basileus, made, having paid for the work by making a living with my mind" (*IGUR* 1176).

One aspect of life that tombstones bring to light is the strong emotions that tied together spouses, family members, or friends. One inscription, for example, testifies to a particularly close friendship between two men that began when both were slaves and continued even after both achieved freedom: "Aulus Memmius Urbanus erected this memorial for his very dear friend and fellow freedman, Aulus Memmius Clarus. The two of us never argued and I held you in the highest regard. By this memorial, I call upon the gods of heaven and the underworld to witness that you and I were sold as slaves at the same time, we became freedmen at the same time in the same household, and that nothing has ever separated us, until the day that death took you" (*CIL* 6.22355a).

One grave marker records a husband's grief for his young wife: "To the eternal memory of Blandina Martiola, a most blameless girl, who lived eighteen years, nine months, five days. Pompeius Catussa, a Sequanian citizen and a plasterer, dedicates this monument to his wife, who was incomparable and very kind to him. She lived with him five years, six months, eighteen days without any shadow of a fault. You who read this, go bathe in the baths of Apollo as I used to do with my wife. I wish I still could" (*CIL* 1.983). In addition to the touching detail about the couple's favorite baths, this inscription also illustrates the early ages at which some women were married, since the couple had apparently lived together

Figure 6.6 Funerary monument of a Roman man, his wife, and their child.

since she was only 13. Another tombstone commemorates a woman who was married at an even younger age: "When alive, my name was Aurelis Philematium. I was chaste and modest, unsoiled by the common crowd, and faithful to my husband. My husband whom I have now left was a fellow freedman and was truly like a father to me. We were married when I was seven. Now I am forty and death has me. Through my constant care, my husband flourished" (*CIL* 1.2.1221).

Another inscription expressing deep affection reads, "Erected by Lucius Aurelius Hermia, freedman of Lucius, a butcher on the Viminal hill. She who preceded me in death was my one and only wife. She was chaste in body with a loving spirit. She lived faithful to her devoted husband and was always optimistic. Even in bitter times, she never shirked her duties" (*CIL* 1.2.1221). One poignant epitaph preserves the history of a love that was cut short: "Furia Spes, freedwoman of Sempronius Firmus, provided this memorial for her dearly beloved husband. When we were still boy and girl, we were bound by mutual love as soon as we met. I lived with him for too brief a time. We were separated by a cruel hand when we should have continued to live in happiness. I therefore beg you, spirits of the dead, that you look after the loved one I have entrusted to you and that you be well disposed and kind to him during the hours of night, so that I may see him, and so that he, too, may wish to persuade fate to allow me to come to him softly and soon" (*CIL* 6.18817).

While these funerary inscriptions emphasize the deep passion that existed between some couples, others are more restrained, although still listing qualities that one partner found congenial in the other. For example, one from Rome reads, "Here lies Amymone, wife of Marcus, most good and most beautiful, wool-spinner, dutiful, modest, careful, chaste, stay-at-home" (*CIL* 6.11602). Modesty and the ability to sew are common positive attributes ascribed to women by their husbands, as in the following inscription: "Stranger, my message is short. Stand and read it through. Here is the unlovely tomb of a lovely woman. Her parents named her Claudia. She loved her husband with all her heart. She bore two sons; of these, she leaves one above ground, but one has already been laid within the earth. She was charming in conversation and gentle in manner. She kept the house, and she spun wool. That is all there is to say. Go now" (*CIL* 1.1211).

The affection that some parents felt for their children is also reflected in these inscriptions. "Spirits who live in the underworld, lead innocent Magnilla through the groves and the Elysian fields directly to your places of rest. She was snatched away in her eighth year by cruel fate while she was still enjoying the tender time of childhood. She was beautiful and sensitive, clever, elegant, sweet, and charming beyond her years. This poor child who was deprived of her life so quickly must be mourned with perpetual lament and tears" (*CIL* 6.21846).

As a number of these tombstones have illustrated, there were often bonds of affection between masters and their former slaves, and some monuments were constructed to house both together: "Gaius Calpenius Hermes built this tomb for himself and his children and his freedmen and freedwomen and their children and for his wife, Anitistia Coetonis" (*CIL* 14.4827). One man who paid for his freedman's tomb went into detail about what he liked about his former slave: "To the spirits of the departed. Here lies Marcus Canuleius Zosimus. He lived 28 years. His patron erected this to a well deserving freedman. In his lifetime he never spoke ill of anyone, he did nothing without his patron's consent, there was always a great amount of my gold and silver in his possession, but he never stole any of it. He was a skilled master of Clodian engraving" (*CIL* 6.9222). Some masters, however, did not view their former slaves with such affection: "Marcus Aemilius Artema built this tomb for his honored brother Marcus Licinius Successus and for Caecilia Modesta his wife, and for himself and for his children and his freedmen and freedwomen and their descendants, with the exception of his freedman Hermes, whom he forbids, because of his ungrateful and obnoxious behavior, to approach, walk around, or come near to this tomb" (*CIL* 6.11027).

Some Romans seemed more concerned with ensuring that their bodies lay undisturbed in their graves after death than with recording their accomplishments while alive. An inscription of this type states, "Gaius Tullius Hesper had this tomb built for himself, as a place where his bones might be laid. If anyone damages them or removes them from here, may he live in great physical pain for a long time, and when he dies, may the gods of the underworld deny entrance to his spirit" (*CIL* 6.36467).

Graves were situated along the roads leading into cities, and some people chose to use their tombstones to give advice to travelers or simply to express their beliefs. One man erected a monument that declared, "To the spirits of the departed. Titus Flavius Martialis lies here. What I ate and drank is with me here, what I left behind is gone forever" (*CIL* 6.18131). An athlete included on his grave a reminder of the fleeting nature of life: "Passer-by, you see me now a corpse. My name was Apollonis. Eight times I won in athletic games, but in the ninth boxing match, I met my end. Passer-by, play and laugh, but know that in the end, you too must die" (Lewis and Reinhold, eds., *Roman Civilization* 284). A similarly pessimistic stone reads, "Do not walk by this epitaph, traveler, but stop, listen, learn, and then proceed. There is no boat in Hades, no ferryman Charon, no caretaker Aeacus, no dog Cerberus. All those who die become bones and ashes—nothing more. I speak the truth. Go now, traveler, lest even though I am dead, I seem to you long-winded" (*CIL* 6.14,672).

A number of remarkable stones do not even record the names of the deceased but instead offer comments that, after all, perhaps do preserve something of their author's temperament. One terse inscription states, "I was not. I was. I am not. I care not" (*CIL* 5.2893). Finally, a man who clearly enjoyed life left a tombstone that simply read, "Baths, wine, and sex ruin our bodies. But what makes life worth living except baths, wine, and sex?" (*CIL* 6.15258).

WILLS

Romans were very concerned with leaving their property to the desired person. Twenty percent of surviving Roman legal writings are about wills and what made them valid. The main purpose of a will was to designate somebody as the heir, which is different from modern wills, whose main purpose is to distribute property. The heir not only inherited some or all of the deceased person's property but they also almost literally assumed the testator's identity and status. Thus, normally the oldest son was made the heir. The first duty of the heir was to see to the funeral of the deceased. An heir not only assumed the property and the rights of the testator, but also inherited any debts. This did not mean that debts were paid out of the estate and that the heir got what, if anything, was left over. Instead, he became legally responsible for the debts of the deceased, even if these exceeded the value of the inheritance.

The shortest will consisted of just four words: "Be X my heir." (X *mihi heres esto.*) This accomplished all that was necessary. The first line of a will was always the designation of the heir. If a man had multiple children or did not want any of his children to be his heir, he next had to specifically list their names with the formula "Let X be disinherited." To be valid, a will had to name an heir, disinherit anyone who might be eligible, and be signed at a special ceremony with seven witnesses observing. The witnesses had to be adult males who were neither blind nor insane. One of the witnesses was designated the *libiprens,* who held up a set of scales while the will was being written and signed; all witnesses had to sign for the will to be valid. The one exception to this required procedure was that soldiers on the eve of a battle were allowed to orally declare their wills before three comrades, and this would function as a legally binding will. If the heir was someone who could legally refuse to accept the inheritance, the testator had to list a time limit and a secondary heir in case the first one did not accept. If a will was defaced, it was rendered invalid.

As time went on, the Romans became concerned that too many people were leaving their property to persons other than their children and that as a result, families were falling into ruin. Therefore, laws were instituted that declared that if children were disinherited in favor of "base persons" they could challenge the will and try to have it declared invalid.

If in your will you wished to include specific gifts of money or property to people other than the heir, you had to add a line called the legacy in which you described the property or the amount of money and the person to whom you wanted it to go. There were two types of legacies. A simple legacy immediately transferred the property or money to the designated person. The second type ordered the heir to pay out the legacy from his inheritance. This was called a damnation legacy, and its formula was "Let my heir be damned to give X to Y." Again, so many people were giving away large portions of their estates through legacies that the laws were changed so that a testator could bequeath no more than three-quarters of his inheritance in legacies. Another very common part of a will was the posthumous manumission, or freeing the testator's favorite slave or slaves.

A will could include a variety of other statements. One standard item was directions for the type of funeral, in particular, the size and expense of the funeral monument that the heir was required to provide. If you really hated someone, in your will you would leave that person a legacy of a rope and a nail; the message was to tie the rope to the nail and then hang yourself from it. It was illegal, however, to slander the emperor in your will in any way.

Finally, someone making a will could include requests. The most famous of these requests occurred in the poet Virgil's will; he demanded that his great epic poem *The Aeneid* be burned and all copies destroyed because he had not quite finished it. The emperor Augustus ordered that this request be ignored, and for this reason we still have *The Aeneid* today.

7

Dangers of Life in Ancient Rome

FIRES

One of the most common hazards faced by city residents was fire. Everyone had to cook over open flames, and for poor apartment dwellers, this might have been a fire kindled on the floor of their apartment or in an improvised stove. Olive-oil lamps, the main source of light, were easy to knock over. Not surprisingly, under these circumstances, fires were extremely frequent. In addition, due to the narrowness of the streets, the widespread use of wood as a building material, and the lack of effective fire-fighting techniques, once started, fires spread easily and caused enormous destruction.

The impression given by ancient authors is that not a night went by without a serious fire somewhere in Rome; larger fires that destroyed entire neighborhoods seem to have struck roughly every other year. One source describes a group of friends climbing up the Cispian hill and seeing a multistory apartment building ablaze. As they watched, the fire spread to the neighboring structures, creating a mighty conflagration. It is interesting that they seem to regard this dramatic spectacle as a routine occurrence, and rather than being shocked or alarmed at the sight, they instead engage in a scholarly conversation about literary allusions to fire-proofing methods (Aulus Gellius, *Attic Nights* 15.1).

To combat the fire menace, Augustus set up a brigade of approximately 7,000 watchmen known as *vigiles,* who patrolled the city at night carrying buckets and attempting to extinguish any fires before they could spread.

They were organized into seven cohorts so that each was responsible for 2 of the 14 regions of the city. Eventually, each cohort was housed in its own barracks in the appropriate part of the city. Their presence in the streets at night may have served as a deterrent to crime, but their principal duty was fire fighting rather than policing. Their equipment consisted of buckets, ladders, axes, and some sort of siphon device for spraying water. In addition, each cohort had several pieces of artillery that could be used to destroy buildings and create a firebreak.

The most destructive fire of all was the Great Fire of AD 64. It began near the Circus Maximus and rapidly spread to other areas of the city. It raged for six days, after which it appeared to have been brought under control, but it then broke out again and burned for an additional three days. By the time it was all over, 10 of Rome's 14 districts had been severely damaged, with 3 of these districts completely leveled. After this fire, the city was rebuilt with wider streets and using more fireproof materials. However, these efforts do not seem to have really curbed the frequency of fires, although they perhaps helped to inhibit their spread.

FLOODS

Floods and civilization have always been companions. The very earliest civilizations, such as those in Mesopotamia, arose along rivers in floodplains. The reasons for settling in such hazardous regions are obvious: by definition, floodplains are flat and near water and, hence, well suited for agriculture. Also, rivers offer routes of communication and transport, and the floods themselves deposit sediments that renew and enrich the soil. The very factors that caused these areas to be attractive for settlement are the same ones that make them vulnerable to the devastation caused by floods. Rome developed where it did because there was a natural ford across the Tiber just below Tiber Island. Rome is built on a series of small but fairly steep hills, but between the hills are valleys that were originally swampy marshland, as was the entire Campus Martius. The Tiber is a turbulent river whose waters, when swollen by rain or snowmelt, routinely inundated these low-lying areas of Rome.

There are accounts of nearly three dozen major floods that struck the city of Rome between 414 BC and AD 400, and later records show that such floods have continued unabated into the modern era. Research suggests that, at a minimum, there has been a severe flood about once every 20 years on average. The normal level of the Tiber is between five and seven meters above sea level. The greatest flood ever recorded was that of 1598, which reached a height of nearly 20 meters above sea level. Any flood over about 13 meters above sea level would have inundated nearly all the low-lying regions of the city, including the Campus Martius, the Roman Forum, the Forum Boarium, the valley of the Circus Maximus, the Emporium district, and the Transtiberim. These areas include nearly all the

Figure 7.1 Map of the flood-prone areas of Rome. These include almost all the major political, commercial, and entertainment structures of the city. (Adapted by the author and David West Reynolds, Phaeton Group, Scientific Graphic Services Division, from map of Rome in *The Urban Image of Augustan Rome* by Diane Favro, 1996, with the permission of Cambridge University Press.)

major political, commercial, and entertainment districts and buildings of the city.

Ancient sources record instances of floods lasting so long that the streets had to be traversed by boat for an entire week. Both ancient and more modern data suggest that the typical flood lasted five days overall, of which two to three days were the period of high water. The Tiber is highest in winter and spring, when it becomes swollen by the winter rainy season and the spring snowmelt. Almost all recorded floods have occurred during these seasons.

The most obvious effect of the floods would have been the disruption of daily life in the city. The low-lying areas of Rome would probably have been inundated by several meters of water, making travel impossible. No fewer than nine of the descriptions of ancient floods specifically mention that it was necessary to travel through the streets in boats. Floods would have had serious disruptive consequences on the movement of people and on the economy. Naturally, any property in those regions reached by the waters would have been destroyed, damaged, or lost. There are many substances that could be damaged or ruined by exposure to water, but probably even more property loss would have been caused by the force of the water, which would have swept through buildings and streets, carrying away everything in them. This would have included even quite large objects, as observed during modern floods, in which less than half a meter of water is sufficient to carry away entire automobiles.

The most dramatic immediate effect would have been the spectacular collapse of large buildings. While monumental architecture was usually built fairly solidly, Rome was full of rickety high-rise structures. There are numerous sources attesting to the shoddy construction techniques of the often seven- or eight-story apartment buildings erected by unscrupulous slum-lords such as Cicero. These precarious structures often collapsed of their own accord, and the stresses placed on them by floodwaters would certainly have brought many toppling down. Not surprisingly, this is one of the most common effects of flooding related by the primary sources. Almost half the accounts of floods, even very brief one-line descriptions, mention buildings collapsing.

The final immediate consequence of a flood is, of course, loss of life, caused by drowning, exposure, and trauma from objects being tossed around in the floodwaters. When deaths are mentioned in ancient sources, it is usually to say that large numbers lost their lives in the waters, although specific figures are never given.

When floodwaters finally receded, this was not the end of the city's problems. One very unpleasant side effect of most floods is that they leave behind a viscous and foul-smelling layer of mud and debris. While no specific mention of this is found in ancient sources, the appearance and effect of this slimy deposit can be inferred from records of modern floods. The 1966 flood in Florence left behind 600,000 tons of stinking mud coating everything up to a depth of one meter.

The detrimental consequences of a flood lingered long after the waters receded. One of the most frequently mentioned delayed effects was the subsequent collapse of buildings that had suffered damage or weakening during the flood. Buildings constructed out of bricks were singled out as being particularly susceptible to damage due to floods. Most of the huge warehouse complexes, which housed Rome's food supply (and, above all, its grain), were quite logically located near the river for ease of unloading. This unfortunately also meant that these warehouses would have been among the first structures to be inundated by floods. The storage of grain is a tricky matter since it needs to be kept cool and dry to deter the growth of fungus, which will ruin it as a comestible product. Even the moisture from humidity can be enough to cause grain to go bad. Naturally, a major flood would have resulted in the complete loss of all grain that was reached by the water.

Another delayed effect of flooding would have been an increased incidence of disease. Those suffering due to food shortages or famine would have had a lowered resistance to illness. Those who had lost their shelter would have been more susceptible to infection and pestilence. Due to the common practice of dumping one's excrement in the streets, another nasty consequence of floods would have been the spread of this waste throughout the flooded areas, contaminating everything it touched and rendering the water in the city unfit for drinking. Floods would also have caused the drains and sewers to back up, depositing their contents throughout the buildings and living spaces of the city. Any food products not ruined outright by the water would at the very least have been contaminated by this filth, severely sickening whoever ate them. Last, the corpses of human and animal victims of the flood would have further added to the omnipresence of contamination and disease.

It is testimony to the importance of floods in Roman history that perhaps the first great public work to be built in the city of Rome was a drainage sewer. According to legend, the Tarquins constructed the first version of the Cloaca Maxima in order to make the forum area habitable. The best way to protect the city from Tiber floods was to build embankments to contain the river. The Romans had probably begun this process by the second century BC, and we have confirmation of such projects preserved on stones from 55 BC onward put up by the magistrates charged with overseeing the river (the *curatores riparum*). The Romans also deliberately dumped fill in key low-lying areas such as the Roman Forum to raise the ground level and make these regions less prone to flooding. By the end of the Roman period, many areas had been raised two or three meters higher than they had been originally. One final ancient response to the problem of flooding was a supposed scheme of Julius Caesar's to divert the course of the Tiber along the Vatican hills. However, this project was never carried out.

Rome did not receive reliable protection until the flood of 1870 prompted the government to construct the current set of high embankments, which reach about 18 meters above sea level all along both sides of the river. Since then, there have been no destructive floods in the city.

SANITATION

The streets of Rome were breeding grounds for numerous disease-causing organisms due to the widespread presence of human and animal cadavers in various states of decomposition as well as the copious quantities of raw sewage deposited in the streets.

The normal course of events produced enormous numbers of dead bodies, many of which were not properly disposed of. The truly impoverished

Figure 7.2 Roman street. Each of the rectangular doorways would have housed a different shop selling goods.

who could not afford to join a burial club or who lacked nearby family members to cremate or bury their bodies, along with Rome's large population of homeless and beggars, simply lay where they dropped or else were thrown into the Tiber or into open pits just outside the city. It has been estimated that the city of Rome produced perhaps 1,500 such unclaimed bodies per year.

A number of literary anecdotes vividly illustrate the presence of both bodies and scavenging animals in the streets of the city. The poet Martial describes the gruesome death of a beggar whose last moments are spent trying to fend off the dogs and vultures that have gathered to feed on him (Martial, *Epigrams* 10.5). Suetonius mentions an incident when a stray dog ran into the room where the emperor Vespasian was dining and deposited a human hand beneath the table (Suetonius, *Life of Vespasian* 5.4), and a partially eaten corpse was hauled through the Roman Forum itself by a pack of scavenging canines (Orosius, *Against the Pagans* 7.41–2).

Although Rome possessed some sewers, their purpose was more to provide drainage than to actually carry away waste. While latrines were sometimes present in buildings, *domus,* and *insulae* at Rome, most often they were not, suggesting that people relieved themselves in the streets or in chamber pots. Unfortunately, most city inhabitants appear to have emptied their chamber pots by simply dumping them out the windows of their dwellings. Much of Rome's garbage and sewage seems to have ended up in the streets. This was no small problem since, at its height,

Figure 7.3 Reconstruction of a typical street in Rome. This drawing captures a sense of the squalid nature of the city's roadways, with mud, overhanging buildings, animals running loose, and poor tenement buildings juxtaposed with monumental marble structures. (From G. Gatteschi, *Restauri della Roma Imperiale*, 1924, p. 27.)

Rome's human inhabitants were producing about 50,000 kilograms of excrement each day. Roman law offers an insight into sanitation and living conditions through laws that attempted to regulate what was obviously a common practice: pouring feces and garbage from one's window into the streets (*Digest of Roman Law,* 9.3.1; 43.10.1). Rome's animals certainly also contributed to the general level of filth. Thus the streets of the city probably more closely resembled open sewers than our modern notion of roadways.

The garbage and excrement deposited onto the roadways would have been trampled together with mud and refuse to form a layer of sludge coating the street surface. The continual flow of water from street-side fountains and basins may have washed this waste into the sewers to some extent, but it would also have covered the surface of the streets with a perpetually moist and unpleasant muck. It is perhaps worth noting Martial's description of the steps leading up from the Subura district as being always wet and filthy and Juvenal's account of a trip through the streets during which his legs (not merely his feet) become entirely splattered with mud (Martial, *Epigrams* 5.22; Juvenal, *Satires* 3.247).

Life in the city would not merely have assaulted one's senses of sight and smell but also one's hearing. The stoic philosopher Seneca, whose apartment was above a public bath, vividly described the annoying sounds that emanated from below, including the grunting of weight lifters, noisy athletes yelling at one another, people who liked to sing while bathing, and merchants hawking snack foods (Seneca, *Moral Epistles* 56). Nor did night offer any relief from the noise; in an effort to reduce congestion in the streets, it was decreed that all supply wagons had to bring in their goods at night, thus filling the night with the noisy rumble of carts on stone roads, the braying of pack animals, and the shouts of drivers.

DISEASE

Not surprisingly, the inhabitants of ancient Rome suffered from a wide assortment of diseases. Malnutrition and the lack of a varied diet would have caused diseases such as scurvy, pellagra, beriberi, and rickets.

The poor level of sanitation would have encouraged many other diseases as well. The presence everywhere of carcasses and excrement, both animal and human; the scavenging dogs, birds, rats, flies, and other vermin; the contamination of the water supply; and the general overcrowding would all have combined to foster the growth of diseases and to rapidly spread them throughout the city. These unsanitary conditions would have made four groups of diseases very common.

One group of organisms frequently found in excrement consists of enteric viruses, such as rotaviruses, parvoviruses, and at least 67 different varieties of enteroviruses. The most common health hazard posed by these viruses is gastroenteritis. Some of the enteroviruses also cause meningitis, which can cause blindness, brain damage, and, frequently, death. Also in this category is the virus causing hepatitis A, a highly infectious form of the disease that produces episodes of fever, lassitude, vomiting, and jaundice, which can persist for weeks.

The second group of disease-causing organisms abundantly present in feces is bacteria. These include the common *Escherichia coli* bacterium, which causes the familiar "traveler's diarrhea" form of gastroenteritis. Another common bacterium found in feces is salmonella, producing salmonellosis, which results in the usual array of gastrointestinal ailments but can sometimes invade the respiratory, cardiovascular, and nervous systems as well. Yet more serious is typhoid fever, which is caused by a bacillus of the salmonella family. Victims of typhoid are struck with fever, malaise, and diarrhea, and the disease can damage the spleen and intestines.

The third category of organisms is certain parasitic protozoans, which, when transmitted to the gastrointestinal tract, produce diarrhea and infection. These include *Giardia lambli* (which causes giardiasis), *Entamoeba histolytica* (causing amebiasis), and *Balantidium coli* (which causes balantidiasis).

The final group is parasitic worms. The most common of these are the nematodes, such as hookworms, threadworms, roundworms, pinworms, and whipworms, and the cestodes, which are various species of tape-worm. While the majority of these parasitic worms are usually not fatal to their hosts, their presence can result in a variety of health problems and substantially weaken infected individuals. On occasion, death might even result, as when roundworms sometimes collect in sufficient quantity to produce a fatal obstruction in the bowels.

One of the most dangerous waterborne diseases, cholera, does not seem to be definitively attested in ancient Rome. The vagueness of ancient descriptions of illnesses makes it difficult to identify diseases for certain, but if cholera were present in ancient Rome, the resulting mortality rates would have been quite high. Dysentery caused by contamination of the water supply would also have been common.

Rome's location near swampy ground and the low-lying areas of the city itself would have offered breeding grounds for mosquitoes, and malaria clearly was a problem. When a carrier mosquito bites a human, parasites are transmitted to the bloodstream and establish themselves in the liver, where they multiply and further infect the bloodstream. While malaria is usually not a fatal disease, bouts are often lengthy and debili-tating, and those stricken suffer recurrent episodes of enervating fever and malaise.

The inhabitants of the ancient world formed strong associations between marshes and diseases, although they usually ascribed this connection to "bad air" rather than to insects. Columella, for example, warned that dwellings should not be placed near marshes, "from which are often con-tracted mysterious diseases whose causes are beyond the understanding of physicians" (Columella, *On Farming* 1.5).

Malaria has sometimes been identified as the principal agent in the decline of various ancient civilizations. While this view is probably too extreme, the disease was plainly a serious problem whose victims may have included such notable individuals as Julius Caesar and Augustus. In Rome, malaria seems to have been a major health threat that killed large numbers of the city's inhabitants outright and weakened many more, leaving them susceptible to other diseases. Studies of the seasonality of deaths in the city of ancient Rome reveal a strong peak in mortality from August to October, which probably correlates to the malaria season.

While ancient Rome was inferior to modern cities in so many aspects of public health and engineering, in terms of the vulnerability of the water supply to contamination and the speed with which it could recover, the peculiar nature of Rome's water-supply system may actually have made the ancient city both unusually resistant and resilient.

First of all, the continual-flow nature of Rome's water-supply system would have ensured that contaminants did not linger in the pipes and basins but were instead flushed out fairly rapidly and prevented from set-tling in standing pools of water within the system. The volume of water passing through Rome's water-supply system was enormous, exceeding

Figure 7.4 Model of the center of Rome, giving a nice impression of the densely packed buildings and narrow streets that formed the heart of the city. The Imperial Fora are in the center, and the infamous, lower-class Subura district is immediately behind them.

the per capita water consumption rates of most modern cities. Another quirk of Rome's water supply was that the majority of water did not originate locally but rather was transported a considerable distance to the city by aqueducts. Most of these aqueducts brought water directly from springs located on high ground up in the foothills of the Apennines. These water sources would have been completely unaffected by local disasters such as floods, so their water would have remained pure and uncontaminated.

One sometimes hears that the Romans were relatively healthy because of the public baths where people could bathe frequently. While this might have helped keep them free of dirt, it probably did not improve their overall health, since a standard prescription given by Roman doctors to those suffering from diseases was to go soak in the baths. The warm waters there would have provided an ideal environment for transmitting diseases to the other bathers. The ancient physician Celsus records in his medical writings that he advised his patients suffering from skin diseases, boils, rabies, tuberculosis, fevers, diarrhea, and parasitic worms to go soak in the baths frequently.

While the Romans did not seem to be upset at the thought of sharing bathwater with the diseased, they do seem to have been bothered by having to look at people with diseases while bathing. There are references to those with illnesses having to keep their clothes on while bathing and to healthy bathers making fun of their unfortunate bathing companions who had visible ailments. In one instance, the bath attendant allowed a disease-ridden old woman to enter the baths but first extinguished the lamps so that her affliction would not be visible.

It is estimated that under these conditions one-third of babies died before they were one year old, and half never survived childhood. Even the rich were not immune, as evidenced by Cornelia, the mother of the Gracchi brothers, who gave birth to 12 children, yet saw only 3 of them reach adulthood.

CRIME AND THE LAW

Rome had no police force, at least not in the way that we tend to think of it today. This lack was not unusual or unique to Rome, since the police force in its modern sense did not develop until the eighteenth and nineteenth centuries. The job of the modern police is to prevent crime, investigate crimes that have been committed, and apprehend criminals. Up until recently, none of these activities was perceived to be the particular responsibility or duty of the state. Rome did possess a legal system and, by the end of Roman history, an extraordinarily sophisticated and complex law code, but this system was only applied to cases that were, on the whole, brought before magistrates by private citizens.

During the republic, it was strictly forbidden to have military forces within the *pomerium*, the sacred boundary of the city. Dealing with day-to-day crime was very much a do-it-yourself system in which individuals had to protect themselves and their property. If Romans became victims of a crime, they or their friends and family had to capture the criminal and drag him before a magistrate. While the state did not take a very active role in regulating criminal activity among individuals, it did intervene in cases in which a crime was perceived to have threatened or been committed against the state. Thus, many of the famous trials during the republic had to do with accusations of treason or disputes among public officials. The only crime among individuals that the magistrates took an active role in investigating was the special crime of parricide.

The earliest law code, the Twelve Tables, emphasized this do-it-yourself nature of Roman justice. If a thief broke into your house at night or was armed, you were allowed to kill the thief, although if the break-in occurred during the day and the thief was unarmed, you were supposed to summon your neighbors and apprehend him. In practice, the slaves and clients of powerful men acted as bodyguards to protect them and their property.

The streets of the city at night were considered to be particularly dangerous due to muggers, and wealthy men returning home from dinner parties took care to be accompanied by a retinue of slaves with torches and often weapons.

Spontaneous mob violence seems to have been permitted or at least ignored and was seen as a way of settling particularly egregious disputes. There are multiple instances of people being torn to pieces by an angry mob if they were generally thought to be guilty of some offensive crime. In 82 BC, the governor of the province of Africa was burned alive in his home by an angry mob of citizens, but no retaliatory action was taken by the authorities because it was generally agreed that he had deserved it.

During the empire, the situation in the city changed a bit due to the establishment of several military and paramilitary groups stationed within the city limits. These included the Praetorian Guard, whose primary function was to protect the emperor; the Urban Cohorts; and the *vigiles*, who fought fires. While the presence of all of these groups may have had some deterrent effect on crimes, and while they were clearly used to keep order and suppress riots at public events such as games, none of them was specifically charged with the prevention, detection, or investigation of ordinary crime.

There were a variety of magistrates whose duties involved supervising judicial-type actions. Praetors had general jurisdiction to conduct trials and pass judgment when criminals were brought before them. The urban aediles may have had some responsibilities in connection with their general oversight of urban affairs. During the empire, an official known as the urban prefect could conduct trials. Finally, there was a board of three junior magistrates known as the *triumviri capitales* who, assisted by a staff of slaves, carried out the torture and execution of convicted criminals.

One of the praetors was responsible for sitting in the Roman Forum and dealing with legal cases that were brought before him. A few crimes, such as treason, required trials before one of the assemblies, but for most day-to-day crimes, he had power to settle the case. Praetors were supposed to follow legal precedents in making judgments, but the system was not formal, and there was room for arbitrariness.

Law cases were judged out in the open, often in the forum itself, so that anyone could gather and watch. Trials therefore often took on the nature of public spectacles, particularly in the Late Republic, when a number of high-profile Roman citizens were involved in a series of sensational public trials. At this time, law cases became almost a form of entertainment. People came and watched the speakers perform. Rome had no professional lawyers, and men like Cicero who were gifted public speakers could make their political careers by presenting celebrity cases. Because of the public nature of trials, speakers like Cicero played as much to the audience as to the jury. Audiences were very vocal and would shout out comments, abuse, and praise.

The punishments inflicted on criminals varied according to their status. Upper-class individuals were penalized by a loss of status, exile, or, in severe cases, by execution, although this would usually have been carried out in private. Lower-class people were more frequently subject to beatings and the humiliation of public execution. Slaves could suffer a variety of cruel tortures and forms of execution.

Rome did not have a prison system. The only jail in Rome was a single cell that was used to hold people until they could be executed. The standard punishments were fines, flogging, decapitation, crucifixion (for incest, treason, and for slaves who had revolted), or burning (for treachery and arson). Citizens could also be stripped of their status as citizens and become slaves or gladiators. Another punishment was to be sent to the mines, which entailed incredibly hard and dangerous labor; this really amounted to a delayed death sentence. A final option was exile. The Romans termed this to be "interdicted from fire and water." It was a capital offense to help or harbor an exile, and if an exile returned, he could be killed with impunity.

The Romans had a couple of special punishments for crimes they found especially offensive. Given the reverence, status, and power accorded to fathers, it is not surprising that the Romans were particularly horrified by children who killed their fathers. The punishment for this crime was to be sewn up in a sack together with a live rooster, dog, snake, and monkey; the sack was then thrown into the ocean.

If a defendant owed money as punishment for a crime and was unable to pay the debt, his body became the property of the wronged person—in other words, he became the slave of that person. If you killed someone else's slave or animal, you had to pay the highest value that the property had possessed in the past year. If you burned, broke, or smashed anything, you had to pay its highest value in the last month. For theft, the wronged party received double the value of the object stolen. If the theft was accompanied by violence, the victim received four times the value. For personal injuries such as one person hitting another, an estimate was made of the damage and a money award was given to the injured person. This type of crime had a one-year statute of limitations, meaning that if you did not bring your suit within one year, you could no longer do so. There were four cases in which the injured party got extra money because of the outrageousness of the crime: First, if the injured person was of high rank, such as a senator; second, if the act was unusually brutal, such as clubbing with a heavy stick; third, if the crime took place in a very public place, such as the theater; and fourth, if the injured body part was particularly sensitive, such as an eye. One of the most frequent sources of lawsuits was people being struck by objects thrown out of windows, and in such cases, the punishment was a fine amounting to two times the loss or damage incurred.

There were even specific laws concerning losses caused by animals. If a domesticated animal caused harm or injury, the owner was liable. However, if a wild animal escaped and caused harm or damage, the owner was not punished as long as he had not shown negligence, since the assumption was that the animal was just being true to its wild nature. There was a special provision, however, that if someone kept a wild or dangerous animal such as a boar or a lion in a place where the public walked, the owner could be held responsible for double the damages.

The Romans liked to keep records, and one of the things they kept very good records of was the law and law cases. From these, we know a great deal about Roman law. In the 500s AD, the emperor Justinian collected vast numbers of these cases and had them compiled into what became known as the *Digest of Roman Law*. It took several years to amass all of these, and it was finally published in AD 533. This collection of cases and commentaries by jurists became the basis for many of the world's legal systems. Nearly every country in Europe and many others around the world can trace their law codes directly back to Justinian's *Digest*. England, however, developed its own code called English Common Law, and the United States copied this code, although most of the terminology and concepts were still derived from Roman law.

The *Digest* represents the end point of Roman law; by this time, Roman law was fully as extensive as our modern legal system, with laws and precedents to cover nearly every possible situation. This complex legal system did not spring up overnight but was the result of hundreds of years of accumulated legal practice. Despite the sophistication of Roman law, the lack of a well-developed enforcement arm of the state ensured that the streets of Rome were the scenes of frequent crimes, and, especially after dark, few wealthy persons would venture outside their homes without bodyguards.

Living in a large city offered a variety of experiences, excitement, and the opportunity to enjoy luxurious public amenities, but there was a darker side to this existence as well.

8

Pleasures of Life in Ancient Rome

GARDENS

The homes of wealthy Romans often contained enclosed outdoor areas that were elaborately landscaped. These private gardens typically featured flower beds, shade trees, marble benches, artworks, ponds, and sometimes plots of herbs, fruits, or vegetables. The frequency with which these gardens appear in Roman houses demonstrates that the Romans had a great love for this sort of natural environment and would go to considerable lengths to provide one for themselves.

During the republic, the wealthiest Romans began to construct estates immediately outside the central built-up portion of the city. These generally included a large expanse of land that was attractively landscaped, within which would be their villa. Julius Caesar, for example, owned a large estate in the Transtiberim. Thus the city of Rome became surrounded by a kind of greenbelt. Over time, many of these estates passed into the hands of the emperor and were opened up to the public for their use and enjoyment.

The generic Roman term for a garden was *horti*, although this is a somewhat ambiguous term because it was applied to a range of things from large estates, including the villas within them, to much smaller garden patches. One of the earliest of the elaborate gardens, constructed by the fabulously wealthy Lucullus, was known as the Horti Luculliani. Covering the top of the Pincian hill and stretching down into the Campus Martius, it featured a number of separate dining rooms, each of which had a fixed budget for the dinners served in it. One of the more expensive of these was the Apollo dining room. Lucullus's gardens also included large libraries that he made available to the public, and these libraries became a kind of unofficial headquarters for literary-minded Greeks who were living in Rome.

The most famous republican gardens were the Horti Sallustiani, constructed by the historian Sallust. They were situated on and around the Quirinal and Pincian hills, and he is said to have spent much of his accumulated wealth on them. Nestled in and around the elaborately landscaped gardens were fishponds, baths, a *porticus* (covered walkway) supposedly a mile in length, an obelisk from Egypt, works of art, and a vault containing the bones of two giants said to be three and a half meters tall. The gardens of both Lucullus and Sallust eventually became imperial property and were made available to the public.

Eventually, green spaces open to the public showed up in even the heart of the city. This trend seems to have been started by Pompey, who attached an enclosed garden to his theater in the Campus Martius. Thus theatergoers could stroll about the covered walkways beneath shade trees and view ponds, flower beds, fountains, and statues. Agrippa similarly seems to have had some sort of gardens surrounding his bath complex, which he willed to the people of Rome upon his death.

The presence of such beautiful and peaceful gardens so close to the city, and which were open to the general public, offered the poor inhabitants of Rome a pleasant escape from the squalor of their apartments, and the gardens were probably one of the areas where they would choose to spend their idle time. Even more luxurious surroundings were made available to the people of the city by the emperors, who constructed gigantic and sumptuous public bath complexes.

BATHS

By the early empire, bathing had become an important social ritual for the Romans that was closely associated with the whole concept of Romanization. Wherever the Romans went, they constructed bath complexes, so these structures have been found even in outposts on the very fringes of the Roman Empire. For example, baths are cited by the author Tacitus as one of the hallmarks of Roman civilization in the distant province of Britain and additionally as a method by which savage barbarians were "softened" through exposure to such cultured luxuries.

For a Roman, a trip to the baths involved far more than simply bathing. Baths were a place for exercise, relaxation, education, grooming, socializing, eating, conducting business, showing off to your peers, and even engaging in sexual activity. Bath complexes included facilities for all of these activities as well as for bathing. An important aspect of baths is that the large, public ones were either free or else charged only token admission fees. Thus, these experiences were open to all levels of Roman society. Unlike public entertainments, which were also provided to Rome's populace by its rulers, baths were available every day, not just on special occasions. Romans of all ranks probably spent as much time as possible at baths.

The gigantic public baths constructed by the emperors were known as *thermae,* while the numerous smaller public or private baths were termed *balnea.* By the fourth century AD, the city of Rome boasted 11 *thermae* and 856 *balnea.* Many of these *balnea* likely served as neighborhood social centers, where a relatively small group of regular clientele would gather and socialize with their acquaintances in much the same way that neighborhood bars today are often popular with a group of locals. Some of these may even have been private baths open only to a small group of dues-paying members.

The grand public *thermae,* on the other hand, while being more anonymous, would have offered a greater range of activities and services as well as being attractive simply due to the magnificence of their construction. Baths both big and small would all have included a standard set of basic bathing facilities. When patrons entered, they would probably have first gone to a dressing room where they would remove their clothes. Surviving examples often feature a series of wall niches where each person could stash his or her belongings, and some may have had cabinets or lockers into which you could put your possessions. Judging from incidents mentioned in literature and in Roman law, theft of belongings or clothes seems to have been a problem. Those who did not trust the bath attendant to safeguard their possessions might bring a slave with them whose job was to stand guard while he or she bathed.

All Roman baths included at least three basic types of rooms for bathing. The *tepidarium* contained a pool of warm water. The *caldarium* featured a pool or tub of hot water. And the *frigidarium* had a pool of cold water. One common bathing sequence seems to have been to go first to the *tepidarium,* then to the *caldarium,* and then to end with a quick plunge into the *frigidarium,* although bathers could go from one room to the other as suited their individual preferences. Sometimes there was an additional room that was heated to a high temperature but did not contain water and thus functioned as a kind of dry-heat sauna. It was also common for the larger bath complexes to have an outdoor swimming pool, which was known as a *natatio.*

The baths were heated by a furnace system, which heated hot water in tanks that was then directed to the appropriate pools and which forced hot air under the floors and between the walls of rooms such as the *caldarium.* Rooms that were supposed to be hot were constructed with a double floor, with the one floor separated from the other by columns of tiles. Hot air was then forced into this space between the two floors, heating the entire room and causing the marble floors to be pleasantly warm to the touch. Such an arrangement was known as a hypocaust system.

Figure 8.1 Ruins of the Baths of Caracalla. The size of the remaining walls suggests the massive scale of the original structure.

The first large public baths were built by Agrippa in 25 BC in the Campus Martius, and to provide sufficient water, he also built a new aqueduct, the Aqua Virgo. In the next several hundred years, the emperors Nero, Titus, Trajan, Caracalla, Diocletian, and Constantine would all construct major public baths for the city's populace, and it is these buildings that were known as the *thermae*. All of these tended to have roughly the same general design.

The best-preserved of these baths was also one of the largest—the Thermae Antoninianae, or, as it is popularly known, the Baths of Caracalla. Built in a relatively short period during the third century AD, it was located along the Via Appia farther down the valley from the Circus Maximus. The ground floor covered an area of over 100,000 square meters, and the baths could accommodate probably around 10,000 people at one time. The foundations for this bath consumed 280,000 cubic meters of tufa, 330,000 cubic meters of landfill, and 15 million pieces of brick, while the walls required 210,000 cubic meters of concrete and some 6 million bricks and parts of bricks. The ornamentation of this structure required 6,300 cubic meters of fine marble and decorative stones and 252 columns, and the work is estimated to have employed nearly 10,000 men laboring every day for five years. The floors were completely covered in elaborate mosaics and artworks adorned the entire complex. The *caldarium* was a gigantic, circular room topped by a dome some 35 meters in diameter—fully four-fifths the size of the great one on the Pantheon.

The central bath complex included dozens of rooms and a *natatio* 23 by 52 meters in size and 1 to 1.5 meters in depth. This main building was almost 250 meters long and over 100 meters wide but in addition was itself completely surrounded by vast fields and tracts where people could play ball games and run. Finally, these fields were themselves enclosed within walls containing yet more rooms, perhaps including eating establishments and libraries. The complex was stocked with equipment so that people could lift weights, play a variety of games, receive massages, purchase and dine on various foods, get manicures and haircuts, and view artwork. Today the extensive ruins are used to stage operas, including, at one time, a production of the opera *Aida* featuring live elephants.

Romans bathed in the nude. Women either had separate bathing facilities, or, in some cases, there was a designated time of day when men were allowed in and a separate time when women were admitted. There are some references, however, that indicate that at least at times, mixed bathing was permitted. Not all Romans approved of baths, and some thought they had a degenerative effect on morality. Baths were sometimes seen as sites of overindulgence in luxury, food, or sex. Some Roman medical writers claimed that too much bathing led to a weakening of the body and condemned the practice. Like today, Romans were cautioned not to swim after eating a heavy meal, and one Roman poet relates a story, perhaps satirical, of a person who died as a consequence of bathing with a stomach full of undigested peacock.

People coming to the baths would either bring their own towels, oil, and strigils, or else they could rent these items. A strigil is a curved, metal tool. After Romans exercised or bathed, they would rub olive oil over their bodies and then scrape it off using the strigil. This was the Roman equivalent of using soap, as dirt and grime were scraped off along with the old oil. Rich men would bring their personal slaves to oil and then scrape them down. Others could hire attendants at the bath to perform these services, whereas the impoverished had to do the best they could themselves. On one occasion the emperor Hadrian was in the baths and saw an old veteran of Rome's wars scraping himself against the wall of the building because he was too poor to hire someone to do it for him. Shocked at this scene, Hadrian gave the man several slaves as well as money for their upkeep. The story of the emperor's generous gesture seems to have spread, and the next time he visited the baths, he was greeted by the sight of a bunch of old men energetically rubbing themselves against the walls, plainly hoping to similarly benefit from the emperor's generosity. Hadrian, however, simply remarked that they should scrape one another.

FOOD AND BANQUETS

The diet of the vast majority of people in the ancient Roman world consisted of a simple routine of grain, olive oil, and wine. The grain was usually consumed either in the form of bread or as a kind of porridge or gruel. This diet was sometimes supplemented by fruits or vegetables when available. Meat, especially red meat, would have been a rarity. Pork was the most readily available red meat product. Fish and poultry were probably more commonly eaten than animal meats.

Adding some flavor to this diet was a kind of fish sauce called *garum* that appears to have been much loved by the Romans. The recipe for making *garum* was to take many of the undesirable parts of the fish, such as the entrails, heads, and fins, and mix them together with herbs and olive oil. This concoction was placed in a barrel or pot and put in the sun, where it was allowed to ferment. The resultant smelly paste was strained and served hot over bread or added to other foods. There were even the Roman equivalent of fast food restaurants where pedestrians could come up to a counter and purchase a bowl of *garum* with some bread.

While the culinary lives of most Romans were monotonous, rich, upper-class Romans were able to eat a vast array of exotic comestibles and to hold lavish banquets. Breakfast and lunch were usually light meals, while dinner, or *cena,* was the principal meal of the day and the occasion for sometimes very elaborate meals.

At a formal Roman dinner party, the guests arrived, removed their shoes, and were led to a dining room called the *triclinium.* Romans lay down on couches when they ate, leaning on their left elbows. Around three sides of a square table were placed low benches or beds called *triclinia.* As the name suggests, each held three diners, so a full dinner party consisted of nine people. If there were more guests, the host had to set up another group of *triclinia.* Romans used knives and spoons but not forks. The first course of appetizers consisted of little treats such as olives, snails, vegetables, eggs, or shellfish. Main courses were elaborate meat dishes. Pig udders and boar meat were very popular, while eels and lampreys were particular delicacies. Many wealthy Romans owned heated fishponds where eels were raised, and aristocrats competed to see who could grow the biggest and tastiest eels. Dessert consisted of nuts or fruit, such as apples, pears, and figs.

There might have been entertainment at the meal; music, jugglers, magicians, actors, and literary readings of poetry or history were frequent accompaniments to a dinner party. After the meal was eaten, there would be drinking and conversation. The host determined the ratio of wine to water that would be drunk and often selected a topic of conversation. There were guidebooks for hosts that listed suggested topics ranging from serious philosophical ones such as "What are the characteristics of the noble man?" to lighter subjects, including, "Why is fresh water better than salt for washing clothes?" "Is Wrestling the oldest sport?" and "What came first, the chicken or the egg?" Finally, the guests went home, but first they might wrap up uneaten food in their napkins to save as a snack for later.

Some wealthy Romans were famous for their gluttony, and there are many well-known instances of ostentatious banquets. The best source for elaborate Roman recipes is a cookbook written by a famous glutton named Apicius. He is said to have spent 100 million sesterces on food, and, when he realized that he only had a few million left, he decided that he could no longer dine properly so he committed suicide. He left behind a book of recipes that range from familiar dishes such as omelets and sweet and sour pork to more exotic fare like ostrich brains, flamingo tongues, sheep's lungs, and pigs' wombs.

Roman gourmands paid enormous sums for the perfect fish, such as the 8,000 sesterces that were spent on one mullet, and periodically the Roman state actually passed laws making it illegal to spend more than a certain amount on one meal or to make overly elaborate dishes. Julius Caesar sent soldiers and lictors into people's dining rooms to make sure that their meals were not too ostentatious and to confiscate excessively elaborate dishes. As an indication of the heights to which luxury could ascend, the emperor Caligula once spent 10 million sesterces on a single dinner party.

Wine was the Roman's drink of choice. The Romans, like the Greeks, usually diluted their wine with water before drinking it. Romans also enjoyed some wines that were served warm, which often had spices added. A popular hot drink was *mulsum,* which was wine sweetened with honey. Fine wines were allowed to age before being drunk, and the Romans recognized that some vintages were superior to others. Imported wines from Greece, such as Chian or Lesbian, were regarded highly. Among Italian wines, Falernian was particularly prized, as well as being considerably more expensive than run-of-the-mill vintages.

Water was also drunk, although even relatively poor people probably had access to some amount of wine. Consuming beer was frowned upon and indeed was considered to be the mark of a northern barbarian. Mediterranean-based peoples such as the Romans defined themselves by their diets so that a Roman governor of a northern province along the Danube was driven to bitterly complain that the locals led a wretched existence because they did not cultivate grapes to make wine.

SEX AND SEXUALITY

During the old Roman Republic, the Romans took a very stern attitude toward sex. At least, this is the impression they tried to give in idealizing literature. Public manifestations of emotion were frowned upon. As an example of such censure, a distinguished senator running for the consulship was not only kicked out of the race but actually expelled from the senate itself for immorality simply because he was seen giving his wife a kiss in public. A person who had sex in the daytime was considered immoral since sex was only supposed to be done at night and secretly. Using a lamp to provide light during sex at night also labeled you as an unhealthy, immoral person. Finally, any woman who took off all of her clothing while having sex was seen as being plainly debauched and immoral. Women were supposed to keep on as much clothing as possible.

These attitudes began to change after the introduction of Greek culture. By the Late Republic and early empire, Romans had become much more open about sexuality and seemingly much more adventurous as well. This more open attitude did not extend to marriage, however. Husbands and wives were obligated to produce children, but there often seems not to have been much affection between them. Marriage was viewed as a social and political relationship, not a romantic one. Some of this lack of affection was no doubt due to the fact that most Roman men and women did not choose their own spouses and were often separated by a vast age difference. Married couples did not share a bed; instead, both husband and wife had their own suite of rooms and their own servants in different parts of the house. This remoteness seems to have led to a certain degree of resentment on the part of Roman wives. An example of this occurred when there was a rash of aristocratic deaths at Rome. Upon investigation, it was discovered that many wives were poisoning their husbands. Some of the women claimed that they had been giving their husbands aphrodisiacs to win their love, but the aphrodisiacs had unfortunately turned out to be toxic. Whether this was their true motivation or they were simply getting revenge on their unfaithful husbands, 170 women were convicted of poisoning.

Oddly enough, it was sometimes seen as dishonorable if a husband was deeply in love with his wife. The Roman general Pompey was in love with his wife and enjoyed spending time with her. He and his young wife would walk for hours together in the gardens and watch the peasants working on their country farms. As a result, Pompey was widely ridiculed and made fun of. Some even ascribed his defeat at the hands of Julius Caesar to the fact that Caesar spent his time plotting and raising armies whereas Pompey dallied away the hours with his wife.

Despite the frequent lack of affection between husband and wife, there was a lot of sex going on in Roman households. All slaves were regarded as fair game by the free members of the household, and it was not uncommon for a master and other members of his family to be simultaneously sleeping with several generations of their slaves. This was not regarded as shameful, at least not for the males.

The entire Roman concept of sexuality was very different from our modern one. They did not categorize people as being homosexual or heterosexual; in fact, there are not really words in Latin that correspond with our modern definitions of *homosexual* and *heterosexual*. Romans could and did have sex with men, women, and children, and it was regarded as normal that one would have relations with people both of one's own gender and of the opposite one. Just as the Romans did not have our modern category of sexual orientation, they were also not as concerned with the types

Figure 8.2 Erotic wall painting from Pompeii.

of sexual acts that people practiced. There were verbs to describe the different sexual acts, and the three main ones were for what we would now term vaginal sex, oral sex, and anal sex. Again, it was expected that a Roman might practice all of these.

The Roman attitude toward sexuality is currently a much debated topic among scholars. Some contend that there was one classification that the Romans were obsessed with. What mattered to them was not the sexual act or the gender of one's partner, but the role one played. In Roman society, passivity or submission was equivalent to inferiority, so to be active was to be superior. In this interpretation, what the Romans were obsessed with was penetration. If you were the penetrator, you were superior and there was nothing shameful about what you were doing. Who or what you penetrated did not matter nearly as much as the fact that you were the active partner. On the other hand, if you were penetrated, it implied that you were like a woman and, therefore, in the Romans' view, inferior, submissive, and bad. Other scholars argue that what was more important to the Romans was the degree to which one exerted control over one's desires and practiced moderation.

One of the greatest insults for a Roman man was to call him effeminate, but this was not necessarily a comment on his demeanor. Julius Caesar had an extremely active sex life, but there was always additional suspicion about him because it was suspected that he played the inferior role at times. A popular Roman witticism claimed that Caesar was "every woman's man and every man's woman" (Suetonius, *Life of Julius Caesar* 52). The first half means that he was promiscuous, but the second half was insulting because it implied his inferiority.

   With Roman men seeking relationships outside of marriage and with most women being married, by necessity there was a great deal of adultery in Rome. Our best source for these affairs comes from Roman poets, two in particular.

   The first of these was the poet Catullus. He lived during the Late Republic at a time of civil war, and although the topic of his poetry was love, his troubled attitude toward it reflects the turmoil of the times he lived in. Catullus fell in love with a married woman named Clodia, and his most famous poems record the course of their affair, ranging from celebrations of passion and the euphoria produced by love to bitter and angry poems recording his hatred of her when she rejects him. Since she was married, he could not refer to her by her real name, so his poetry is addressed to a woman he calls Lesbia. Catullus's poetry captures the extremes of emotion produced by love—happiness, jealousy, and hatred—as exemplified by one of his shorter poems, "I hate and I love. How can this be, you ask. I do not know, but I feel it and am in torment" (Catullus, *Poems* 85). Catullus's intense emotions, particularly when he was ultimately rejected, perhaps wore him out, and his lifestyle also caused him to become bankrupt. He died at the age of 33, leaving behind a small but powerful body of work.

   Another important poet of love, Publius Ovidius Naso (Ovid), lived during the empire. Ovid's work *The Art of Love* is basically a practical manual of advice on how to seduce women. To Ovid, love was a game whose goal was seduction, and he offers tips on how to win this game. He describes good places where one can go in Rome to pick up women, such as the law courts and the colonnades where many likely women could be found. He offers a considerable amount of practical and modern-sounding advice for hopeful lovers, including to wear clean, well-fitting clothes, comb your hair neatly, wash your hands, trim your nostril hair, and avoid bad breath and body odor. He also comments that a tan always looks nice.

   Morality was unimportant to Ovid, so he recommends that, no matter what the truth, men should shower the women they are wooing with flattery and praise and compliment them constantly on their physical appearance. He advises the reader to be persistent and not give up when a woman rejects him, since often one can wear down her defenses. He suggests that getting her drunk can hurry things along and that another good strategy is to cry; if real tears are not forthcoming, one can induce them artificially. To seduce a woman, Ovid says that you should become friends with the woman's maid and her servants because this will help enormously in getting secret love letters to her and sneaking into her house. His solution for mending a lovers' quarrel is to try to get the woman into bed.

   Ovid suggests taking a woman to the circus to watch chariot races as a good date. He tells the lover to find out what horse she is cheering for and then, no matter what his own preference, to cheer loudly for her favorite. He should buy her a cushion to sit on and prevent the people sitting behind her from poking her in the back with their knees. The crowded benches on which the audience sat also gave opportunities to press up against her, and the dust thrown up into the air by the chariots would create an excuse to fondle her while pretending to brush dirt off of her clothes.

The emperor Augustus was very concerned with public morality and consequently was quite offended by Ovid's *Art of Love*. Indeed, he was so outraged that he banished Ovid and sent him to live in exile north of the Black Sea. For someone who thrived on the sophisticated, urban culture of the city of Rome, this amounted to torture, and Ovid spent the rest of his life writing bad poetry praising Augustus in the hope that Augustus would allow him to return to Rome. Unfortunately for Ovid, Augustus never forgave him, and Ovid died alone and miserable far from the city that he loved.

The attitude of the Romans toward Ovid and people like him is hard to determine. Roman literature is filled with moralizing against adultery, yet it is clear that many people practiced it. With all the sexual activity, contraception was obviously a concern. The Romans did have the idea to use sheep's intestines as condoms, and this was probably at least somewhat effective. However, the most common type of contraception was magic potions and charms. A Roman encyclopedia records one charm that was thought to be highly effective. Women were instructed to find a certain species of large, hairy spider. It was believed that if the head of the spider was cut open, one would find two small worms, and if a woman wore these worms on her body, it would prevent pregnancy. This contraceptive was thought to be effective for one year, after which a woman would have to find another spider (Pliny the Elder, *Natural History* 29.27.85).

Rome had its share of prostitutes. The term for prostitute was *meretrix*. Prostitution was legal in Rome, and all prostitutes were required to register themselves with an aedile (urban magistrate), who would collect taxes from them. The tax, computed on a daily basis, was intended to be equal to the amount she got from her first client of the day. Some prostitutes roamed the streets of the city, and a good place to find them was around the *Circus Maximus,* but most were based in brothels.

In the third century AD, Rome had 45 brothels. By law, a brothel could not open before 3:00 P.M. Many of these brothels have been excavated, particularly at Pompeii. They consisted of a lot of little rooms, each one containing a rather narrow, stone bed on which was placed a mattress. The walls were decorated with graphically obscene paintings. In addition, many inns and hotels would provide prostitutes for their guests, which was regarded as a normal service. One hotel bill lists the charges run up by a guest, including his room, meals, hay for his mule, and the price of a girl (*CIL* 9.2689).

Finally, there was a great deal of what we today would classify as pornography in Roman culture, although the Romans did not see it as

Figure 8.3 Bronze good-luck charm in the shape of an erect penis with legs, tail, and wings.

such. Many Roman lamps and bowls were decorated with graphic erotic scenes. The large numbers of these that survive indicate that they were mass-market items used in everyday life by average Romans. There was a healthy market in erotic artwork, and many private homes contained sexually explicit paintings and mosaics. The Romans were a superstitious people and wore many charms to ward off evil. The most popular of these was cast in the shape of an erect male organ.

9

Entertainment in Ancient Rome

HOLIDAYS

The Roman calendar included a large number of public holidays, called *feriae,* that increased in number as time went on. (See Appendix II for more on the calendar.) On some of these days, there would have been private rituals of worship, but more common were religious rites performed by state officials at mass ceremonies, often accompanied by public entertainments held as a part of the religious observances.

One popular Roman holiday was the Saturnalia. Originally an agricultural festival held during the winter solstice, it was meant particularly to honor the god Saturn, who was associated with grain and the growing of wheat. The Saturnalia initially was held just after the last wheat crop of the year was sown. Eventually the Romans settled on December 17 as the date to celebrate the Saturnalia, but as the festival grew in popularity, they kept adding days until, by the high empire, the Saturnalia was a full, weeklong holiday beginning on the 17th. The official component of the Saturnalia was on December 17, when the senators performed a mass animal sacrifice at the temple of Saturn, and afterward there was a huge banquet to which everyone was invited. The rest of the week was taken up with nonstop parties and feasts. All shops, law courts, and schools were closed. Normal moral restraints were loosened and everyone was expected to engage in all forms of revelry and fun. This was the only time of year when people were legally allowed to gamble in public. Bands of revelers ran through the streets drinking and shouting *"Io Saturnalia."*

Some of the customs of this festival involved inversions in status. Thus, for one day of the week, slaves were treated as equals, and often at the banquet that day, masters would wait on their slaves and serve them their food. During the festival, everyone wore liberty caps, symbolizing either that for the moment everyone was equal or that everyone was expected to behave with freedom and abandon. Each family would select a *princeps*, or "leader," of the Saturnalia, who presided over the parties. Often this was someone normally of low status, such as a child. Another custom of the Saturnalia was exchanging gifts. People gave dolls made out of clay to children and wax candles to their friends. Not all Romans approved of such merrymaking, however. The senator Pliny the Younger supposedly had a special soundproofed room constructed at his villa, and while everyone else in his household was having a good time and partying, Pliny would retreat to his room for the week and work.

Another popular holiday, which fell on the 15th of February, seems to have been a festival somehow associated with the story of Romulus and Remus, the legendary founders of Rome who were raised by a wolf. The name of this festival was the Lupercalia. Since the Latin word for wolf is *lupus*, this is one of the reasons it was thought to be associated with the legend of Rome's founding. On the 15th of February, priests gathered at a cave believed to be the lair of the wolf who had raised Romulus and Remus. There, the priests sacrificed several goats and a dog. Two young men of aristocratic families then came forward and had their foreheads smeared with the bloodstained knife. Other priests wiped away the blood using wool that had been soaked in milk. Next, the skins of the goats were sliced up into long leather strips, and everyone indulged in a rowdy feast. After the feast came the highlight of the celebration: Young men stripped naked, took the goatskin strips in their hands, and ran through the streets of the city, whipping bystanders. Women in particular would line the streets to watch the naked men and to invite the runners to beat them. It was believed that a woman who was whipped by one of the Lupercalia runners would become more fertile.

One of the more serious festivals, held on the 9th, 11th, and 13th of May, was called the Lemuria. This was a ceremony intended to appease spirits of the dead who were walking the earth, often because they had died an untimely death. These wandering ghosts were called *lemures*. Rather than being a big public ceremony, this was a private one performed by each family. Each head of a family had to get up at midnight. His feet had to be bare, and he could not have any knots anywhere on his clothing. He first made an apotropaic gesture with his thumb held between his closed fingers. Then he washed his hands and walked through the entire house, spitting out black beans. As he did so, he repeated nine times the phrase, "With these beans I redeem me and mine." He washed his hands again and clanged together bronze vessels, repeating nine times, "Ghosts be gone." Throughout this entire ceremony, he was forbidden to look behind him because presumably the ghosts were following him and picking up the beans. After the ninth repetition of "Ghosts be gone," he finally looked behind him, and this ended the ceremony.

GLADIATORS

On some holidays, the state provided public entertainment, of which there were two broad categories. The first was *ludi*, meaning "games." These took many forms, including theatrical performances, dances, and circus races. The vast majority of entertainments were *ludi*. Much rarer were *munera*. These were spectacles such as gladiatorial combats, wild animal shows, and other unusual exhibitions. The biggest difference between the Romans' concept of entertainment and our own is that all of these events had a religious component. The Romans regarded them as a form of worship, and prayers and sacrifices to the gods were a part of all of them.

Gladiatorial combats have a very ancient history in Roman society. They probably originated with the Etruscans, the predecessors of the Romans in central Italy. Among the Etruscans, when a king or war leader died, as part of the funeral ceremony a pair of warriors fought to the death as a way to honor the warlike spirit of the leader. Over time, this practice became institutionalized, and the Romans subsequently imitated it. Throughout the next 800 years of the Roman Republic, gladiator games remained very rare and on a small scale and were always held as part of a funeral service.

Like many other things, this began to change in the Late Republic. Julius Caesar is regarded as the man who began to transform them from primarily a religious ceremony into a form of entertainment. At an early point in his career when he was trying to gain fame, Caesar put on a gladiatorial show that featured an unheard-of 320 pairs of gladiators. This was supposedly in honor of his father, despite the fact that the elder Caesar had been dead for over 20 years. Whatever the effects on the ghost of Caesar's father, these games made Caesar popular with the people of Rome.

During the empire, by law the senate could sponsor no more than two gladiator shows per year. There was no limit, however, to the number the emperor could hold. Despite this, they always remained rare and unusual events. In his 60-plus-year reign, the emperor Augustus put on gladiator shows only eight times. Thus, the popular image in movies and on television of Romans spending all their time at gladiator shows is erroneous.

There were three sources for gladiators. The first and most common was slaves who were condemned to be gladiators because they either had committed some crime or else seemed likely to be good fighters. This latter category included prisoners of war captured in Rome's campaigns. Second, criminals were sometimes condemned to be gladiators. The third (and by far the rarest) category was free people who volunteered to become gladiators in a quest for fame and money.

When one became a gladiator, he (the vast majority of gladiators were men, although there are a few attested instances of female gladiators) was sent to gladiator school, where the first thing he did was abandon his old name and take a new stage name. During the republic, most of these schools were privately owned businesses, but under the empire, they all fell under the control of the emperor and the state. The staff of the schools included weapon makers, guards, masseurs, doctors, and most important, the trainer, called a *lanista*. This was the man who actually taught novice gladiators how to fight.

The new gladiator first underwent general training with wooden weapons until he became familiar with basic fighting techniques. At this point, the *lanista* evaluated him and assigned him to different programs of specialized training depending on his abilities. There were at least 14 different varieties of gladiator, divided up according to their type of weapons and tactics. The Romans liked to see battles of contrasts, and thus nearly all gladiator contests matched a heavily armed and armored man against a lightly armed but more mobile opponent.

The heavily armored types of gladiators included the Gaul, Hoplite, Samnite, and *secutor*. All of these were armed with a sword and helmet that completely covered the face. Some were totally covered in armor, while others had lighter armor but possessed huge, five-foot-tall shields. In all these cases, the gladiators were well protected but slow moving.

The lighter-armed opponents came in two main categories. The first was the Thracian. He wore little or no armor and carried in one hand a small shield made only of wood or wicker and in the other a short, curved sword. The Thracian would dart back and forth, looking for a gap in his enemy's armor. In turn, his heavily armed enemy would laboriously pursue him, trying to trap him against a wall where he could not use his agility to escape. The other type of lightly armed gladiator was perhaps the most skilled of all and provided the greatest battle of contrasts. This was the *retiarius*. The *retiarius* was completely naked except for a loincloth. In one hand, he held a net with weights at the corners and in the other, a trident. His strategy was to dance around an opponent and try to entangle him in the net, where he could be skewered by the trident. In the final stages of his training, the gladiator would switch from wooden weapons to real steel ones.

When someone wished to put on a gladiatorial show, he would rent the desired number of gladiators from one of the schools. The prices seemed to range from about 1,000 sesterces for a first-time or not very talented gladiator to around 15,000 for an experienced veteran of many combats. The most famous gladiators could command gigantic fees for their every appearance, and some are attested whose fee was over 100,000 sesterces.

Figure 9.1 Relief of two gladiators fighting.

One rather odd part of the ritual leading up to a contest was that on the night before the fight, all the gladiators who would be attempting to kill one another the next day ate dinner together. Curious or morbid fans could pay to come and watch these dinners.

Some gladiators, particularly enemy soldiers captured in war, when faced with the prospect of fighting each other, would choose to commit suicide. On one famous occasion, 29 Germans who were supposed to fight the next day strangled each other. An even more horrible method of suicide was employed by another German who found a way to kill himself when he was allowed to go to the bathroom. Romans did not have toilet paper, but in its place each bathroom was equipped with a sponge on a stick. The German took one of these sponges and crammed it down his throat, thereby suffocating himself.

On the day of the show, the festivities began with a big parade of all the participants. At the head of the parade was the person providing the funding, who was accompanied by lictors as if he were a magistrate. During this parade, and indeed all throughout the day's activities, there was a band playing. Such bands included flute players, horn players, and often a water organ. In the morning, there might be exhibitions of beasts and beast hunts. These continued until noon, when there was an intermission.

During this intermission, the spectators could choose to either go get some lunch or stay and watch executions. During this interval, particularly bad criminals were led into the arena, where they were lined up and had their throats cut. These criminals were known as *noxii*. When Christians were persecuted during the later empire, they were often executed during the intermission. Once at some games at which he was presiding, the emperor Caligula became bored because there were no criminals to be executed during the intermission. His solution was to order his guards to throw an entire section of the crowd into the arena to be eaten by animals.

In the afternoon came the main event, the gladiator fight. According to one tradition, the gladiators came out and raised their weapons in salute to the giver of the games while shouting the phrase *Morituri te salutant* (We who are about to die salute you). The gladiators started off by yelling abuse at one another and then, at a signal, they would begin to fight. Most fans had a favorite type of gladiator that they would root for and enjoyed arguing with each other over the merits and drawbacks of the different varieties of fighter. In these combats, there were no referees, no rules, and no time limit. Whenever a gladiator received a wound, the crowd would shout out *Habet*, meaning a hit. A gladiator could ask for mercy by dropping his shield and raising a finger of his left hand. The crowd then either called for him to be killed or, if he had fought well, asked that he be spared. They did this using both shouts and gestures. Hollywood has decided that the thumbs-down gesture meant that he should be killed and thumbs up that he should be spared. In Latin, the relevant passage does not specify which way the thumb was turned, only that the gesture involved the turning of the thumb. Many scholars believe that the thumbs-down sign was actually a way of calling for the victorious gladiator to drop his weapon and spare his enemy, whereas the thumbs up meant to stab him in the throat. If the crowd demanded death, then the winner plunged his sword into his enemy's throat. The victor received the palm of victory, a crown, and prize money.

It is hard to determine how many contests ended in death; sources mention some games in which nearly every contest resulted in the death of the loser, while at other games nearly everyone was spared. Each gladiator probably fought only a couple of times a year, but nonetheless to win more than 10 combats seems to have been exceptional. Perhaps the record was held by one gladiator who was said to have been the victor in no fewer than 88 combats over the course of his career. If a gladiator fought extraordinarily well, he could be freed, although it seems that many of these continued to fight even though they no longer had to. When they were freed, they received a wooden sword, called the *rudis*, which was the symbol of their freedom.

Champion gladiators were celebrities with status similar to that of rock stars today. Women threw themselves at them, and there are many stories of even rich aristocratic women having affairs with gladiators. The gladiator functioned as a symbol of virility in Roman society. At the same time, they were also one of the most despised groups in society; it is an interesting contradiction of the Romans that they both glorified and looked down on the same figure. Even though gladiator games always remained relatively rare, by the second century AD, they could involve huge numbers of participants. In one of the greatest spectacles, the emperor Trajan gave games lasting 123 days, during which 10,000 gladiators fought.

THE FLAVIAN AMPHITHEATER (THE COLOSSEUM)

The earliest gladiatorial games seem to have been held in the Roman Forum, and this practice continued throughout nearly the entire republic. For some of the larger, more elaborate games toward the end of the republic, temporary wooden amphitheaters were constructed.

The basic amphitheater form, as implied by the name, seems to have been inspired by simply attaching two theaters back-to-back. This created a central arena where combat took place that was entirely surrounded by stepped seating for the audience. The sandy, oval area at the center was called the arena, literally meaning "sand," and the seating area was known as the *cavea*. The oldest known stone amphitheater is located in the city of Pompeii on the Bay of Naples. The first permanent stone amphitheater at Rome was not built until 30 BC, when one was constructed in the Campus Martius by Statilius Taurus.

The largest and most famous amphitheater is, of course, the one today known as the Colosseum, although its proper name is the Flavian Amphitheater after the family of emperors who built it in the late first century AD. The founder of the Flavian Dynasty was the emperor Vespasian, who came to power in AD 69 by emerging as the victor in a civil war. By the mid-70s AD, Vespasian had begun construction on his great amphitheater.

Some of the motivation for the project seems to have been a public relations ploy to win popularity for the new dynasty among the city's inhabitants. Even the location chosen for the amphitheater was symbolic since it was built on the grounds of Nero's fantastic palace; it thus symbolized a return of this land to the public rather than its being used exclusively for the emperor's pleasure. Vespasian had the artificial lake of Nero's palace drained, and this site below the Oppian hill became the place upon which the new amphitheater rose.

Figure 9.2 Model of the Flavian Amphitheater (the Colosseum). (Scala/Art Resource, NY.)

To support the great weight of the structure, a large area was excavated, and concrete foundations an impressive 12 meters deep were poured. The footprint of the building was 188 meters on the long axis by 156 meters wide. The actual space occupied by the arena where the gladiators fought was 86 meters by 54 meters. In its final form, the outside ascended four levels. The bottom level was a continuous ring of 80 arches of the Tuscan order (Doric with square bases). On top of this was another colonnade of Ionic arches. Above this was yet a third level consisting of an arched colonnade of the Corinthian order.

The third level seems to have been as far as the construction had progressed by the time of Vespasian's death, but his son Titus, the next emperor, finished the building by adding a fourth level and inaugurating it in AD 80. The fourth level was a solid layer with Corinthian pilasters. The total height of the four layers of the exterior wall was 48.5 meters.

The whole edifice was composed of a mixture of concrete core with brick facing and tufa and travertine stone. It has been estimated that over 100,000 tons of fine travertine stone were used in the facing of the amphitheater. This covering was attached to the structure with iron clamps, which themselves weighed around a total of 300 tons.

Upon entering one of the 78 ground-level entrances, each of which was marked by a number, spectators found their way to their seats through an extraordinarily complex network of ramps, stairs, and corridors. Those destined for the upper levels made use of different corridors from those whose seating was in the lower *cavea*. In all, there were four tiers of seats and an additional standing-room-only gallery at the highest level. Altogether, the Flavian Amphitheater could probably have accommodated

Figure 9.3 Interior of the Flavian Amphitheater. The floor of the arena is missing, revealing the network of rooms, cages, passages, and elevators that lay beneath it.

about 55,000 spectators. Roman spectators appear to have been given tokens similar to modern stadium tickets that listed the number of their gate, the level, the section, and the row where they would sit.

The seating within the *cavea* was arranged as a microcosm of Roman society, with the spectators placed according to their status. The emperor or the presiding magistrate, along with his coterie, was seated in a special box, and other prime seats at the lowest level were reserved for other important figures, including the Vestal Virgins. The lowest rows of seats were reserved for senators, and those immediately above were similarly set aside for equestrians. The poor women and slaves seem to have been relegated to the highest level in the gallery.

Beneath the floor of the arena were two subterranean levels that contained as least 32 cages for wild animals as well as rooms for gladiators and equipment. This underground maze also included an elaborate system of trapdoors and elevators to raise scenery up into the arena or, perhaps most spectacularly, to disgorge combatants or wild animals, which would appear to spring forth unexpectedly from the ground itself. The exact number and operation of these trapdoors and elevators are a matter of some scholarly debate. There seem to have been at least 32 of them but possibly many more. The much smaller amphitheater at Capua, for example, featured no fewer than 62 trapdoors and elevators of varying sizes.

One of the unpleasant trials of attending an event in the Mediterranean can be the hot sun, but the amphitheater even provided for this contingency.

Attached to the top level was a forest of 240 wooden masts from which was suspended a retractable cloth covering called the velarium. This cover could be deployed or pulled back as needed to provide shade for the spectators in various parts of the *cavea*. Precisely how this enormous retractable roof was rigged is another hot topic of scholarly contention, but apparently a contingent of sailors was stationed in the city to operate the ropes and pulleys. This feature seems to have been included even on earlier versions of amphitheaters; there is a reference to its abuse by the emperor Caligula, who delighted in locking the exits and pulling back the velarium on an especially hot day, causing audience members to faint from the heat.

Along with the Pantheon, the Flavian Amphitheater is perhaps one of the most influential Roman buildings since the features of nearly all modern sports complexes can be traced back to it.

Just to the east of the Flavian Amphitheater was a complex known as the Ludus Magnus. This was one of four gladiator training schools set up by the emperor Domitian to ensure an adequate supply of gladiators for the amphitheater. It included barracks, training facilities, and a small amphitheater that could hold about 3,000 spectators. The entire complex was directly connected to the substructure of the Flavian Amphitheater by an underground tunnel.

CHARIOT RACING AND THE CIRCUS MAXIMUS

The largest stadium in Rome was not the Colosseum but the Circus Maximus. This was the site of chariot races, which were the favorite entertainment of the average citizen of Rome. The Circus Maximus was situated in the long, narrow valley between the Palatine and Aventine hills, which formed a natural stadium for chariot racing. The Etruscans seem to have first held races here, and crowds likely gathered on the natural slopes of the hills to watch. Over time, the creek in the bottom of the valley was drained and a wooden structure erected. By the empire, this seems to have been largely replaced by a stone one, and by the time of Trajan it had become a gigantic and awe-inspiring marble stadium. Races continued to be held here through at least the sixth century AD.

The Circus Maximus was by far the largest stadium in Rome. It was a third of a mile long and could seat potentially up to 350,000 spectators. Unlike the Flavian Amphitheater, whose 55,000 seats would have been largely occupied by the upper classes, the size of the Circus Maximus meant that all segments of Roman society could attend races. Admission was free or for a nominal fee. In addition, chariot races were held frequently. Whereas there might have been only two or three gladiator contests per year, each of the over 100 holidays per year would have included chariot racing. All these factors ensured that chariot racing was the most popular form of entertainment for the average inhabitant of the city as well as the most accessible.

Organizations called factions trained, equipped, and entered teams in the races. Originally, there seem to have been just two of these, the Reds and the Whites. Later, two more were added, the Blues and the Greens. One of the emperors tried to create two new groups, the Golds and the Purples, but these did not catch on, and for most of racing history, the four big groups dominated. They were large and powerful organizations; each one owned extensive stables and breeding farms for their horses and highly organized training centers and schools for their charioteers. Naturally, they also maintained a number of grooms and veterinarians. On one occasion, the factions refused to provide horses unless they were paid more. The praetor in charge of games threatened to substitute dogs instead, but the emperor Nero then intervened with a cash gift.

The Circus Maximus was an impressive building whose design affected the course of the races. It enclosed a long, oval-shaped track, and the entire structure in its final form was about 600 meters long and 180 meters wide. One end of the oval was flat rather than curved and the starting gates *(carceres)* were located along the flat side of the oval. There were 12 of these gates; thus, a race could have a maximum of 12 chariots. Down the center of the track was a long, narrow divider known as the *spina,* meaning "spine." At each end of the *spina* were placed three cones, known as the *metae.* These were the posts around which the chariots turned. Along its length, the *spina* was decorated with several Egyptian obelisks as well as various statues and monuments. Among these were the mechanisms used to mark laps. One way this was indicated was with large, golden eggs that were lowered or raised as each lap was completed. This method was supplemented by Agrippa, who had erected seven golden dolphins. These were used to indicate when each lap had been finished, probably by being tipped. The Romans regarded the dolphin as the fastest creature, so this was a symbolically appropriate device for a horse race. Also, dolphins were associated with the god of the sea, Neptune, who was himself associated with horses. A standard race consisted of seven laps, and as the lead chariot crossed the finish line on each lap, one of the dolphins was tipped. The area between the turning posts also featured pools of water and fountains, and on at least one occasion an emperor replaced the water with wine. Painted lines delineated the lanes and the finish line. The surface of the track was probably sand over another, firmer substance. Some emperors had pigments added to the sand to create a spectacular appearance, including instances when the track was colored red or green, or when shiny rocks such as mica were added to the sand to give a glittering effect. The total length of a standard race was about eight kilometers and probably took less than 15 minutes to complete.

There were many varieties of races. One employed two-horse chariots, which were called *bigae.* The most popular and common races involved four-horse chariots called *quadrigae.* Nearly all races were of one of these two main types, although for the sake of variety there were odd vari-

Figure 9.4 Reconstruction drawing of the northern half of the Circus Maximus, seen from behind the starting gates. (From G. Gatteschi, *Restauri della Roma Imperiale*, 1924, p. 53.)

Figure 9.5 The valley of the Circus Maximus today, viewed from approximately the same perspective as Figure 9.4.

ations. The Romans experimented with different numbers of horses, sometimes using odd numbers of horses, such as in three-horse chariots, and other times yoking large numbers of horses to a single chariot. The largest recorded example of the latter was a race held with chariots each drawn by no fewer than 10 horses. One unusual type of race was the *pedibus ad quadrigum*. The exact nature of this race is debated, but it clearly incorporated a footrace element into the chariot race. One theory holds that there was a passenger in each chariot in addition to the driver, and as soon as each chariot crossed the finish line, the passenger jumped out and had to run one additional lap around the circus to win. This would certainly have been a hazardous situation for the runner with all the other rival chariots still on the track, and one can readily imagine frequent "accidents" as the runner was trampled under the hooves or wheels of competing *quadrigae*.

In a *quadriga* race with 12 chariots competing, each faction would have entered 3 chariots of its color. The factions drew lots to determine the order in which the drivers would select their starting gate. The signal for the start of the race was when the emperor or presiding magistrate dropped a cloth called the *mappa*.

On the straightaways, each charioteer would urge his horses to go as fast as possible, and the points of greatest tension were the turns around the *metae* at either end of the *spina*. In modern racecourses, the turns are very gradual, but in the circus, each chariot actually had to complete a 180-degree turn. Naturally, the chariot that turned closest to the *metae* would travel the shortest distance and would therefore have the inside track on the next straightaway. This led to the chariots bunching together, and crashes were frequent. The actual stadium seems to have been designed to maximize carnage, and crashes were often fatal. Making races even more competitive was the fact that all the chariots from a single faction might work together as a team. To ensure the victory of one chariot from the faction, the other two might possibly sacrifice themselves by obstructing chariots from the other factions or even intentionally ramming them.

There were 24 races per day; thus, one could spend an entire day at the Circus Maximus. The winning charioteer received a crown of palm leaves and the winner's prize money. These prizes seem to have ranged between 5,000 and 60,000 sesterces for first place, and there were also lesser prizes for second, third, and fourth place. The inhabitants of Rome were truly fanatical spectators. Just as modern sports fans follow specific teams, Romans would choose a faction and live and die with the fortunes of that group. An example of the extremes to which this fanaticism could reach happened when one of the most successful charioteers for the Whites died in a crash; at his funeral when the body was being cremated, a distraught fan flung himself on the pyre. Even fans who didn't go to such lengths were rabidly enthusiastic about their factions. Dressed in the appropriate

Figure 9.6 Sculptural relief of a chariot race in the Circus Maximus. The turning posts *(metae)* and dolphin lap markers are visible on the *spina*.

Figure 9.7 Wall painting of the riot of AD 59 in the amphitheater at Pompeii, which resulted in a ban on amphitheater events for 10 years.

color, they went to the Circus Maximus in large groups and sat together. They developed elaborate cheers and songs that tens of thousands of fans would chant and sing in unison. Often these chants deteriorated into abuse directed at the fans of other factions, and riots were not infrequent.

The most violent of these riots occurred not at Rome but at Constantinople. By the time it was over, most of the city had been burned down and 30,000 people were dead. Since one common chant of the factions was *Nike*, meaning "victory," this riot became known as the Nike Riot. Another famous riot, although this time at a gladiator game, happened in AD 59 at Pompeii, when a large group of spectators from a neighboring city got into a fight with the locals. In the ensuing riot, many people were killed, and the city of Pompeii was banned from holding any games for the next 10 years.

The most popular faction among the poor people seems to have been the Greens, who were also favored by most of the insane emperors, including Caligula, Nero, Commodus, and Elagabalus. Zealous fans sometimes placed curse tablets in the stables of their rivals. One of these that has been found featured on one side a number of magical words and on the other the injunction, "Demon, I demand and ask of you that from this day, hour, and moment forward that you torture the horses of the Greens and Whites. Kill Them! Kill also the charioteers Glarus, Felix, Primulus, and Romanus. Cause them to crash and leave no breath in their bodies!" (Sherk, *Roman Empire* 217). Concern over this practice actually led to a law being passed declaring it illegal to use magic against charioteers.

The most successful charioteers became phenomenally wealthy as well as famous. They were celebrities who even had poems written about them. A number of monuments put up in honor of these charioteers have been found, erected after their deaths by mourning fans. Typical of these charioteers was a man named Crescens. He was an African who began racing at the age of 13 and who died in a crash at 22. His monument notes that during this time, he won victory purses totaling 1.5 million sesterces (*CIL* 6.10050). One of the most successful charioteers was a man named Gaius Apuleius Diocles. He was from what is now Portugal and began racing at 18 for the Whites, although he did not win a race until he was 20. He later switched to the Greens and then again to the Reds. His racing career lasted 24 years, and he participated in 4,257 races, 1,462 of which he won. The prizes he earned were worth a total of 4 million sesterces. More than 1,000 of his victories occurred in races in which there was only one team from each faction; he won 347 times when there were two teams from each faction and only 51 times when there were three teams from each faction. The inscription recording his life contains the information that 815 of his victories came in races in which he led from the start, 67 were in races in which he came from behind, and 36 were in races in which he managed to win even after another racer had passed him at some point.

Figure 9.8 Mosaic of a charioteer of the Red faction with his horse. Successful charioteers could become wealthy and attain a celebrity-like status.

On 42 occasions, he emerged victorious in other ways, perhaps due to his opponents crashing. Finally, it is mentioned that he won races at various times while driving two, four, six, and even seven horse chariots (*ILS* 5287).

Many charioteers died not directly as the result of a crash but from being dragged around the track after one. This happened because charioteers habitually tied the reins to their arms. All charioteers carried a knife during races with which they hoped to be able to cut themselves free, but this may have been wishful thinking rather than a practical solution.

BEAST HUNTS

The Romans seem to have had a real fascination with exotic animals. Oddly enough, however, a proper zoo was never established at Rome; instead, they seem mostly to have enjoyed just watching these animals kill or be killed. As with gladiatorial combat, this form of entertainment grew popular in the Late Republic. Pompey started the trend with some games at which several hundred lions and leopards were killed. The Roman conquest of North Africa and Egypt made all sorts of exotic animals available. The first hippo and crocodile were seen at Rome in 58 BC. How quickly this type of entertainment expanded can be seen by considering a single day during the empire when the following animals were slaughtered at Rome: 32 elephants, 10 elk, 20 mules, 10 tigers, 40 horses, 60 lions, 30 leopards, 10 hyenas, 10 giraffes, 6 hippos, 1 rhino, and several dozen gazelles and ostriches.

There were four main ways in which animals were used for entertainment: an armed man versus a wild animal or animals, animals versus other animals, people being fed to animals, and trained animals performing tricks.

This last category was unusual in that it was the only one that did not focus upon the death of the participants. The Romans enjoyed watching performing bears and seals do tricks, much as people at modern circuses do. They also had trained elephants that were tightrope walkers. One celebrated dog would apparently lick up a bowl of poison. It would then go into violent convulsions, after which it flopped over, apparently dead. This was all an act, however, and at the end the dog was revealed to be alive. There was also a group of trained monkeys dressed as soldiers, some of whom rode goats as if they were horses, and others who drove chariots pulled by teams of goats. One of the consuls in 35 BC had a pet elephant that he rode to dinner parties.

A beast hunt, called a *venatione*, usually pitted a man called a *bestiarius*, armed with a dagger or spear, against one or several animals. To make these hunts more exciting, sometimes little natural settings were built in the arena, including forests, hills, caves, and streams. Some emperors seem to have enjoyed displaying their prowess as hunters before the Roman public. The emperor Domitian liked to show off his skill as an archer and would shoot animals in the head with a pair of arrows in such a way that the arrows protruded from the animal's head like horns.

The mentally unbalanced emperor Commodus, who considered himself a mighty hunter, had specially made arrows with curved tips. He liked to shoot these at ostriches while they were running because the arrows would neatly cut off the ostriches' heads, but the bodies would go on running for a while before they collapsed. On another occasion, he had 100 lions released into the amphitheater and killed them all using exactly 100 spears. His bravery did not match his skill, however, since he had walkways placed above the floor of the amphitheater, and it was from these elevated and safe platforms that he killed the animals rather than confronting them down on the surface of the arena. On one occasion a beast hunt provided Commodus with a way to intimidate the senate. He despised the senate and had many of the senators put to death. After killing some ostriches in the arena, he picked up one of the severed heads, walked over to where the senate was sitting, and shook the head at them—a clear message that he would like to do the same to the senators. This bizarre and ridiculous image provoked humor rather than fear in some of the senators. One who described the scene resorted to stuffing the laurel leaves of the crown he was wearing into his mouth and desperately chewing them to avoid bursting out in laughter, which probably would have resulted in his death.

Figure 9.9 Mosaic of a *bestiarius* fighting a leopard. These men were rarely armed with more than a simple spear or dagger.

One creative variant on a beast hunt occurred during the reign of the emperor Septimius Severus, who had an enormous ship built in the Circus Maximus. It was designed so that it would collapse and release 700 animals of seven different species, which were then hunted down. This was apparently intended as a kind of shipwreck scenario. Coins were issued during this set of games that bore the legend "*laetitia tempore*," or "happy times."

When animals were pitted against each other, the Romans often tied them together with a chain to make sure that they would fight. Favorite pairings of this sort included a bull versus a bear and an elephant versus a rhino. The last form of beast show was perhaps the most sadistic. The Romans had special little wagons built that had a stake projecting up from them. Criminals were tied to these stakes and then the wagons were wheeled into the arena. After the handlers had left, they released starving animals, which proceeded to chew on the helpless victims at their leisure.

Perhaps the most amazing beast hunt took place during the 123-day-long games of Trajan, which, in addition to featuring 10,000 gladiators, saw no less than 11,000 wild animals slaughtered in the arena. In view of statistics such as this, it is no surprise that in about a century, the Romans had caused most of the wild animals of North Africa to become extinct.

SPECTACLES

In addition to these regularly scheduled entertainments, occasionally an emperor would sponsor a special spectacle. One example was a naumachia (naval battle). These could be held on an existing lake, or an artificial lake might be dug. Squadrons of ships manned by slaves or criminals might be pitted against each other. The biggest naumachia ever was held on the Fucine Lake by the emperor Claudius. In this colossal battle, two complete fleets of ships were manned by 19,000 men.

Another category of spectacle that was always popular was reenactments of famous historical battles or mythological stories. Simple spectacles might involve dressing a few gladiators up as Greeks and Trojans to have a Trojan War, or as Spartans and Athenians to stage a Peloponnesian War. More creative reenactments told mythological stories. A favorite one was the myth of Orpheus. Orpheus was a Greek musician so skilled that wild beasts would docilely listen to him play. Naturally, in the Roman version, the beasts were only soothed initially and the spectacle ended with the poor slave dressed as Orpheus being eaten by wild beasts. Another popular myth was that of Icarus, a man who supposedly constructed wings out of wax and feathers and flew. Foolishly, Icarus approached too close to the sun and the wax melted, causing his wings to fall apart and Icarus to crash to his death. To recreate this myth, a slave was outfitted with wings and then flung off the top of the stadium. On one occasion, the man playing Icarus crashed so close to the couch of Nero that the emperor was splattered with blood. The Romans also liked to recreate scenes from their own history. A popular one was the story of the Roman hero Mucius Scaevola, who burned off his own hand to demonstrate his bravery.

Sometimes, rather than using special effects to simulate violence in plays, they would simply insert a slave and inflict real violence. Nero once attended a play called *The Fire*. A full-size wooden house was constructed onstage and filled with valuable objects. It was then lit on fire, and people were told that they could keep whatever they could save from the burning, collapsing building. Entertainments such as these destroyed the fundamental distinction between theater and real life.

The violence and cruelty of many Roman spectacles have prompted much debate regarding their purpose and morality. Even among the Romans, there were some who questioned them and were disgusted by them. One traditional justification the Romans gave is that they were a warlike people and should therefore be accustomed to violent death. Others, both ancient and modern, have suggested that the games served as a symbolic assertion of Roman dominance since many of the entertainments featured foreigners whose fate was determined by the will of the crowd representing the Roman people. Another suggested interpretation summed up by the phrase "bread and circuses" is that the games served as a way of keeping the masses distracted and uninterested in politics. The truth may be a complex mixture of all of these factors, but regardless, gladiator games and fantastic spectacles remain one of the best-known aspects of Roman civilization.

THEATER, DANCE, AND PANTOMIME

There were some popular forms of entertainment that did not involve violence. In ancient Rome, theater, music, and dance were often combined as one synthetic experience rather than presented as independent art forms. From the third century BC on, plays were performed on the model of Greek theater, with masks and without women actors. The male actors, who were usually slaves or freedmen who had been specially trained for the stage, played the female parts as well. Roman playwrights are best known today for their comedies, which relied on stock characters, coincidences, and mistaken or hidden identities.

For a long time, the Romans made do with temporary, wooden theaters. Some of these could be quite elaborate, with marble columns and statues. The first stone theater at Rome, built in the southern Campus Martius by Pompey the Great in 55 BC, could hold approximately 11,000 spectators. This theater was quickly supplemented in the next 50 years by two others, the Theater of Balbus and the Theater of Marcellus, which could hold an estimated 14,000 spectators.

From the first century BC on, mimes and pantomimes surpassed plays to become the most popular forms of theatrical entertainment. Ancient mime was different in style from what is currently practiced, since the performers had speaking roles. Mimes sang, danced, and acted without masks, while pantomimes wore masks, acted, and danced but didn't sing; instead, musicians or a chorus offered musical accompaniment. Also, women were permitted to act in mimes and pantomimes. In a general sense, the two forms can be distinguished by subject matter; mimes tended to be realistic, comic, and even vulgar and could deal with any topic, whereas pantomimes resembled ballet productions of themes and stories from myth and evolved into impressive spectacles full of elaborate staging, costumes, and special effects.

Mime did not require a special setting; it was often used as entertainment between acts at the theater, so mimes would perform in front of a linen screen pulled out to hide the stage scenery. Mimes were considered more lowbrow than pantomimes, as they were meant to produce laughter by any means, including physical comedy and beatings, while pantomimes were often tragic in character. Songs heard at mimes sometimes became popular among the public at large. The popularity of these forms of entertainment was probably at least partly due to the relative unimportance of language; Rome's diverse populace and its many foreigners could appreciate the stories being told through the actors' use of gestures and sign language, which were crucial to conveying the action.

Ancient Roman dance was not completely like dance in the modern sense in that it often focused on stylized rhythmic and expressive move-

Figure 9.10 Reconstruction of the Theater of Pompey. (From G. Gatteschi, *Restauri della Roma Imperiale*, 1924, p. 89.)

ments of the head and hands. There are mentions of athletically strenuous motions such as leaps, twists, quick turns, jerks, and suddenly freezing in place—all of which were intended to help illustrate the story being told.

Dance and dramatic performances were accompanied by music, and choral singing and solos existed in ancient times. Poetry was usually set to music (played on stringed instruments), and musicians were often also poets who did the musical arrangements for their own poems.

The most popular instruments for "artistic" musical performances were the flute and the cithara (resembling a harp without a fret board), which could be played with either the hands or a plectrum, a tool like a small wand (similar in function to a guitar pick). Other instruments were reserved for more specialized uses. Horns and trumpets, such as the *cornu* (similar to a large French horn) and the tuba (a trumpet over three feet long), were employed by the army for martial music and giving commands, and noisy instruments, such as cymbals and drums, were used in cult festivals. The hydraulic, or water, organ, invented in Hellenistic times, was played as popular entertainment and was said to induce strong emotional reactions in audience members.

Despite the ubiquitousness of music in everyday life and the admiration afforded to those who were musically skilled, the Romans had a mixed reaction and contradictory attitude toward music and dance. Stern Roman tradition dictated that music, singing, and dancing were morally suspect, improper pursuits for freeborn Roman citizens that should be relegated to slaves and freedmen, who already suffered from lowered status. Over time, attitudes relaxed so that an amateur interest in music was acceptable; even the emperor could indulge in music. What was scandalous was to pursue music as a professional, which Nero did, to the shock of his subjects.

10

Religion in Ancient Rome

ROMAN RELIGION

The religion of the Romans was different in a number of profound ways, not just from modern Christianity, but from the very ways in which we today tend to think about the purpose, function, and characteristics of religion. The most obvious difference is that Roman paganism was a polytheistic religion, meaning that there were many gods. For the Romans, the world was a place inhabited by an infinite number of gods, including many that they had not heard of. When the Romans encountered other religions, they were very open about adding these new gods to the list of those they already worshiped. Thus the Roman pantheon was constantly expanding due to the addition of new gods. This attitude is vividly illustrated by a ritual called the *evocatio*. This occurred when the Romans were about to attack and possibly destroy an enemy city. Before launching the assault, the Roman priests would formally invite the gods of the city to abandon it and take up residence and be worshiped at Rome.

The pantheon of Roman gods included deities who resembled humans (such as Jupiter), personifications of abstract qualities (such as Victoria, the personification of victory), nature spirits or deities usually associated with geographic places or bodies of water (such as Father Tiber), and a variety of gods imported from foreign cultures (such as the Egyptian goddess Isis). Each individual would pick one or more gods to worship as his or her particular guardians. Since certain gods were associated with specific cities and professions, these gods would probably have received particular attention from people of that profession or who lived in that city.

Roman religion did not possess a standardized sacred text like the Bible. While there were certain rituals, such as sacrifice, that were commonly prescribed for worshiping the gods, there was no central and all-encompassing theology. Roman religion was a loose collection of diverse gods and practices allowing a great deal of variety and personal choice. There were hundreds—perhaps thousands—of divinities that were worshiped in Roman polytheism. Further adding to the complexity of Roman religion was the fact that there were different types of gods whose powers, inclinations, and areas of influence varied greatly. The state religion was based on worshiping a subset of all the gods who were thought to be particularly concerned with the success and preservation of the Roman state, but individuals could choose any combination of gods to pay homage to.

The most prominent Roman gods were what might be termed the Olympian gods. This set of deities, derived from the Greek gods said to live on Mount Olympus, included Jupiter, Juno, Mars, Venus, Neptune, Apollo, Diana, Ceres, Bacchus, Mercury, Minerva, Vesta, and Vulcan. The most important of these for the Romans were Jupiter, the king of the gods, and Mars, the god of war, both of whom were thought to be especially interested in the success of Rome.

Often, however, these major gods were multiplied through the addition of epithets that identified some particular aspect of the god. These epithets were usually related to either a location or an activity. For example, there were Jupiter Capitolinus (the Jupiter who lived on the Capitoline hill) and Mars Ultor (Mars the Avenger), to whom Augustus dedicated a temple in commemoration of his avenging the assassination of his adoptive father, Julius Caesar. Jupiter alone had at least 19 different epithets.

In addition to these gods, there were what might be called demigods, who were often men who had attained divine status, such as the Greek hero Hercules and Romulus, the founder of Rome. There were many entities that might be called gods as well, such as spirits of streams, rivers, and trees. Such a god was a *genius loci*, literally "the spirit of the place." Some gods were personifications of abstract qualities. The most important of these to the Romans were Fortuna, or luck, and Victoria, victory. Finally, there were all the gods borrowed from other cultures, including Egyptian, Etruscan, and Germanic ones. The Romans were extremely open to adopting new gods that they encountered and adding them to their pantheon. Further complicating Roman religion was the fact that, when encountering new foreign gods, the Romans sometimes decided that these gods were simply local variants of gods they already knew.

Thus, it is almost deceptive to speak of a single notion of godhood in Roman culture since there was such a variety of forms that divine beings or spirits could take. Nor did they fit into any clear hierarchy. Any attempt to create such a hierarchy would quickly run into contradictions and problems in logic; even to try to do so is a modern concept and something that the Romans themselves never attempted.

PRIESTS AND RITUAL

In ancient Rome, there were very few professional priests. There was a great variety of types of priests, but with a few exceptions, this was not a full-time occupation. Nor did priests receive any specialized training. Priests mainly performed certain public rituals and sacrifices. The most prominent priests, who were almost exclusively male, were members of several important priesthoods called colleges. Each college had a fixed number of positions. When one member died, a new one was selected to take his place. The existing priests nominated several names to fill the vacancy. An election was then held and the winner joined the college. Once elected to a priesthood, one held the office until death.

The most important of these colleges was the pontifical college. It contained 16 men called *pontifexes* and 15 called flamens. The leader of this college was known as the Pontifex Maximus, or the "Great Priest." He was considered the head of religious affairs, and it is from this title that Christianity derived its title of pope. The *pontifexes'* main duties were to preside over various religious festivals.

Each of the flamens was associated with one particular god. Of these, 12 were known as minor flamens. The remaining 3, the major flamens, were associated with the three gods thought to have special links to the Roman people: Jupiter, Mars, and Quirinus. In keeping with the importance attached to these gods, each of their flamens had special rules and regulations governing his behavior.

The flamen of Jupiter was known as the Flamen Dialis, and since Jupiter was the king of the gods, he was the most important flamen. Jupiter was particularly linked to the city of Rome; therefore, his flamen could never spend the night outside the city, nor could he sleep away from his own bed for more than three nights. To connect the Flamen Dialis with the earth, the legs of his bed were coated in clay. To avoid contamination, he could not eat beans; touch fermented flour, raw meat, or a dog; or see a dead body, a horse, or the Roman army. He could never have any knots on his clothing. At all times, even in the privacy of his own home, he had to wear a special hat called the *apex*, which was like a circular disk with a rod protruding from the middle. The Flamen Dialis was the link between the city of Rome and the most potent aspect of Jupiter, Jupiter Optimus Maximus, or "Jupiter the Best and the Greatest."

The next most important college was the college of augurs, of which there were 16. These priests had a specialized job. They had to discern the will of the gods through the interpretation of various signs. Much of Roman religious ritual practice, including augury, was derived from the Etruscans. The three main categories of augury were the observation of the flight and feeding habits of birds; the inspection of the internal organs of sacrificed animals; and the interpretation of portents, such as lightning, natural disasters, and bizarre occurrences in general.

There was a special site on the Capitoline hill called the *auguraculum.* The augur would sit here and designate one of the four quarters of the sky for observation. Any birds that flew through this zone were thought to carry a message from the gods. For ravens, crows, and owls, they studied the cries of the birds; for eagles and vultures, they noted the direction of their flight and their number. There were also augurs who studied specific avian behaviors. One of the most famous of these was the *pullarius,* who observed how a group of sacred chickens ate. The more eagerly the chickens ate their food, the better, and the best omen of all was when the chickens ate so greedily that bits of food fell from their beaks. Conversely, the worst sign was if the birds refused to eat at all.

This type of augury was frequently used as a test of the gods' favor before a battle. The most famous incident concerning the sacred chickens involved an admiral named Appius Claudius Pulcher, who, just before a naval battle, consulted the esteemed birds. The chickens absolutely refused to eat anything. Pulcher became enraged, saying, "If they won't eat, then let them drink." He then threw the sacred chickens overboard, drowning them. Needless to say, he lost the battle.

Another type of augur was the haruspex, who specialized in examining the internal organs of sacrificed animals, especially the liver. The emperor always had a haruspex on his staff. The haruspex examined the color, size, and shape of the liver. If the liver was diseased or malformed, it was a terrible omen. Archaeologists have discovered a liver made out of bronze, which was probably used as a training device to instruct novice haruspices. The bronze liver was divided up into 40 sections, each of which had a certain god associated with it. The worst omen of all involving a liver was if part of it was missing. Supposedly such a liver turned up at a sacrifice at which Nero was presiding shortly before he was assassinated. By law, all important public acts or events had to be preceded by some form of augury, and if the omens were unfavorable, the event had to be canceled.

The final form of augury was the interpretation of prodigies. Whereas the examination of birds and organs was a form of men asking questions of the gods, prodigies were unsolicited messages sent from the gods. The most common of these was lightning. As lightning was the symbol of Jupiter, it held special significance for the Romans. Any site struck by lightning became holy. If lightning was seen before a public assembly, it had to be called off. This rule was much abused and manipulated for political purposes during the Late Republic. In this period, a remarkable number of magistrates seemed to see lightning that no one else noticed. On the other hand, if, when a magistrate first took up his office, he saw lightning on the left, it was a good sign.

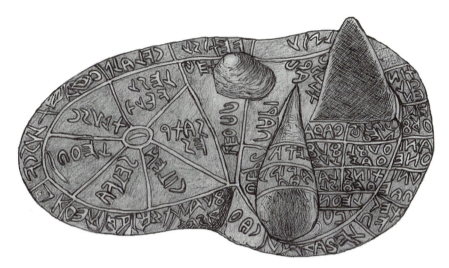

Figure 10.1 Etruscan bronze liver of Piacenza marked into quadrants. Roman priests would study the livers of sacrificed animals to determine the will of the gods. (Drawing by Alicia Aldrete, Phaeton Group, Scientific Graphic Services Division.)

Any exceptional or bizarre event was a sign from the gods and had to be interpreted by the augurs. All Roman authors report such portents as having occurred before most important events. Some of the types of portents listed include the following: cows talk; it rains stones; statues weep tears or blood; it rains blood; spears, statues, or swords burst into flame; swarms of bees settle on battle standards; a bull kicks over an altar; the sky bursts into flames; animals are born with multiple heads; an ox climbs up a building and commits suicide by throwing itself off; and mysterious voices speak.

Particularly dramatic omens were associated with the death and deification of emperors and famous men. Toward the end of Augustus's life, lightning struck one of his statues and melted off the first letter of the word *Caesar* inscribed on the base. Since C is the Roman numeral 100 and *aesar* was the Etruscan word for "god," this was interpreted to mean that in 100 days he would die and become a god. When Julius Caesar died, a comet appeared in the sky, which was also interpreted as a sign of his divinity. This interpretation was strengthened by the fact that the Romans called comets "hairy stars" and the word *caesar* in Latin means "hairy." Dreams were also thought to be messages from the gods, particularly useful as predictions of the future.

In times of great disaster, when the state itself seemed threatened, the third of the colleges, the Decemviri, was called upon. They were the custodians of a group of ancient scrolls called the Sibylline Books. These were a series of manuscripts supposedly given to the Romans in the earliest days of their history by a prophetess known as the Sibyl. The Decemviri would randomly pluck a page from these books and read it, and whatever it instructed, they would do. Usually this involved the introduction of a new god or ceremony.

Another type of specialized religious ritual was the *lustratio.* This was a purification ceremony to cleanse of impurities a plot of land that was about to be used for some purpose and to protect it from future hazards. The way this was accomplished was by taking a pig, a sheep, and a bull and leading them in a procession all around the perimeter of a territory. The three animals were then sacrificed in a rite known as a *suovetaurilia* (*sus* = pig, *ovis* = sheep, *taurus* = bull).

Another important priestly college was the *fetials.* This priesthood, with 20 members, performed religious rites involving international relations, including declarations of war and the signing of treaties. When the Romans went to war, they were very concerned that it be a just war, at least in their eyes. To make it a just war, one of the *fetial* priests had to perform the following actions: He traveled to the land of the people against which the Romans were considering declaring war. To the first person he met after crossing the border, he said, "Hear me, Jupiter and Quirinus and all the gods of the sky and all the gods of the earth and of the underworld. I call you to witness that these people are unjust and do not make reparations." He then wandered around for 33 days, saying the same thing to the first person he met whenever he entered a city or marketplace. If, at the end of this time, the demands of the Romans had not been met, then a vote was taken and the Romans declared war. The *fetial* then took a bloody spear and, in the presence of three adult men, recited another formula stating the war to be a just war, at the end of which he threw the spear into enemy territory. This was the formal procedure by which the Romans declared war. When the Romans signed a treaty with another nation, the *fetials* again played an important role. To formalize the treaty, they recited a very long prayer to call the gods' attention to what was happening. The prayer ended with the phrase, "If the Romans shall break this treaty, then on that day great Jupiter smite the Roman people as today I smite this pig." With these words, the priest bludgeoned a pig.

When the Romans addressed a prayer to one of the gods, they usually first addressed it to all the different names associated with that particular deity and then to the geographic locations with which he or she was thought to be linked. Finally, just to make sure they had not left anything out, they would add the phrase, "Or whatever name you care to be called."

Sacrifice was a major part of religious worship. The Romans sacrificed many different animals to their various gods, including goats, cows, bulls, sheep, pigs, birds, dogs, and horses. Male animals were sacrificed to male gods and female animals to goddesses. White animals were sacrificed to gods of the sky, and black animals to gods of the underworld. The animal

Figure 10.2 Animal being led to sacrifice by temple attendant carrying the axe that will be used to kill the animal.

had to be perfect. Any deformities or unusual coloration or characteristics rendered it unsuitable. If the animal had horns, ribbons were tied around them. If the sponsor of the sacrifice were rich, he or she would have the horns gilded with gold.

When the animal was led to the altar, it was a good sign if it went willingly. If it struggled a lot, the officiant was supposed to get another animal and start over. All temples had their altars located outside, which was where the sacrifices actually occurred. Before the sacrifice, worshipers would go inside the temple and, if making a vow, would write it on wax tablets and attach these to the cult statue. At the sacrifice, everyone involved had to be sure they had washed their hands, and the priests had to cover their heads. Except for the prayers, everyone was expected to remain silent. Throughout the course of the sacrifice, one person played a flute.

Once the animal had been led to the altar, a prayer was recited following the usual prayer formula of invocation of the deity's name, the geographic locations associated with the deity, and the actual request being made. If it was a large animal, one of the priest's attendants struck it on the head with a hammer or axe, and then another cut its throat. They cut upward if it was for a god of the skies, downward if it was for a god of the underworld. The kill needed to be done cleanly and efficiently. If it was performed sloppily, it was a bad omen. The worst thing that could happen was if the wounded animal broke free and ran off. This once occurred at a sacrifice Julius Caesar was presiding over, and because he ignored it, he received much criticism.

The internal organs were then removed, in particular the heart, liver, and intestines. These organs were cut up and burned in a fire on the altar. This comprised the actual offering to the gods, and as they were burned, the priest directed the following phrase to the god being honored: "Be you increased by this offering." If an error was made at any stage of this process, the whole thing had to be repeated, along with an extra prayer and sacrifice to make up for the error. Sometimes the priest would make a preliminary sacrifice to atone ahead of time for any error he might make.

These sacrifices could be on a gigantic scale. When Caligula became emperor, to celebrate his accession, 160,000 cows were sacrificed at Rome over a three-month period—nearly 2,000 per day. This must have created quite a gory scene, since each cow would have contained over two gallons of blood.

RELIGION AND MAGIC

Some aspects of the Romans' religion we might consider more superstitions than formal religious beliefs. Many of the current superstitions that people follow today are directly traceable to ancient ones, including black cats crossing your path and stepping under ladders as harbingers of bad luck.

Superstitions were widespread in the Roman world and were not limited to uneducated or unsophisticated Romans. The Roman general Sulla always carried around a little statue of the god Apollo, and whenever he got in trouble, he would kiss it and pray to it. Even many emperors were highly superstitious. If the emperor Augustus put the wrong shoe on upon getting out of bed, he thought it was a bad omen for the day. If dew was present when he started a long journey, he considered it a good sign. At all times, he carried around a piece of sealskin, which he thought would protect him from thunderstorms. He also liked to repeat stories about omens that had foretold his rise to power. One of these claimed that as a very young child on the family farm, he once ordered some frogs to stop croaking; to everyone's astonishment, they promptly stopped and never croaked again. Some superstitions were associated with good-luck icons.

Augustus's successor, Tiberius, was particularly superstitious as the following anecdote suggests: Tiberius had a favorite pet snake that he took with him everywhere. One time, when he had just set out on a journey for Rome, he opened up its box and discovered that his snake had been eaten by ants. Seeing this, he immediately turned around and canceled his journey. Tiberius was an enthusiastic follower of astrology, and during the latter half of his reign, he spent all his time on an island with his personal astrologer, Thrasyllus. Many people believed that Thrasyllus really ran the empire since Tiberius would not do anything without consulting his astrologer; if he received a negative horoscope, he would cancel that activity or decree.

Another aspect of Roman religion that seems akin to magic is that the Romans tried to place curses on their enemies to bring them bad luck. Individuals would invoke magical powers to place curses on their enemies. Oddly enough, the exact details of many of these curses are known to us today because of the way they were created. The text of the curse was written on a tablet, often by a professional sorcerer. It was then in essence mailed to the gods of the underworld by being dropped down a well, thrown in a cave, or buried. The usual form that the curse took was to address one or several of the gods of the underworld (such as Pluto), promise him or her something in exchange for helping you, and then consign your enemy to him or her. To make the curse even more explicit, it was common to list all of your enemy's body parts that were to be affected by the curse. One such curse tablet reads, "Spirits of the underworld, I dedicate and hand into your power, Ticene of Carisius. Let everything she attempts turn out badly. Spirits of the underworld, I dedicate to you her limbs, her face, her body, her head, her hair, her shade, her brain, her forehead, her eyebrows, her mouth, her nose, her chin, her cheeks, her lips, her speech, her breath, her neck, her liver, her shoulders, her heart, her lungs, her intestines, her stomach, her arms, her fingers, her hands, her navel, her entrails, her thighs, her knees, her calves, her heels, her soles, her toes. Spirits of the underworld, if I witness her wasting away, I promise that I will joyfully present to you a sacrifice every year" (*CIL* 10.8249).

In addition to general curses condemning an entire person, there were also curses that asked for specific actions. Archaeologists have found a number of these hidden in the walls of horse stables. Chariot racing was an extremely popular sport, and fans apparently tried to curse the horses of opposing teams. Inevitably, another way that people used magic was to attempt to make others love them. A large number of magic spells and incantations survive, testifying to desperate people's attempts to make the objects of their obsession return their love or lust. Curses were made not just on an individual level, but even on a national one. After the ritual of *evocatio*, by which the Romans invited the gods of a city they were attacking to come over to the Roman side, they then usually followed up with the *devotio*, which was in essence a curse pledging the enemy city to the gods of the underworld.

Foretelling the future has always been a topic of interest. The various forms of prophecy connected to reading signs from the gods have been described in the section on priests and ritual. However, there even exists a reference to the Roman equivalent of a Ouija board. A group of people who wanted to know the future made a magic device. They fashioned a tripod of laurel twigs, from the top of which they suspended a ring on a fine, cotton thread. The tripod was placed over a metal dish whose outer rim was engraved with the 24 letters of the Greek alphabet. This object was consecrated with spells and magic rites. They then asked it a question that they wanted answered and put the ring into motion; the ring swung in the direction of individual letters, spelling out an answer. One of the questions they asked was who the next emperor would be, and when word of this came to the current emperor, he had them tried for treason and executed.

TEMPLES

The modern word *temple* is derived from the Latin word *templum*, but, strictly speaking, a *templum* was not a building but rather a sacred precinct where augurs (a type of priest) looked for signs from the gods, especially by observing the flight of birds. Because of the link between sacred precincts and observing birds, most early Roman temples were situated facing south on sites with an unobstructed view. When a building was constructed within a *templum*, it was referred to as an *aedes*; therefore, most of the buildings that we now refer to as temples were known by the Romans as *aedes*. Thus, it was possible for there to be a *templum* that did not have an *aedes*, but not an *aedes* without a *templum*. The two most significant areas of an *aedes* were the altar, where sacrifices were performed, and the room that contained the cult statue of the god or sometimes a collection of sacred objects. Such a room, usually the innermost one at the back of the structure, was termed the *cella*. An altar was called an *ara*, and these were always located outside, not in the interior of the building. The most common position for the *ara* was on the front steps of the structure. Today we tend to think of religious services as taking place inside a building, but nearly all Roman religious rituals took place outside; this reflects the public nature of Roman religion in general as opposed to the more private focus of modern monotheistic religions.

The earliest temples at Rome followed Etruscan models. They were characterized by being set on a high platform called a podium and had a frontal orientation, meaning that stairs were often only at the front. Unlike in many Greek temples, the columns did not go all the way around the building, but were instead only at the front or at the front and sides. Like Etruscan temples, early Roman temples were built with wooden columns, mud brick walls, and terra-cotta roof tiles. Eventually, during the republic, temples began to be made out of stone, and by the end of the republic, temples were constructed out of high-quality, decorative marbles. The first all-marble temple was built in 146 BC. After the conquest of the East, Roman temples were influenced by Greek architectural styles and became a fusion of Italic and Greek elements. On a number of sites in the city, the Romans built a row of temples lined up with the same orientation, as, for example, in the Area Sacra di Largo Argentina, where four small temples were erected in a row between the fourth and second centuries BC.

Since the interiors of temples were not used to hold congregations of worshipers, this space was frequently employed to store objects. Over time, votive dedications such as statues and valuable items piled up in the interiors of these temples. In addition, booty from successful military campaigns was deposited in temples as a way of giving thanks to the gods for granting victory. These objects ranged from weapons and armor to crowns and other items made of precious metals. It was not uncommon for the Romans to seize artworks, and bronze and marble statues as well as paintings found their way into temples. After generations of such dedications, the interiors of many temples resembled treasuries due to the valuable nature of these offerings. With their massive stone construction and restricted entrances, temples did indeed constitute fairly secure vaults for storing such items. The clutter within temples stuffed with dedicatory offerings could eventually become a problem, and periodically items had to be cleared out. Such was the case in the main temple on the Capitoline of Jupiter Optimus Maximus when the many shields that had been affixed to the interior columns became such a nuisance that they were cleared out in 179 BC. The riches housed within Roman temples could arouse the greed of thieves, and there seems to have been at least one instance when robbers broke into a temple and stole some of the dedications. The Temple of Saturn was used to house the state treasury and served as the headquarters of the magistrates who were in charge of financial affairs. In this instance, the state treasury was probably not in the main room of the temple itself, but instead was kept in vaults located within the podium of the temple.

SOME FAMOUS TEMPLES AT ROME

This was the famous temple to Jupiter on the Capitoline hill. It was unusual because it was dedicated to three gods, together known as the Capitoline Triad, each of whom had his or her own *cella* (inner room) and cult statue. Jupiter was in the center; on one side was his wife, Juno, and on the other side, his daughter, Minerva. The original cult statue of Jupiter was a famous one made of terra-cotta depicting a standing Jupiter holding a thunderbolt, the symbol of his power as king of the gods. He wore a purple toga trimmed in gold, and on special occasions, the statue's face was painted red. This attire was imitated by the special costume worn by generals celebrating a triumph.

Temple of Jupiter Optimus Maximus

Construction of this temple seems to have originally begun under the kings, but it was not dedicated until 509 BC, the year of the founding of the republic. It was struck by lightning and burned down on a number of occasions but was rebuilt using increasingly more-costly materials. The roof was always decorated with elaborate statuary, including a *quadriga*, a four-horse chariot, being driven by Jupiter. One of the temple's most spectacular reconstructions was the one undertaken by Domitian after it burned down in AD 80. This version boasted fine, white, Pentelic marble columns and doors that were covered with gold plate. The roof was also

Figure 10.3 Reconstruction of the Temple of Jupiter Optimus Maximus on the Capitoline. This temple was famous for its gold-plated roof and doors. (From G. Gatteschi, *Restauri della Roma Imperiale*, 1924, p. 3.)

Figure 10.4 Depiction of the Capitoline Triad of Jupiter, Minerva, and Juno. Each deity has his or her associated bird next to their throne (from left to right: an owl for Minerva, an eagle for Jupiter, and a peacock for Juno).

gilded, which supposedly cost 12,000 talents. The pediment featured a depiction of the Capitoline Triad seated on thrones over an eagle with outstretched wings.

This temple, with its shining roof, must have been visible from all over the city, and it seems to have been regarded as one of the most impressive monuments of Rome. It always played a central role in Roman politics and religion. When the new consuls for each year were elected, they began their terms by sacrificing a pair of white bulls at the altar on the steps of this temple. This altar was also the final destination for generals celebrating triumphs; it was on this spot that the ritual of the triumph reached its climax, with the dedication to Jupiter of triumphal crowns and victory spoils by the generals.

When Rome's political power began to falter in the later empire, this temple became a target for looters. In the fifth century AD, the gold plating of the doors was pried off and carried away, and half the gilded roof tiles were stolen.

Temple of Castor (Aedes Castor)

According to legend, during one of Rome's early battles, the Greek gods Castor and Pollux supposedly appeared, inspiring the Romans to victory. As a result, a temple was vowed near the site of their appearance. It was dedicated in 484 BC. Like most Roman temples, it was repeatedly rebuilt.

This temple is famous as a frequent meeting place of the senate and also as the place in which the official standards for weights and measures were kept. The imperial treasury was stored within a number of small rooms carved into the podium, and private individuals could apparently also place valuables in these repositories.

Temple of Concord (Aedes Concordia)

This temple was located at the foot of the Capitoline hill facing the Roman Forum. It was vowed by Camillus in 367 BC but may not have been constructed until considerably later. This temple was most famous for being the site where the senate frequently met during the Late Republic, particularly in times of internal unrest. This role was in keeping with the nature of the goddess Concordia, who was the personification of agreement and harmony among members of the state.

The dimensions of the temple were unusual as a result of its having to be squeezed into the available space backing up against the Capitoline hill. It was rebuilt a number of times, most famously by the emperor Tiberius. Tiberius's reconstruction was lavish and featured a thick forest of statues of deities on the roof, among them the Capitoline Triad, Ceres, Diana, and multiple personifications of victory. Tiberius also filled the interior of the temple with an assortment of famous artworks, including at least 11 famous statues as well as a number of paintings by renowned artists. Finally, the interior also boasted four elephants carved out of obsidian.

Temple of the Deified Caesar (Aedes Divus Iulius) After the assassination of Julius Caesar, who had been popular with the people of the city, Mark Antony read his will in the Roman Forum, and the people rioted and cremated his body at its eastern end. After Caesar's death, he was posthumously declared to be a god, and this deification was lent credence by the appearance of a comet in the night sky. If the manifestation of this omen was not convincing-enough evidence of Caesar's godhood, the Roman term for comet is "hairy star," and the name *Caesar* itself means "hairy." It was therefore decided to erect a temple to the deified Caesar on the spot where he had been cremated. The building was actually not finished for some time, so Augustus did not dedicate it until 29 BC.

The temple itself had six columns across the front, and inside the *cella* was a large statue of Caesar. In reference to the comet that had confirmed his divine status, a star was placed either on the head of the statue or on the pediment of the temple. Two ramps ascended the sides of the temple and led to a large platform in front. This platform was used as a *rostra*, or speakers' platform, and was a favorite site from which the emperors addressed crowds in the Roman Forum. The platform itself was about 3.5 meters high and was decorated with the rams taken from Antony and Cleopatra's ships captured at the Battle of Actium.

Shrine to Janus Geminus This is an example of a sacred area rather than a true, fully formed temple building and was dedicated to the god Janus. Janus was the god of beginnings, gates, and doorways. He was depicted as a male figure with two heads facing opposite directions. In connection with his status as god of beginnings, any time a prayer was made to a list of gods, he was named first and received the first portion of the sacrifice. Also, the first month of the calendar was named after him—January.

The original shrine was located in the forum area and perhaps included a set of bridges that carried the Sacra Via (Sacred Way) over the ditch of the Cloaca Maxima. According to legend, the enclosure, said to have been founded during the reign of King Numa, also contained walls, double doorways, and a statue of the deity. Also according to legend, when the Sabines were attacking Rome, a flood of hot water spewed forth from the shrine of Janus and repelled the invaders.

It became traditional for the doors of the shrine to be closed during times when Rome was at peace and to be opened during times of war. It is a testament to the warlike nature of the Romans that the doors were nearly always open. The doors were shut during the reign of King Numa. Then, aside from one brief closing in 235 BC, they remained open for an astounding stretch of approximately six centuries until 30 BC, after the Battle of Actium. Under the reign of Augustus, they were shut two additional times and then were open and closed intermittently during the Roman Empire.

Most Roman temples were rectangular, but there were a few exceptions, the most famous being the round Temple of Vesta. This was located at the southeast corner of the Roman Forum near the Palatine hill. It was

Temple of Vesta (Aedes Vesta)

close to the House of the Vestals and was the central focus of their religious activities.

Vesta was the goddess of the hearth, and hence of the home, and as such was worshiped by a group of six female priests, known as the Vestal Virgins. In keeping with the idea that women could not be priests, when a woman became a Vestal, she in essence gave up her gender. Part of this belief was the requirement that the Vestals be virgins and that they remain virgins the entire time they served the goddess.

Vestals had to serve for 30 years. In the first 10 years, they learned their duties; in the second, they performed them; in the third, they taught others. Ideally, the Vestals were staggered in age so that there were always two at each of the three stages. After 30 years, they had the option of resigning from the priesthood and getting married, but few did this. The most important duty of the Vestals was to tend the sacred fire located in the Temple of Vesta. If this fire was allowed to go out, it was considered an omen foretelling the destruction of the city. Each year on March 1, the fire was relit in a ritual by rubbing two sticks together.

Figure 10.5 Reconstruction of the interior of the House of the Vestals near the Roman Forum. The Vestals' house was adjacent to the round Temple of Vesta, where the sacred flame was kept. (From G. Gatteschi, *Restauri della Roma Imperiale*, 1924, p. 21.)

The ultimate crime for a Vestal was to lose her virginity. If one did this and was discovered, she was dressed in funeral clothes and carried in a funeral procession with her friends and relatives lamenting her. She was then placed in an underground room and buried alive. The Romans actually invoked this punishment, as, for example, under the emperor Domitian in AD 83, when three Vestals were executed for immorality and the chief Vestal was buried alive.

The round shape of the Temple of Vesta is thought to reflect its original form as a primitive hut, like the famous hut of Romulus. In addition to containing the sacred fire, it served as a repository for various items of great sanctity, including the *palladium,* an object that supposedly originally resided in Troy but was brought to Italy by Aeneas.

This temple was repeatedly destroyed or burned down, and a number of heroic stories are associated with efforts to rescue the sacred objects. It was demolished when Rome was sacked by the Gauls in 390 BC, although the sacred items were first removed. In 241 BC, it burned down, but the holy objects were rescued by Caecilius Metellus, who lost his sight achieving this deed. In 210 BC, it caught fire, and the loss of the objects was only prevented by the fire-fighting efforts of 13 slaves, who as a reward received their freedom. In 48 and 14 BC, it again caught fire, and yet again the objects were salvaged. During the empire, it burned down at least three additional times. Throughout all these tribulations, it was consistently rebuilt as a circular structure surrounded by columns, although details of the roof and decorations varied. Today, only three of the columns remain standing and can be seen by visitors to the Roman Forum.

The Pantheon   The Pantheon is one of the most famous, best preserved, and most influential Roman buildings. Its design is unique among Roman temples and was a revolutionary innovation. The term *pantheon* means "temple to all the gods." The structure that can be seen today is not the original version of the Pantheon, which was built in 27 BC by Agrippa in conjunction with a number of other buildings that he erected in the Campus Martius, including his baths. Agrippa's structure seems to have possessed a fairly conventional rectangular design, judging from the foundations of his Pantheon, which have been discovered several meters beneath the current one. The structure was damaged and restored several times but was entirely rebuilt to a new design and on a grander scale by the emperor Hadrian. Evidence from stamps on the bricks suggests that Hadrian's Pantheon was built between AD 118 and 128.

When viewed from the front, Hadrian's Pantheon has an entirely conventional appearance. There is a podium with steps that lead up to a porch with several rows of columns. Above this is a typical triangular pediment. Hadrian kept the original inscription, so even though this building has almost nothing to do with Agrippa's, the inscription still reads, "*M. AGRIPPA L F COS TERTIUM FECIT*" (Marcus Agrippa, the son of Lucius,

Figure 10.6 The Pantheon seen from the front. From this angle, with its unique dome concealed, the structure resembles an ordinary temple.

consul three times, built it). The only odd feature, when it is viewed from the front, is that the pediment is unusually high in proportion to its width. After entering the building through a set of massive bronze doors, one would expect to find oneself inside the usual cramped and dark rectangular interior of a temple. Instead, visitors to the Pantheon step into an enormous circular space some 43 meters wide. Even more astonishing, the space overhead is topped by a colossal dome of equal height. The dome itself is a perfect half-circle so that a sphere of the same diameter would fit exactly in the structure. The only source of light is a circular opening in the top of the dome nine meters wide called an *oculus* (eye), which creates a dramatic circular shaft of light that moves about the interior over the course of the day.

The engineering of this marvel is particularly impressive. One secret to its success is that the architects employed a wide range of materials. The lower levels are constructed of thick, dense substances best able to bear the weight of the dome, and the materials grow increasingly lighter at progressively higher levels of the structure. The lowest sections are made of solid stone, travertine, and tufa, which gives way to tufa and brick, and then just brick at the middle levels, while the dome itself is of concrete made with the light volcanic stone, pumice, mixed in. The concrete of the dome steadily narrows in thickness from about 6 meters at the top of the drum that supports it to only 1.5 meters at the *oculus*. The whole thing was so well made that, despite having to support such a huge expanse of roof

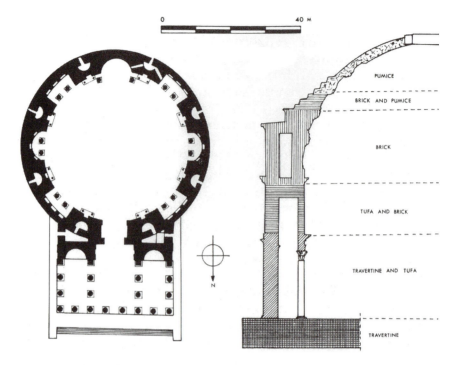

Figure 10.7 Plan and section of the Pantheon. (Reprinted from Frank Sear: *Roman Architecture*. Copyright 1982 by Frank Sear. Used by permission of the publisher, Cornell University Press.)

without any internal struts, it remains standing intact today, some 2,000 years later. The dome remained the largest such concrete span until 1958. One reason for the Pantheon's survival is its reconsecration as a Christian church in AD 608. For a while, it sported two rather unsightly bell towers (known by the derisive nickname, "the ass's ears"), which were not removed until the late 1800s.

The Pantheon is arguably one of the most influential buildings of all time. Its formula of a square facade with columns, surmounted by a triangular pediment fronting a huge dome and a circular internal space has become a stock design for innumerable government buildings, including the U.S. Capitol building in Washington, D.C., as well as nearly every state capitol building across the United States.

MYSTERY RELIGIONS

As Rome's population grew, many foreign cults, particularly from the East, began to show up in the city. People who, for one reason or another, came to Rome from the East, whether as slaves captured in war or as merchants establishing trade links or bringing supplies to the city, brought their religions with them. Also, Rome's wars resulted in many Italians going off for decades to fight in the army in distant provinces, and when they returned home to Italy, they brought foreign customs and cults with them as well.

Such cults, which became known as mystery religions, tended to address spiritual or mystical concerns more heavily than did standard Roman paganism. These cults often centered around mysterious gods such as Isis, Mithras, and Serapis, all of whom were involved in processes of renewal. Initiates had to go through an elaborate and secret initiation ceremony. Such cults appealed to people looking for a more spiritually satisfying religion. Members were attracted by promises of immortality and the appeal of belonging to a group of holders of secret knowledge.

Archaeological evidence for a huge range of foreign religious cults has been found in every region of the city. Syrian cults had shrines in the Transtiberim, on top of the Janiculum hill, and near the Horrea Galbana (a major grain warehouse). Serapis was worshiped on the Quirinal hill. Three of the most popular mystery religions centered around the gods Isis, Mithras, and Magna Mater. There was a temple to Magna Mater on the Palatine hill. Shrines to Isis have been identified in the Transtiberim, near the Circus Maximus, and in the Campus Martius. At least 25 different sanctuaries to the god Mithras have been identified, scattered throughout the city.

Isis was originally an Egyptian goddess. A crucial myth in traditional Egyptian religion, which helped to explain their funerary customs and ideas about death, involved Isis, her brother and husband, Osiris, and their brother, Set. Osiris was initially ruler of Egypt, much beloved by his subjects for his goodness and wisdom. He taught human beings about agriculture, the arts, and other life-improving knowledge. As a result, Set became jealous and decided to murder his brother. He built a chest specifically tailored to Osiris's measurements and at a party offered it to whoever best fit inside it. When Osiris tried it out, Set slammed the chest shut and threw it into the Nile. Isis searched for the chest and eventually found it, but Set again interfered, dismembering Osiris's body and scattering the pieces throughout Egypt. The grieving widow Isis tirelessly searched for the pieces and then reassembled them (all except for the penis, which had been swallowed by a fish). Isis thus managed to make the first mummy and through magic resurrected her husband and conceived a son, Horus. Osiris then went to the land of the dead to reign as its king.

Isis in the meantime raised Horus in secret to keep him safe from Set. The son's goal was to avenge his father, and he engaged in a violent fight with his uncle in which both were grievously wounded; Set stole one of Horus's eyes, sometimes said to be the sun. The rest of the gods held court in order to settle this bitter feud and ultimately decided in favor of Horus and Osiris. Since Osiris had assumed the role of king of the underworld and judge of the dead, Horus took over his father's former role as king of the living. He gave his restored eye to his father and replaced it with the *uraeus,* a divine snake. Set, now called "the Evil One," was exiled.

Converts to the cult of Isis could find analogies between their own daily struggles and the arduous journey of Isis to find Osiris, and the implicit promise of an afterlife that this myth held was also appealing, particularly since most standard Roman beliefs did not have a well-developed notion of an afterlife. The cult of Isis at Rome took the Egyptian myth as its beginning but built upon it. Isis worship, which became particularly popular among women, involved complex initiation ceremonies. Initiates were taken to a room in a temple of Isis where they chanted and performed rituals. Dream interpretation also played an important role. Initiates were purified by baptism and ten days of fasting before being led to the most secret and sacred part of the temple. The rites that took place there have remained a secret, but some think that they symbolically passed through death and rebirth, like Isis's husband.

Priests of Isis shaved their heads. A famous symbol of Isis that was often carried by her worshipers was the *sistrum,* a sort of rattle. Isis was sometimes depicted in art holding her son Horus on her lap, which became a popular image of maternal love and may even have influenced later Christian iconography of Mary with the baby Jesus.

There were a number of sites at Rome that were either temples or shrines to Isis, and the archaeological remains show the strong Egyptian influence that this religion retained. For example, the Sanctuary to Isis in the Campus Martius featured an obelisk like those found in Egypt.

Isis was popular with women, as were most mystery religions, but one mystery religion was exclusively for men—the cult of Mithras. Mithras remained very popular for centuries into the Roman Empire. The religion emphasized order, hierarchy, and duty, which made it especially popular with soldiers. Many Roman soldiers became initiates into Mithraism. Mithraism seems to have originated in Persia but really took off in the second century AD in the Roman Empire. In Persian mythology, Mithras was sent by the god Ahura Mazda to kill a divine bull. He eventually slew the bull in a cave, and from the bull's blood all living things were created.

In Italy, Mithraism was most popular in Rome and Ostia, which was clearly a result of the great numbers of foreign immigrants to these places. It was also popular in several frontier zones, particularly in the northern region along the Rhine and Danube Rivers and in Britain, but it does not seem to have been nearly as prevalent in most other areas around the Mediterranean. Since large contingents of the Roman army were posted on the Rhine, the Danube, and the British frontiers, the geographic distribution suggests a link with the religion's popularity among soldiers.

Prospective members went through grades of initiation before becoming full-fledged followers. The first grade was the Raven, followed by the Male Bride (Nymph), the Soldier, the Lion, the Persian, and the Runner of the Sun; the ultimate grade one could aspire to was Father. Mithraism had

Figure 10.8 Roman sculpture of the dog-headed Egyptian god, Anubis. Many Egyptian gods such as Isis became popular at Rome.

lots of links to the zodiac and the stars, and the sun also seems to have played an important role. The seven stages of initiation might also be linked to astronomical bodies. The matching bodies, from the lowest to the highest grade were Mercury, Venus, Mars, Jupiter, the moon, the sun, and Saturn for the Father. Raven initiates may have had to wear a bird mask, while nymphs may have had to wear a veil like that worn by Roman brides. Soldiers had a mark either tattooed or branded on their foreheads. Lions were associated with fire, and their hands and tongues were purified with honey. They may have worn lion masks. The Phrygians may have worn a Phrygian cap, and their symbol was a sickle. The symbol of the Runner of the Sun was a crown with rays; the Father wore an ornately decorated cap and carried a staff of authority as well as a liba-

Figure 10.9 Roman *mithraeum* in Ostia with standard sculptural image of Mithras slaying the bull. Worshipers would have sat on the long benches to the right and left of the central aisle.

tion cup. There were different colored cloaks for the different levels: Lions wore bright red, Persians silver, and Nymphs yellow.

Worshipers of Mithras gathered in a sanctuary called a *mithraeum*. These sites are readily identifiable because they were remarkably standardized both in form and decoration. *Mithraea* were almost always underground and consisted of a long, cavelike room or tunnel. Both sides of this passage were lined with benches, and at the end was either a painting or a statue of Mithras killing the bull. Many of these statues have survived and contain a specific and consistent iconography. Mithras, wearing a Phrygian cap, kneels on top of a bull, which he is stabbing with his right hand. He averts his face to the right. Grain sprouts out of the bull's tail, a raven appears over Mithras's shoulder, a dog drinks the blood from the wound, a serpent and a cup rest below the bull, and a scorpion is attached to the bull's testicles. At each side of the scene is a torchbearer, and the sun and moon float overhead.

The cult of Mithras was indeed a true mystery religion; because it was very secretive, we know very little of its practices today. Clearly a focal point of Mithraic worship was a ceremonial feast held in the cavern, and the benches were dining benches. There also seem to have been elaborate rituals associated with the initiates' progress from one level to the next.

Few dependable details of these ceremonies survive, however, and some later Christian sources that describe them have to be regarded with skepticism. These include accounts of fasts lasting 50 days and ordeals of endurance, such as lying within snow for 20 days. Also mentioned was a ritual in which the initiate was blindfolded and had his hands tied together using chicken entrails; in this state, he had to leap over a series of pits filled with water.

Women seem to have been excluded from most Mithraic ceremonies and memberships, and one text goes so far as to classify them as "noxious hyenas." This attitude does not seem to have been completely uniform, however, since there is evidence of some dedications to Mithras by women, and individual Mithraic cult groups may have followed varying policies regarding women.

As previously mentioned, there is evidence for dozens of Mithraic sites at Rome and Ostia, including a number of complete *mithraea*. Several of the most famous and best preserved of these are, ironically enough, located beneath Christian churches, such as the churches of San Clemente and Santa Prisca in Rome. The largest *mithraeum* found at Rome, which is 23 meters long, was discovered lying beneath the Baths of Caracalla.

A third popular mystery religion centered around the deity Magna Mater. This goddess's name literally means "Great Mother," and indeed her worship focused on her role as the mother of all things. This religion seems to have been a Roman variant of the Phrygian cult of the goddess Cybele.

The worship of Magna Mater featured a number of dramatic rituals, among them a special form of sacrifice in which a worshiper stood in a pit over which a grate was placed, and then a bull was led on top of the grate and killed so that its blood drenched the worshiper below. There were different categories of worshipers of Magna Mater, including a group called the Dendrophori, literally the "Tree Carriers." The most famous category, however, was certainly the priests, known as Galli, who in a frenzied state castrated themselves using crude implements such as pieces of flint.

One high point of the year for worshipers of Magna Mater at Rome came on April 4, when there was a festival with a parade that issued from her sanctuary on the Palatine and wound through the streets of the city. The Galli marched and danced while playing various instruments including cymbals and tossing flowers and coins before a statue of the goddess that was borne through the streets.

CHRISTIANITY

From a Roman perspective, Christianity initially was just one more strange mystery cult from the East. It is only through hindsight that we know its eventual importance and role as the official religion of the Roman state. The key characteristic of Christianity that would eventually separate it from other mystery religions was the Christians' insistence that their god was the only god. At the time, this was a unique perspective, shared only by Judaism, from which Christianity had branched off. Even devout followers of mystery religions such as the worshipers of Mithras would never have thought to assert that their god was the only god. This clash of perspectives between the predominant polytheism practiced by pagans and Christian and Jewish monotheism initially caused the martyrdom of some Christians but ultimately resulted in the religion's emergence as the dominant one in Europe.

Early Christianity began as an offshoot of Judaism. Jesus was born and raised as a Jew; despite our dating system, he was probably actually born around 4 BC, so our calendar is likely off by several years. He lived during the reigns of Augustus and Tiberius and was crucified around AD 27. Perhaps the most important figure in the spread of Christianity after Jesus's death was the apostle Paul. He was a Greek, a Jew, and held Roman citizenship and thus was heir to many of the main cultural movements of the period. After his conversion to Christianity, he spent the rest of his life constantly traveling around the Mediterranean, preaching and attempting to convert others. In this way, he also was responsible for the spread of the religion beyond Judea.

Christianity spread very slowly. It was most successful in the most strongly Romanized areas of the empire, particularly in cities and in the eastern Mediterranean. Very gradually, with its promise of immortality and its emphasis on morality and good behavior, the religion gained converts, especially among those who occupied low status positions in Roman society, such as slaves and women. One of the very earliest references to Christianity in a non-Christian source (a letter of the Roman governor of Pontus and Bithynia, Pliny the Younger, written in the early second century AD) contains the interesting detail that the leaders of a local congregation of Christians were two slave women (Pliny the Younger, *Letters* 10.96).

Romans were generally very tolerant of other religions, but the monotheism of Christianity and Judaism created problems. At the core of these conflicts was the Roman state's insistence that citizens occasionally perform rituals directed to the emperor as a kind of civic pledge. This might take the form of saying a prayer before a statue of the emperor and making an offering such as pouring out some wine. To the Romans, this was merely part of good citizenship, but to the Christians, of course, such an action would violate the first commandment, and so they refused. This was to some degree a failure of communication, but the result was persecution.

The first widespread persecution of Christians at Rome occurred in AD 64, though its cause was not so much religious belief as Nero's need to find a scapegoat to blame for the Great Fire. To divert suspicion away from himself, he claimed that the Christians had started it. After this incident, there were sporadic persecutions, but the first empirewide one did not

Figure 10.10 Colossal head of Constantine, the first emperor to convert to Christianity.

come until the late third century AD under Diocletian. Events took an abrupt and unexpected turn early in the next century when the emperor Constantine converted to Christianity. At this time, a full 300 years after the death of Christ, only a tiny minority of Romans, perhaps around 10 percent, had converted to Christianity; but from this point on, all but one of the emperors would be Christian, and within 100 years, the religion would be proclaimed the official one of the Roman Empire.

Probably the most famous and distinctive archaeological remains from the early Christian period at Rome are the catacombs. While most pagans were cremated after death, the early Christians preferred burial, and this led to the development of specifically Christian inhumation sites. All of the catacombs, which consist of networks of underground tunnels and chambers, are located outside the walls of the city. The greatest concentrations of catacombs were built along major roads leading away from the city, in particular along the Via Appia heading south and the Via Salaria heading north. Some of these underground systems are enormous, with up to five levels and hundreds of rooms and passages.

The actual burials are predominantly Christian, although some Jewish ones have been identified, along with a few pagan ones as well. The typical method of burial was to carve out a rectangular niche in the wall of a room or tunnel into which the body, wrapped in sheets, was placed. The opening was then sealed with earth, tiles, or a stone slab, which was often inscribed either with the name of the deceased or simply with a Christian symbol. Typically these niches were excavated in rows, one above the other, and the taller tunnels might have many layers of them reaching to the ceiling. The walls of some chambers were decorated with painted frescoes depicting scenes from the Bible or symbols from Christian iconography. One common image is that of a banquet, which may be a reference to the Last Supper or to the tradition of holding a funeral feast.

The catacombs stayed in active use from the first to around the fourth century AD, and a number of famous people, including the early popes, were buried in them. Although many of the artifacts they once contained have been removed over time, much still remains, and a number of catacombs, such as that of St. Callistus on the Appian Way, are open to visitors today.

11

The Emperors
and Ancient Rome

THE PALACES OF THE EMPERORS

Rome was the official site of the emperor's residence, and various emperors emphatically left their mark on the city and its buildings. The most obvious structures that resulted from the emperor's presence were the imperial palaces. During the republic, one of the most desirable addresses for upper-class Romans was the Palatine hill. During the first century of the empire, the dwelling of the emperors was situated on this hill and gradually expanded until it covered nearly the entire surface of the Palatine.

This process began with the first emperor, Augustus. At the time he became emperor, he was living in a modest house on the Palatine, which had previously been owned by the eminent orator Hortensius. This was supposedly a smallish house with unusually plain decor. Augustus continued to live in these simple surroundings as part of a concerted propaganda effort to portray himself as just another Roman citizen. He also made a point of dressing in unostentatious clothing. There were elements of the house that belied this interpretation, however; part of the property was used to build a temple to Apollo, and a crown was placed by order of the senate over the doorway of the house, with laurel trees (symbols of Apollo) flanking the entrance.

The next emperor, Tiberius, seems to have built a substantial palace on the northern side of the Palatine, which looked down into the Roman Forum. The details of the Tiberian structure are ill understood, as his palace was absorbed into later rebuildings, but it seems to have covered a fairly large area. Subsequent emperors continued to expand the rooms, reception halls, and dining rooms that constituted the imperial palace, and gradually this sprawling complex displaced the remaining private homes atop the Palatine.

Most of the extant ruins visible today on the Palatine are remnants of the version of the palace built by the emperor Domitian near the end of the first century AD. This structure, which was designed by the architect Rabirius, featured several distinct wings on different levels. These included numerous clusters of rooms around luxurious courtyards, grand reception halls, balconies for public appearances, private apartments, banquet halls, fountains, and gardens. Many of the rooms and spaces had a fanciful character, with irregular shapes, octagonal courtyards, and a sunken garden in the form of a hippodrome (an arena for horse racing). The rooms employed a large variety of concrete vaults in different shapes. At the back of the hill, the palace complex overlooked the Circus Maximus, the primary venue for the popular chariot races. Part of the palace may have comprised a sort of imperial box from which the emperor could observe the races and appear before the cheering throngs gathered in the Circus Maximus, all without ever really having to leave his home.

While the palace on the Palatine was the primary residence of most of the emperors, the most famous and notorious imperial dwelling was the Domus Aurea, or "Golden House," constructed by the emperor Nero. The Great Fire of AD 64 devastated 10 of the 14 regions of Rome, and Nero took advantage of some of the space cleared by the fire to construct an extravagant new palace, which stretched from the Palatine to the Esquiline. There were rumors that Nero had started the fire deliberately to make room for his grand project.

At the time of Nero's death, construction had not yet finished, but the parts already completed were impressive enough. These included a triple colonnade that extended for an entire mile, an artificial lake in the valley where the Flavian Amphitheater would later be built, elaborate pavilions and gardens stocked with a variety of exotic wild animals, and a huge complex of over 140 rooms to be used for hosting feasts and dinner parties. At the dedication of this extraordinary set of structures, Nero's comment was, "Finally I can begin to live like a human being" (Suetonius, *Life of Nero* 31).

Part of the dining block survives and nicely illustrates the extravagance of this project. It includes several courtyards, each surrounded by no fewer than 50 dining rooms, where Nero could play host to gigantic feasts. Other dining rooms featured fountains in the ceilings and walls that could pour water down between the guests. One principal dining room was said to have a revolving rotunda, and a number of dining rooms were equipped with panels in the ceiling that could be opened, allowing flowers and perfumes to drift down upon the guests. One of the most dramatic

Figure 11.1 Reconstruction of the interior of the emperors' palace on the Palatine hill. While the details are speculative, this drawing conveys an impression of the sumptuousness of the decor. (From G. Gatteschi, *Restauri della Roma Imperiale*, 1924, p. 41.)

rooms located at the center of the structure is an octagonal dining court with an *oculus* in the middle of the roof. Opening onto this octagonal space were a number of dining rooms with waterfalls flowing down one side of their walls. The entire surface of the walls and ceilings of this wing was covered with fine decorative marbles and lavish wall paintings.

The crowning touch to the whole complex was placed on the hill above it, where Nero constructed a gigantic, 40-meter-tall bronze statue of himself in the nude. This statue, known as the Colossus of Nero, was an appropriate symbol of Nero's egomania. After his death and the condemnation of his memory, it was obviously awkward to have such an enormous reminder of such a reviled figure. The solution that was settled upon was to alter the head of the Colossus, changing the features and adding rays projecting out of the head so that it was transformed into a statue of Sol, the god of the sun. Later, the emperor Hadrian had the statue moved to a new position next to the Flavian Amphitheater to make room for a new temple he wished to build. This relocation was a formidable engineering challenge, and the statue was reportedly transported in an upright position using the muscle power of 24 elephants.

This statue's strange odyssey did not end there, however, since the emperor Commodus once again removed the head and substituted a new one to aggrandize himself. Commodus had an obsession with the mythical hero Hercules and liked to dress up in a lion skin and carry a club to emulate his role model. Therefore, he had a new head with his own features placed on the Colossus and added the attributes of Hercules. Upon Commodus's death, the statue was reworked yet again to restore it as a statue of Sol. The Colossus seems to have survived until at least the fourth century AD, though it was torn down at some point later during the Middle Ages. Its memory was preserved, however, since the adjacent Flavian Amphitheater became popularly known as the Colosseum some time around the year 1000, a nickname that it still retains today. By the mid-second century AD, the Golden House had been abandoned by the emperors and was buried under later structures, such as the Baths of Trajan.

THE IMPERIAL FORA

By the end of the late republic, the Roman Forum had become very crowded due to the many purposes for which this relatively small space was being used, so Julius Caesar constructed a new forum just north of the Roman Forum, which became known as the Forum of Caesar. Roughly the size of the original forum, it consisted of a rectangular open space surrounded all the way around by colonnades, and contained a temple to Venus Genetrix. This area was obviously prime real estate, so Caesar had to spend an enormous amount of money to purchase the land upon which it was built. It is said that just acquiring the land cost 100 million sesterces. This was the start of one of the largest ongoing developments in Rome and would result in some of its most spectacular buildings. A number of emperors constructed additional fora, which, when completed, connected the old Roman Forum with the Campus Martius and dwarfed the original forum in size. Collectively, these areas are known as the Imperial Fora.

The next one to be constructed was the Forum of Augustus. It was built branching off from the side of Caesar's forum and was roughly the same size. The centerpiece of the Forum of Augustus was an enormous temple dedicated to Mars Ultor (Mars the Avenger). After the assassination of his adoptive father, Caesar, in 44 BC, Octavian (later known as Augustus) vowed to construct a temple to Mars Ultor if he were able to successfully avenge Caesar's death. The erection of this temple was delayed for various reasons so that it was not finally dedicated until 2 BC. Acquiring the necessary land again posed a problem. According to one source, Augustus was reluctant to evict people; therefore, the back wall of his forum is irregular in shape because he was unable to obtain all the land he desired.

This forum was a rectangle about 125 meters long by 90 meters wide with an open space in the center containing the temple at one end and a row of columns down each side of the enclosure. One highly innovative feature was two large hemicycles (half-circles) opening off the colonnade at the level of the temple. The scale of the entire forum was impressive, with the columns of the colonnades nearly 10 meters high and made out of high-quality decorative marbles. The temple itself had 15-meter-high

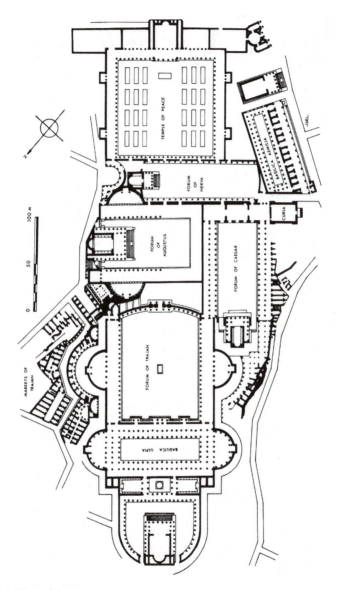

Figure 11.2 Plan of the Imperial Fora. (Reprinted from Frank Sear: *Roman Architecture*. Copyright 1982 by Frank Sear. Used by permission of the publisher, Cornell University Press.)

Corinthian columns and sat atop a high podium. The forum backed up against the densely inhabited Subura district but was separated from it by a massive wall of grey tufa some 30 meters in height. This wall not only insulated the magnificence of the forum from the somewhat disreputable Subura district but also served as a firebreak.

Figure 11.3 The remains of the Temple of Mars Ultor. The high, grey tufa wall that separated the back of the Forum of Augustus from the Subura district is clearly visible.

Figure 11.4 Model of the Temple of Mars Ultor. Octavian vowed to build this temple if he were able to successfully avenge Julius Caesar's death.

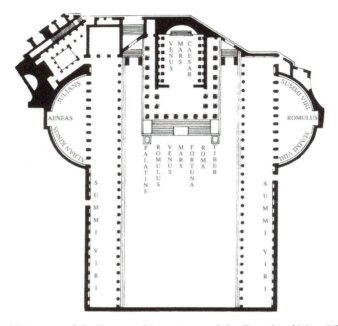

Figure 11.5 Diagram of the Forum of Augustus and the Temple of Mars Ultor showing the arrangement of statues that collectively serve as propaganda for the emperor Augustus. (This diagram is adapted by Gregory S. Aldrete, Phaeton Group, Scientific Graphic Services Division, from Fig. 50 in *The Urban Image of Augustan Rome,* Diane Favro, 1996. Reprinted with the permission of Cambridge University Press.)

Augustus was a master of using propaganda to justify and popularize his rule, and the decoration of the entire Forum of Augustus complex can be read as the assertion of a consistent symbolic message glorifying Augustus, his family, and his achievements. This symbolism began in the temple itself, where the cult statue of Mars was flanked by statues of Venus on one side and the deified Caesar on the other. On the pediment, Mars was again in the center, with Venus to his right and, on her right, Romulus. On Mars's left were personifications of Fortune and Rome, while at the corners were personifications of the Tiber and the Palatine. The pediment was aligned with the deepest recess of the two half-circular exedra. In a large niche at the center of the northwestern exedra was a statue of Aeneas, and filling the remainder of the niches in this exedra were members of the Julian family and the kings of Alba Longa. In the large niche at the center of the southeastern exedra was a statue of Romulus, and in the other niches were *summi viri,* or "great men" from Rome's history. The long corridors on either side of the forum also contained niches with statues of additional *summi viri.* Beneath each of these statues was a plaque listing the man's notable achievements, so the forum became a kind of gallery of all the greatest men in Roman history.

This entire decorative scheme served to link Augustus with the legendary founders of the city, to the great men of its history, and even to the gods themselves. As the adopted son of Julius Caesar, Augustus could lay claim to the lineage of the Julian family, which traced its ancestry to the Trojan hero Aeneas. Aeneas was the son of the goddess Venus, and thus Augustus could claim divine ancestry. The prominence given to Venus inside and on the pediment of the temple would remind viewers of this connection with Augustus, as would the statues of Aeneas and the members of the Julian family featured in the one exedra. Romulus in legend was the son of the god Mars, and while Aeneas may be said to have founded the Roman people, Romulus founded the actual city of Rome. Romulus's mother was a woman named Rhea Silvia, who was the daughter of the king of Alba Longa, and this family was descended from Aeneas. Thus Augustus could be linked to both Venus and Mars, Aeneas and Romulus.

Even the minor figures on the pediment contributed to the connection of Augustus with these pivotal figures of Roman myth. The Tiber naturally played a key role in the history of the city, but the choice of the personification of the Palatine is interesting. The ostensible reason for its inclusion was that this was where Romulus lived, but contemporary viewers would have inevitably made the association that this was also the current site of Augustus's house.

The exedra and the temple formed a kind of intersection of both literal and symbolic axes that tied together Augustus and the founders of the Roman people, the city of Rome, and the important gods Mars and Venus. Given Augustus's desire to be seen as a kind of second founder of Rome, this symbolic emphasis is not accidental. His forum became the scene of a number of rituals, particularly those involving foreign affairs. Governors of provinces were supposed to begin the journey to their provinces from this forum. When the senate was debating whether or not to declare war or whether to award triumphs, they met in Augustus's forum. Military banners and standards that had been seized in battle from Rome's enemies were displayed in the Temple of Mars Ultor. Finally, the ceremony in which Roman boys assumed the toga of manhood took place in this forum.

The last and the largest of the imperial fora was the Forum of Trajan, dedicated in the early second century AD. It was attached to the already existing imperial fora and stretched away from them toward the Campus Martius to the northwest. The Forum of Trajan was a truly colossal complex, over 300 meters long and 180 meters wide at points. There was a gigantic open courtyard surrounded by columns with two hemicyclical exedra opening off of it, obviously imitating the Forum of Augustus. After this came the Basilica of Trajan, a vast structure in its own right with hemicycles at either end mirroring those of the forum. Beyond this was Trajan's Column, which was itself flanked by two buildings, one containing a Greek library and the other a Latin library.

Figure 11.6 Ruins of the Basilica of Trajan. The grey columns are all that remain of the once-imposing structure.

Figure 11.7 Reconstruction of the opulent interior of the Basilica of Trajan. (From G. Gatteschi, *Restauri della Roma Imperiale*, 1924, p. 71.)

The quality of materials used throughout this series of structures was extremely high. The floors were paved with yellow Numidian marble and purple Phrygian marble, forming geometric shapes. The various columns used these same stones as well as elements made of grey Egyptian granite and fine white marble. The basilica had columns of grey Egyptian granite and green Carystian marble as well as ornate, inlaid marble floors. Trajan's forum was built using the proceeds from his military campaigns in Dacia, and the space was used for judicial purposes, providing needed expansion space for law courts.

VICTORY MONUMENTS

The Romans liked to erect monuments commemorating military victories or other achievements. There was a long tradition in Roman society of immortalizing these actions in stone. As time went on, the physical city itself began more and more to symbolize Rome's conquest of the Mediterranean world through its actual structures. The city itself could be considered a giant trophy case for the display of captured objects, since its public spaces were decorated with items stolen from all over the Mediterranean during Roman campaigns. Temples such as those of Mars the Avenger and Jupiter Optimus Maximus were literally stuffed to overflowing with captured enemy flags, standards, armor, and other military trophies. The streets, gardens, baths, and houses of Rome were decorated with works of art seized during Rome's campaigns, particularly in the Greek East. Finally, the very stones that made up the great public buildings of Rome were themselves reminders of Rome's status as conqueror of the known world. Rome imported colored marbles and decorative stones at great expense and effort from all over the Mediterranean. Thus, many of the buildings that made up the city were themselves composed of booty from the conquered territories, and anyone walking around the city of Rome would have been constantly confronted with highly visible reminders of Rome's dominance over the Mediterranean.

One common form of victory monument that the Romans built was the triumphal or commemorative arch. These probably had their origins in temporary decorations that were placed on archways through which generals passed when celebrating a special ritual known as a triumph. A triumph was essentially a parade granted to a victorious general. The day would be declared a public holiday, and the general, his troops, prisoners of war, and captured booty would march through the streets of the city while the people gathered to cheer them. Triumphs were not given to all generals but rather were awarded by the senate as a special honor. In order for a general to qualify for a triumph, at least 5,000 enemy troops had to have been killed during his campaign. Between 220 and 70 BC, 100 triumphs were granted. During the empire, triumphs were limited to the emperor and members of his family.

Figure 11.8 Depiction of a Roman triumph. A slave holds a laurel wreath of victory above the head of the general.

The procession would assemble outside Rome in the Campus Martius and then enter the city through a gate known as the Porta Triumphalis. The route wound through the city, passing by the Circus Maximus, around the Palatine, and along the Via Sacra, and ending up at the foot of the Capitoline hill. It culminated with the *triumphator* climbing up the Capitoline to the Temple of Jupiter Optimus Maximus, where a sacrifice was performed. The *triumphator* was dressed in the *toga picta*, which was purple with gold trim, and his face was painted red so that he looked like the cult statue of Jupiter on the Capitoline. He rode in a gilded four-horse chariot accompanied by a slave who held a gold crown over his head and whispered in his ear that fortune was fleeting. His troops accompanied him, shouting the acclamation *"Io Triumphe."*

An idea of what a triumph was like can be gained by considering the one celebrated by a general named Lucius Aemilius Paullus, who conquered Macedon during the republic. This was by no means the most spectacular triumph ever staged, but it nevertheless took three entire days. On the first day, 250 wagons loaded with all the artworks that Lucius Aemilius Paullus had stolen while in Greece rolled through the streets. On the second day, the crowds witnessed wagons burdened with the weapons and armor of all the foreigners that his army had killed, followed by wagons carrying 2,250 talents of silver. The third and final day began with a parade of 231 talents of gold, followed by the golden plates and tableware of the defeated enemy king, then the golden crown of the enemy king, then members of the enemy king's immediate family, then the enemy king in chains marching before a golden chariot, in which stood Lucius Aemilius Paullus himself, wrapped in a purple toga.

Sometimes, rather than a triumph, a general would be granted a lesser honor known as an *ovatio*. This was also a parade but a less spectacular one; the general had to walk on foot or ride a horse and he wore an ordinary *toga praetexta*.

ARCHES

During the empire, triumphs became nearly the sole prerogative of the emperor, his family, and his close associates. Hoping to leave a permanent reminder of military victories, emperors began erecting monuments to commemorate these accomplishments. One of the most common forms that such a structure took was the triumphal arch. Originally, one of the arches in the Servian Wall through which triumphal parades traditionally passed was known as the Porta Triumphalis, and this gateway probably served as the inspiration for triumphal arches.

The earliest triumphal arches were free-standing ones not incorporated into adjoining walls; these were erected along the path followed by triumphal processions. While the majority of arches were at first placed somewhere along the triumphal route, over time the arch evolved into a form of monument that began to appear in other places throughout the city. Additionally, some arches began to be put up to commemorate individuals and not just those who had celebrated a triumph. Archaeological remains or literary references attest to nearly 50 triumphal or commemorative arches that were built in ancient Rome, although only 3 of these survive today in the central city.

Triumphal arches were surmounted by a bronze statue of a four-horse chariot (a *quadriga*) being driven by the person or persons celebrating the triumph. Arches had either a single opening or else triple passages, with the central one usually larger than the ones to either side. Free-standing arches as monuments were almost always put up by emperors, and nearly all the known ones celebrate either an emperor or a member of the royal family. In addition to having portraits of the person being honored, these arches were frequently decorated with carved reliefs depicting scenes from the campaign, such as Roman soldiers slaughtering barbarians and carrying booty back to Rome. The three most famous arches, which are still standing today, are those of the emperors Titus, Septimius Severus, and Constantine.

The Arch of Titus is a single-opening arch 15 meters high and 13.5 meters wide. Located along the Sacra Via between the Roman Forum and the Flavian Amphitheater, it was built in AD 81 just after the death of Titus in commemoration of Titus's military victories in Judea. The arch features several famous relief panels of Roman soldiers carrying away loot from the Great Temple of the Jews in Jerusalem, including a scene of soldiers bearing a large menorah, the traditional seven-branched Jewish candle-holder.

Figure 11.9 Arch of Titus. This single-opening arch was erected to celebrate the conquest of Judea.

Figure 11.10 Arch of Septimius Severus in the Roman Forum.

The 21-meter-high Arch of Septimius Severus, located at the northwestern corner of the Roman Forum along the triumphal route, has three passageways. Erected in the early third century AD to commemorate the emperor's eastern campaigns against Parthia, it was topped by a statue of the emperor and his sons in a chariot drawn by six horses.

The Arch of Constantine, which stands along the triumphal route adjacent to the Flavian Amphitheater, was dedicated on July 25, AD 315 in celebration of the victory of Constantine over his rival for the throne, Maxentius, in AD 312. It is composed of a triple arcade 21 meters high and 26 meters wide. This relatively late arch is interesting because its builders seem to have cut corners in order to erect it quickly. This was accomplished most notably by recycling statues, reliefs, and materials from earlier buildings and monuments. The decorative marbles used in its construction are a mishmash of different colors and types. Several large statues adorning it depict Dacian prisoners, which must have been stolen from a monument put up by the emperor Trajan. Also clearly taken from a Trajanic structure are carved reliefs showing Romans battling barbarians. Included in these scenes is the emperor himself, but Trajan's head has plainly been recarved to change his features into Constantine's. On the front and back of the arch are round panels that seem to have been looted from a monument to the emperor Hadrian. Finally, there are other reliefs that, by style and subject matter, seem to have originally been part of a memorial to the emperor Marcus Aurelius. Once again, on these, Aurelius's head has been reworked to convert his features into Constantine's.

COLUMNS

Another form that such monuments took was a column topped by a statue of the person being honored. One of the earliest examples of such memorials is a column surmounted by a statue erected in 439 BC honoring Lucius Minucius, who had safeguarded the grain supply. Later monuments resulted in a veritable forest of honorific statues and columns, many of them clustering in and around the Roman Forum.

By far the most spectacular examples of such columns were those erected by the emperors Trajan and Marcus Aurelius, both of which are still standing today. These columns were erected to celebrate military campaigns, and the entire shaft was carved with a spiraling frieze that illustrated the campaigns from beginning to end. These continuous friezes could be read much like a modern cartoon and told the story of the military expedition in visual form.

The Column of Trajan was dedicated on May 18, AD 113, and commemorates a series of military campaigns waged by the emperor in Dacia between AD 101 and 106. It rests upon a square base, and the shaft of the column is 100 Roman feet tall (30 meters) and 3.83 meters wide at the base, tapering slightly as it proceeds upward. The column itself is composed of 17 separate drums of fine Luna marble, and the carved spiral frieze contains 155 different scenes featuring over 2,600 carved figures.

If the frieze were unraveled and stretched out, it would be over 200 meters long. The frieze is meant to be read from the bottom up, and the figures increase in size (from about 0.6 meter tall at the base to around 0.9 meter at the top) as they proceed up from the bottom, presumably giving the illusion that they are all the same size when viewed from below. The emperor Trajan frequently appears, directing the campaign in these scenes; he is carved slightly larger than the other figures to emphasize his status.

A spiral staircase running up the inside of the column has 185 steps and is lit by narrow slit windows. A statue of Trajan originally stood on top of the whole edifice. The column, located adjoining the Basilica of Trajan, was flanked by separate Greek and Latin libraries, and Trajan's successor, Hadrian, added a temple to Trajan on the other side. The column served not just as a victory monument but also as a mausoleum, since after Trajan's death his ashes were put into a golden urn, which was placed within the base of the column.

The later Column of Marcus Aurelius was clearly constructed in imitation of the Column of Trajan and was similarly decorated with a

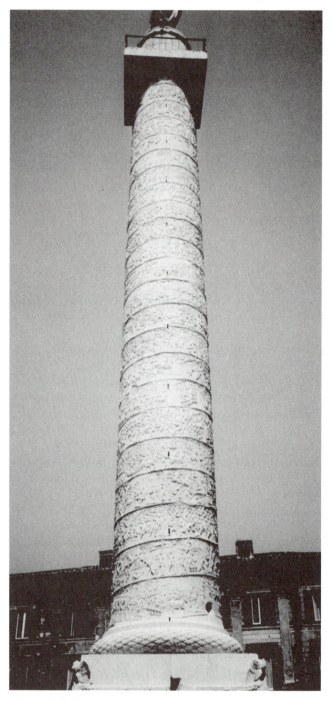

Figure 11.11 Trajan's Column. In addition to celebrating his military victories, this monument also served as the tomb for Trajan's ashes.

Figure 11.12 Scene from Trajan's Column that shows the emperor being presented with the heads of barbarians by Roman legionaries.

carved spiral relief illustrating some of the emperor's campaigns, in this case those that he directed against the Marcomanni and the Sarmatians between AD 172 and 175. This column was also 100 Roman feet high (30 meters) and was composed of 26 drums of Luna marble. It too concealed a spiral staircase within it, this one consisting of 200 steps, and the column was again also used as a mausoleum to house the remains of Marcus Aurelius after his death in AD 180. The reliefs on this column were originally inscribed more deeply than those on Trajan's Column but have suffered greatly from the effects of air pollution, and many of the panels are badly eroded. In the sixteenth century, the Vatican placed a statue of St. Paul atop the column.

The fine details of the carvings on both of these columns have proven to be of enormous use to historians and archaeologists in reconstructing the particulars of Roman military equipment and tactics, as well as the interactions of Romans with barbarians. The panels show every stage of a military campaign, such as the emperor planning strategy with his generals, troops gathering and transporting food and supplies, combat between Romans and barbarians, the emperor delivering speeches to inspire the legionaries, fortified towns being attacked with siege weapons, parlays between Roman and barbarian ambassadors, raiding expeditions, and even refugees fleeing from the danger zone. Many scenes demonstrate the brutality of war and atrocities committed by both sides; for instance, one panel depicts barbarian women torturing Roman prisoners with fire, and another shows Roman soldiers displaying the heads of slain barbarians to the emperor. Other dramatic scenes show defiant barbarians committing suicide rather than being captured by the Romans. Coupled with these violent images are more mundane scenes, including many of Roman soldiers chopping down trees and gathering wood for fires or to build forts. Much of our current knowledge of Roman military equipment is derived from these carvings, which meticulously recorded the details of various types of arms and armor. These columns are as close as we can come to having the equivalent of a motion picture that tells the story of a Roman military campaign.

EMPERORS' TOMBS

Even in death, the emperors prominently left their mark on the city. While the impressive columns described in the previous section served as highly visible monuments to hold the ashes of the emperors who built them, these were by no means the most extravagant emperors' tombs. Augustus and Hadrian erected colossal mausoleums for themselves, which became repositories not only for their own ashes, but for those of their families as well. These tombs became some of the most highly visible monuments in the northern section of the city.

Traditionally, the remains of members of Rome's wealthy families were interred in tombs along the roads leading into the city. A very small number of individuals were granted the special privilege of being buried in the Campus Martius. Very soon after rising to power, the first emperor, Augustus, began the construction of an innovative and gigantic tomb for himself on the very northern edge of the Campus Martius, where it would have been highly visible across the flat and, at that time, mostly undeveloped plain. This building, which came to be known as the Mausoleum of Augustus, seems to have been completed during the 20s BC.

The Mausoleum of Augustus took the form of an enormous cylinder slightly less than 90 meters in diameter. This drum was composed of concentric rings of very thick concrete walls, and the exterior was faced with fine marble. Earth was piled on the top of the drum, and evergreen trees (a symbol of immortality) were planted thickly on this platform. The whole edifice was surmounted with a large bronze statue of Augustus himself, which may have stood on a second, smaller cylinder rising from the center of the trees. The overall height of the structure (not counting the statue) is estimated to have been close to 45 meters. The mausoleum was surrounded by elaborate and beautiful gardens with arbors and walkways.

The entrance to the building faced south toward the city, and the doorway was flanked by two obelisks of Egyptian marble. Also near the entrance were two bronze tablets inscribed with the Res Gestae, Augustus's autobiography. Inside the tomb was a series of circular passageways culminating in a burial chamber at the center, which included niches for other members of his family. This structure became the resting place not only for Augustus's ashes, but also for those of at least 13 other members of the Julio-Claudian family, including his wife, Livia, his friend and assistant, Agrippa, various relatives, and later Julio-Claudian emperors. The round shape was traditional for tombs and burial mounds, but the scale of Augustus's mausoleum and its visibility from the city were unprecedented.

During the Middle Ages, the mausoleum was turned into a fortress and the fine marble was stripped off. Subsequent incarnations of the monument included a bullring, a garden, and a site for theatrical performances. Today all that remains is the concentric interior walls of concrete, but even these are impressive in their scale and solidity.

The other emperor to erect a spectacular tomb close to the city was Hadrian, who built his mausoleum in the second century AD. The Mausoleum of Hadrian resembled the earlier one of Augustus in many ways and, similarly, had a long and varied history. It is today known as the Castel Sant'Angelo.

Hadrian situated his tomb in an unusual location on the right bank of the Tiber River, just before the sharp bend that encloses the Campus Martius. At the time it was built, this was a largely undeveloped region, and one possible motivation for this choice of site may have been to encourage growth of the city in this direction. Hadrian began construction of his mausoleum during his reign, but it was not completed until AD 139, a year after his death, when Hadrian's successor, Antoninus Pius, put the finishing touches on it and interred the ashes of Hadrian and his wife, Sabina.

Hadrian's mausoleum consists of a large cylindrical drum some 64 meters in diameter and 21 meters high that rested atop a square base whose sides measured close to 90 meters in length and that was itself 10 meters high. The walls were faced with fine white marble and covered with extremely ornate carvings. Numerous large statue groups decorated the top of the drum, and the pinnacle of the monument was capped with a huge statue of a *quadriga,* a four-horse chariot, in which rode a statue of the emperor himself. The overall height was probably close to 55 meters.

The interior of the monument contained a complex series of passageways, including a spiraling ramp that led to the top. At the center was the burial chamber for Hadrian and his family. The entrance, like that of Augustus's tomb, was oriented toward the south. The entire structure was surrounded by a bronze grillwork fence that was topped with gilded peacocks (also symbols of immortality). A bridge, the Pons Aelius, led directly from the mausoleum across the river into the Campus Martius and seems to have been constructed in concert with the tomb. The mausoleum continued to be used as the burial site for the remains of a number of subsequent emperors, including Septimius Severus; the last known interment was that of the emperor Caracalla in AD 217.

Figure 11.13 The Mausoleum of Hadrian. Today known as the Castel Sant'Angelo, for many years this structure served as a fortress for the popes.

During the Middle Ages, Hadrian's mausoleum was transformed into a fortress, and outer bastions and other fortifications were added. In 1277, an elevated walkway was constructed, connecting the fortress directly with the Vatican; from this point on, it became the refuge of the popes in times of crisis. The structure was renamed the Castel Sant'Angelo, and today nearly all the visible superstructure reflects these later rebuildings as a castle, although the interior preserves much of the original design.

12

The Economy
and Ancient Rome

AGRICULTURE

Employment for 80–90 percent of the people in the ancient Roman world simply meant being a farmer out in the countryside. The basis of the Roman economy was farming and land ownership. The Latin word for farmer is *agricola*—a revealing word because it is made up of two other words: *ager*, which means "field," and the verb *colere*, which means "to cultivate." Thus, an *agricola* is literally one who cultivates the field. From these terms comes our modern English word, agriculture.

During the republic, farms tended to be fairly small. The average farm was typically as much land as one family could manage. Archaeological evidence suggests that farms may have been on average about 1.6 hectares in area. Roman farmers had a saying that you could not trust anyone whose farm was larger than 12 *iugera* (about 3 hectares). They were suspicious of anyone who farmed more than he needed to, since this indicated that he must be greedy and therefore also dishonest. Cincinnatus, the ideal Roman citizen-hero, worked a farm of about 1.2 hectares.

During the Late Republic, when rich men began buying up all the land and putting together huge estates, the Romans passed legislation stipulating that it was illegal for any one person to own more than 500 *iugera* of land. In practice, this law was either plainly ignored or else people found loopholes to circumvent it, but it nonetheless serves as an interesting indication of how suspicious Romans were of large landholders.

The core of Roman agriculture was what is known today as the Mediterranean triad: wheat, olives, and wine. The cultivation of wheat was a multistep process. Many Romans seem to have used a two-field system, which meant that each year farmers only planted on half their land while the other half was allowed to rest to recover nutrients and moisture. Farmers first had to prepare the land they were going to farm, and this meant plowing. Each field had to be plowed between three and six times before it would be properly ready; this process entailed extremely hard work. Oxen, which were used to pull plows, were quite expensive. Often an entire village would share one team of oxen, which were probably the most valuable things in the village. After plowing, the farmer had to fertilize the fields, which demanded that manure be mixed into the soil, often by hand. It is estimated that it took a family six days working from dawn until dusk to properly manure a single acre of soil. Fertilization was followed by the actual sowing of the seeds. Romans just scattered the seed around by hand, so they ended up wasting and losing a lot. Modern sow-to-reap ratios are very high, about 1:50 or so, but Roman farmers may have had ratios of only 1:4. Thus one-quarter of each crop had to be saved to produce the next one. Once the seeds were sown, the soil had to be worked over with hoes and weeded by hand. At last came harvest time. Farmers walked through the wheat fields with sickles and cut off the wheat stalks. The work was by no means finished yet, however. The wheat stalks were then threshed to separate the grain from the straw. On the threshing floor, farmers beat the wheat with flails or sometimes even had cows trample on it. Threshing was followed by winnowing, in which the wheat was tossed into the air to separate out the heavier grain from the chaff.

If all these stages went well and the crops were neither destroyed by rain, flood, cold, or vermin nor stolen by thieves, then a farmer at last ended up with some wheat. The amount was probably barely enough to feed a family for the coming year; even in a perfect year, the surplus might amount to only 5–10 percent. This was a world always literally on the brink of starvation. The routine of Roman farming had little variation and demanded lots of hard work, and the rhythms of the cultivation process governed life for the vast majority of people in the Roman world.

Other cereal crops grown included barley and millet. Ancient sources seem to have regarded these as less desirable for human consumption. They were primarily used as feed for animals, although in the army a common punishment was to have to eat barley for a while instead of wheat. Despite this bias, many poor people probably depended on barley for subsistence.

Another important crop was olives. The olive is the definitive plant of the Mediterranean, but it is also the one most restricted by environmental factors. Olives were, of course, eaten as food, but olive oil was used for many other purposes, such as in cooking (instead of butter), as a light

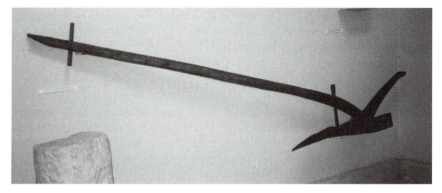

Figure 12.1 A Roman plow. Roman agriculture was a labor-intensive process using only the most basic tools.

source (in lamps that burned olive oil), as a kind of soap (rubbed on the body and then scraped off after bathing), and as the basis for all sorts of perfumes (modern perfumes, in contrast, have an alcohol base). Olives were truly central to the entire Mediterranean lifestyle.

Olives were harvested in the fall. Olive trees were precious resources, since a tree can take 5–10 years to even start producing olives, but they can live for hundreds of years. The trees are biennial, producing a crop every other year. The olives had to be carefully picked by hand, since they are very tender and bruise easily. After harvesting, olives could be transformed into olive oil by putting the olives in a press. The oil yield from this process was one-quarter to one-third the original weight of the olives. The Romans made use of every bit of the olive. The pressing process resulted in a black, sludgelike by-product, which was used for fertilizer, pesticide, sealant, moth deterrent, copper polish, axle grease, and sheep medicine.

Grapes were widely cultivated and were most often consumed in the form of wine. The main labor in grape growing consisted of pruning, grafting, and harvesting. This work could be done by the elderly and by children, leaving the able-bodied adults free for more demanding activities such as wheat farming. Wine was made by pressing the grapes and then allowing the juice to ferment. Vegetables were also grown but were not staples of the average diet. Crops such as vegetables could be grown in and around olive trees. There were no pesticides or mechanical harvesters in the ancient world, so it was possible to cultivate different crops mixed together on the same plot of land, a process known as intercultivation.

The main animals that were raised were sheep and goats, from which were obtained milk and cheese. Cattle herding was relatively rare on the shores of the Mediterranean. Goats and sheep could graze on mountainous terrain that was unsuitable for growing crops, and the lonely goatherd leading flocks around the mountains of Italy was a stereotypical figure in

Roman literature. Beekeeping was common and was especially important since honey was the only sweetener that was widely available to the Romans.

EMPLOYMENT AND COMMERCE

The remaining population who were not farmers and who were not in the army mostly lived in cities, and, for them, there was a variety of ways to earn a living. The upper-class Romans who wrote all the surviving sources had very definite ideas about work and employment. For them, how you earned an income had strong moral overtones. In fact, they believed that most forms of employment were degrading and that truly civilized people should not work at all. This is quite an extreme way of viewing employment, since nearly everything we would consider a form of work today was considered to be morally degrading by aristocratic Romans. Earning a salary, buying or selling goods, manufacturing goods— all of these activities were considered vulgar, and a true aristocrat could not dirty himself with them. Thus, to the upper-class Romans, only those people who were so rich that they did not have to do anything to earn a living were considered fully human and civilized.

The things that aristocrats did that we would consider to be jobs, like serving as a lawyer or being elected to a magistracy such as a praetorship or consulship, were not considered jobs because their practitioners received no pay. Politics and the law were truly the preserve of rich men since these fields entailed spending a lot of money but did not grant any in return. In keeping with the republican ideology of virtue exemplified by Cincinnatus, the only profession that did not degrade someone was farming. Rich men were expected to acquire and maintain their wealth primarily by owning land. By the empire, aristocrats did not do any real farming themselves, however, and in fact spent almost all their time in Rome rather than on their estates. They lived off the labor of hundreds or thousands of slaves who did the actual farming on their estates. The sources are full of expressions of contempt for anyone who made a living by working or through commerce. This was the Romans' ideology, but in reality, the picture was more complex. Many rich Romans gained and maintained their fortunes through means other than farming. Some were moneylenders who charged up to 60 percent annual interest on a loan. Some were in essence factory owners who had shops that produced goods such as lamps, bricks for building, and plates and containers made out of clay.

A few aristocrats got very creative in the ways they amassed wealth. The best example of this was a man named Crassus, who lived during the Late Republic. Crassus became the richest man in Rome at least partially through an original and clever strategy. He prowled the streets of Rome at night, accompanied by a huge band of his slaves carrying buckets and axes. As soon as one of the frequent fires broke out, Crassus and his slaves would rush to the spot, and Crassus would offer to buy the burning build-ing from its owner. He would usually offer between one-quarter and one-third of its real value. The poor owner, faced with the choice of one-quarter of the value or losing everything when it burned down, usually sold it to Crassus. As soon as the document was signed, Crassus would order his well-trained gang of fire-fighting slaves into action, and they would put out the fire. In this way, Crassus ended up owning much of Rome, which he acquired literally at fire sale prices.

While the upper classes could afford to be choosy about employment, the vast majority of people in cities had to work. The working classes can be divided into two basic groups: those whose profession required some sort of training, talent, skill, or capital and those who were unskilled and sold their labor for wages. One of the ironies of Rome is that most poor cit-izens fell into the second category, that of the unskilled wage laborer. The skilled workers were often slaves and ex-slaves. In inscriptions on tomb-stones, about two-thirds of those who identify themselves as some sort of skilled worker are freedmen. Over 200 different jobs are mentioned on tombstones from the city of Rome. Many of these professions listed were specialty jobs manufacturing luxury items, such as the *plumarii,* who apparently made a living doing embroidery exclusively using feathers, or the *fabri ocularii,* whose full-time employment was to manufacture the eyes for statues. There were six or seven different makers of footwear, including those who made only boots, those who made only women's shoes, and those who only wove sandals. Another large category was peo-ple who provided specialized services to the rich. Among these was one full-time job consisting of memorizing the names of a patron's clients. Perhaps one of the most unappealing service specialties belonged to the *alipilus,* whose job was to pluck out underarm hair.

Although aristocrats regarded work and moneymaking with scorn, many freedmen seem to have taken great pride in their work. This can be seen most clearly on their tombstones, which often featured a sculptural relief showing the deceased practicing whatever profession he or she had followed. Even if they lacked a picture, tombstones would often include symbols that indicated the job the owner had held. For example, a butcher might have a selection of knives and cleavers on his tombstone. Some-times, freedmen got quite creative with their funeral monuments. One man named Eurysaces, who owned a shop that baked bread, had his tomb carved into the shape of a giant bread oven, onto the sides of which were carved pictures of the baker overseeing his workers grinding grain, kneading dough, and cooking it. Another famous tomb belongs to a man who owned a construction company, and his monument mostly consists of a carving of a building crane used to erect structures. This pride in work can also be seen in the decoration found in the homes of some of these people: one worker at Pompeii had set into the floor of his house the phrase "Profit is happiness."

Figure 12.2 A Roman *popinae*, or fast food restaurant, from Pompeii. The openings in the counter would have held pots, which were kept warm by fires underneath the countertop.

In addition to tombstones, another way that we know about Roman jobs is that all the people who practiced the same profession formed professional associations. These trade associations were called collegia, and often the members of such a group would put up a monument commemorating their accomplishments. The collegia also seemed to play a role in politics, and much of the graffiti on Roman walls consists of collegia urging other people to vote for a certain politician.

Many Romans owned small shops where they sold goods. One common type of small business was the *popinae*, which was a Roman combination of bar and fast food restaurant. These were housed in small rooms usually located at the intersections of major streets. Across the front was a counter with two or three large clay pots set into it. Underneath the pots were places where small fires could be built to keep the pots warm. These pots probably contained an assortment of gruel, fish stew, and *garum*, and pedestrians passing by who felt hungry could purchase a ladleful of whatever fast food they wanted.

A number of different sites in Rome were identified as a *macellum*, or marketplace, although the location of these varied over time. While individual shops were found throughout the city, these markets would have served as focal points where a dense concentration of goods, particularly foodstuffs, was bought and sold. Early in Roman history, sites including the Forum Boarium, Forum Holitorium, Forum Piscarium, and Forum Cuppedinis seem to have been associated with different types of com-

Figure 12.3 Trajan's Markets. This well-built structure may have functioned much like a modern shopping mall.

merce, and later, a great *macellum* seems to have been established to the northeast of the Roman Forum. This was eventually displaced by the Imperial Fora as they grew in extent.

Constructed at the same time as the imperial Forum of Trajan was the building known today as Trajan's Markets. This is an extensive structure of complex design spanning six levels and including over 170 rooms. It was built up against the slope of the Quirinal hill, a large chunk of which was cut away to make room for the adjacent Forum of Trajan. Trajan's Markets are separated from Trajan's Forum by a high tufa wall that would have prevented direct communication between them, but the markets' shape is nevertheless dictated by the curve of one of the forum's hemicycles, which it reflects. The markets consist of several levels of superimposed curving corridors lined with individual rooms. The large, square doorways to these rooms are trimmed with travertine marble, and the entire structure is built out of brick-faced concrete in a style similar to that seen at Ostia. Several vaulted hallways, themselves lined with more rooms, extend toward the hillside, and other levels of the complex include several streets similarly fronted with rooms. The entire edifice is linked by a complicated series of stairways and passages. Trajan's Markets are an astonishingly sophisti-cated and creative piece of architecture, in which visually striking struc-tures were built in a difficult space with a high degree of quality. A modern visitor to this well-preserved complex cannot help but be struck by the sim-ilarity of the structure to a contemporary multilevel shopping mall, and this may indeed have been the purpose of the building. The construction of the Imperial Fora had displaced a number of shops and markets, so this structure could have served to replace the lost commercial space. Others have argued that it was the site of government offices, but these two functions are not mutually exclusive.

The lowest form of employment was unskilled workers who had nothing to offer except their labor. They hired themselves out for a salary to perform various menial jobs. Such wage labor was considered the most degrading sort because the Romans thought that it was the equivalent of becoming someone's slave. These wage laborers were called *mercenarii,* which is the root of our word *mercenary.* Today, wage labor is usually calculated on an hourly basis, but in ancient Rome, the standard unit of labor for a *mercenarius* was one day's work. A day's worth of work was known as an *operae,* and contracts would specify a certain number of days of labor that the *mercenarius* was selling to his employer. The most common type of day-labor job was simply to carry things around. A sizeable percentage of the free inhabitants of Rome would have found employment in two fields: the supply of food and other commodities to Rome and the construction industry. Especially during the early empire, the emperors built lavishly, and these projects would have employed thousands of people merely to dig the foundations and carry away the dirt. A single construction project of the emperor Claudius employed 30,000 men for 11 years as diggers.

The overwhelming majority of foodstuffs grown, and goods manufactured, in the Roman world was consumed or utilized very close to its site of production. Most items were sold by the growers or manufacturers themselves in their own neighborhoods or villages. The local marketplace was the center for most trade and transactions, and whatever goods were available regionally formed the entirety of most people's economic world.

While small regional markets did a lively trade in local commodities, true long-distance trade was a daunting proposition. Moving anything in large quantities overland was both expensive and hazardous. Bulky cargo could be transported more easily by water, and it is no coincidence that most major cities grew up along coasts or on navigable rivers. However, seafaring technology was rudimentary, there was no effective way to predict storms at sea, and piracy was rampant, so there had to be either very strong motivations or very high profit margins to justify shipping goods across the sea. Despite these hazards, one of the most lucrative businesses in which one could make fantastic profits was the long-distance trade of luxury goods by ship. A single shipload of spices, fabrics, or dyes from the East could make one a millionaire overnight. However, building a merchant ship and buying its cargo required substantial capital up front, and it was an extremely risky investment.

Only the very wealthy would have had enough capital to outfit and equip such a ship and to be able to survive the loss if it did not return. The potential for huge profits tempted many aristocrats into backing such risky expeditions. This sort of activity was dangerously close, in the Romans' eyes, to engaging in vulgar commerce, and the senate became concerned that too many aristocrats were debasing themselves through owning merchant ships. This led to a law called the Lex Claudia, passed in the first century AD, which made it illegal for a senator or the son of a senator to own a large merchant ship. To get around this restriction, aristocrats took advantage of the patron/client system. For example, an aristocrat might free one of his slaves and then provide him with the capital to outfit a ship. Thus the freedman would technically be the ship's owner, but the profits would be funneled back to the patron. Through measures such as this, Roman aristocrats maintained an ideology in which they were all idle and did not dirty their hands with commerce, while at the same time they were getting rich off commercial activity.

ROMAN MONEY

The Romans continued the well-established Greek practice of coinage. Because the Romans were in the habit of minting coins with portraits of their emperors on one side, their money has become one of the most reliable guides to what these rulers looked like. While the widespread use of coinage constituted a great step forward in the development of a complex economy, the ancient world was not free of the problems associated with currency, and there were numerous instances of counterfeiting, inflation, and debasement of the coinage.

At various times, the Romans used many different coin denominations, and the relative values of these denominations also changed over time. Three of the most common coins were the silver denarius, the bronze sestertius, and the bronze as. Much rarer was the gold aureus. The relative values of these coins was as follows: 1 aureus = 25 denarii, 1 denarius = 4 sesterces, and 1 sestertius = 4 asses. Sometimes very large sums were expressed using the Greek denomination of a talent. One talent was equivalent to approximately 6,000 denarii. When writing about the Roman world, most historians express numbers in terms of sesterces, which they abbreviate as HS. It is very difficult to meaningfully translate Roman amounts of money into comparable modern sums, but the annual salary of a Roman legionary was 900 HS, and the minimum wealth qualification to be a Roman senator was 1,000,000 HS.

During the republic, there were no standard designs for coins, but human beings were not supposed to be depicted on coins. During the empire, most coins were minted with the head of the emperor in profile on one side, surrounded by his titles written encircling his head, while the other side was decorated with propagandistic symbols and slogans. Due to the obvious space limitations, the Romans made heavy use of abbreviations on their coinage. Some of the most common abbreviations and slogans are listed in bold below:

S C (SENATUS CONSULTUM) = By order of the senate

IMP (IMPERATOR) = Emperor

COS (CONSUL) = Has been elected Consul

TRIB POT or **TR P** (TRIBUNICIA POTESTAS) = Holder of Tribunician power

F (FILIUS) = Son of

DIVI = Divine

AUG (AUGUSTUS)

CAES (CAESAR)

PIUS = Pious

PONT MAX (PONTIFEX MAXIMUS) = Chief priest

P P (PATER PATRIAE) = Father of the country

S P Q R (SENATUS POPULUSQUE ROMANUS) = The senate and people of Rome

-ICUS (added onto a geographical place) = Conqueror of that place

Sometimes Roman numerals appear. These were used if someone held an office more than once. For example, if a coin bore the inscription COS II, it meant that the person was elected to the consulship twice. These same abbreviations were often used in inscriptions carved in stone. One factor that can make coins and inscriptions hard to read is that the Romans often did not put spaces between words and abbreviations.

> *Example:* A typical coin might have an inscription such as
> IMPDIVIAUGNEROPONTMAXCOSIVPARTHICUS
> This can then be divided up as IMP DIVI AUG NERO PONT MAX COS
> IV PARTHICUS
> Translated, this inscription would mean something like, "The emperor, the divine augustus Nero, chief priest, elected consul four times, conqueror of Parthia."

FEEDING THE CITY

There are few absolute necessities for life. One of these is water, and the Roman aqueduct system has already been described. Another of these fundamental necessities is food, and ensuring that the inhabitants of the city of Rome had enough to eat was one of the major achievements of the Romans and demanded extensive infrastructure.

The diet of the vast majority of people in the ancient Roman world would have consisted of a simple routine of grain, olive oil, and wine. The grain was usually consumed either as bread or as a kind of porridge or gruel. This diet would sometimes have been supplemented by fruits or vegetables, but meat, especially red meat, would have been a rarity. Fish and poultry were eaten when available.

When the city's population began to increase rapidly in the middle republic, local resources began to prove inadequate to provide the huge quantities of food necessary to sustain the populace. To avoid riots and chaos in the capital, the Roman state was compelled to start taking an active role in the food supply. Within a few hundred years, this role would evolve from simple price fixing to a state-run system that distributed free portions of food to the citizens of the city. The earliest known instance of state intervention occurred in 299 BC, when high grain prices caused the aediles to get involved in setting maximum prices and making sure that enough food was reaching Rome. In 123 BC, a law called the Lex Sempronia established the precedent that grain would be sold to the inhabitants of the city at a fixed and subsidized price. The Romans measured grain in a unit called a *modius,* which was equivalent to roughly 6.5 kilograms of grain. This law set a price of slightly more than 1.5 HS per *modius.*

A truly radical development took place in 58 BC, when a rabble-rousing politician named Clodius passed a new grain law that established the precedent of free monthly distributions of grain in the city. Clodius's law also redefined those eligible in ways that increased the number who could draw this ration—for example, by lowering the minimum qualifying age to 10. Under this law, all citizens over the age of 10, even if they were of freedman status, could collect 5 *modii* (32.5 kilograms) of free grain per month.

The amount chosen is interesting because this is really more grain than would be necessary to feed one person for a month; in fact, it was probably almost enough to feed two. The grain dole was not a completely free ride for the recipients, however, since they would still have had to come up with enough money on their own to pay for the grain to be milled and then baked into bread. Various statistics survive indicating the number of grain dole recipients at different points in time, and there seem to have been repeated efforts by the state to pare down the number of recipients in response to the swelling numbers of those on the list.

By 46 BC, 320,000 people were receiving the grain dole. This number was reduced to 150,000 the next year by Julius Caesar but almost immediately seems to have ballooned back to 250,000 in 44 BC. It remained at 250,000 in 29, 24, 23, and 12 BC. By 5 BC, the number of names on the list had crept back up to 320,000, provoking another revision of the rolls by Augustus, so that by 2 BC, the number of recipients was back down to 200,000. In AD 14 and 37, 150,000 dole recipients were recorded, and the system probably continued on at least this scale for the next couple of centuries.

Various emperors had granted occasional largesse of additional foodstuffs to the city's inhabitants, and the emperor Septimius Severus in the early third century AD augmented the grain dole with a regular distribution of olive oil. Later that century, the emperor Aurelian apparently included monthly servings of pork and wine as well.

Keeping Rome's gigantic population fed created a substantial industry dedicated to the collection and shipping of food to the city. Based on comparative data from sources such as studies of Greek peasants, it is estimated that each person in ancient Rome probably consumed 237 kilograms of wheat, 20 liters of olive oil, and 100 liters of wine per year. Multiplied by a million inhabitants, this results in 237,000 tons of wheat and 120,000 tons of oil and wine. Since liquids were transported in large, clay pots, this requires adding another 70,000 tons for the weight of the containers. The result is that over 400,000 tons of food had to be imported each year to feed the city of Rome. Where did all this food come from and how was it transported?

One important characteristic of grain, olive oil, and wine is that these forms of food can be preserved for a considerable length of time. Olive oil and wine, when stored in clay jars and properly sealed, have very long shelf lives, and as long as grain is kept dry, it too can be stored for months or even years. It was not only their suitability to be grown in the Mediterranean climate that made these crops dominant, but the fact that they could be stored for substantial periods of time and therefore moved long distances.

Transportation of bulk goods by land was prohibitively expensive and slow. It simply was not practical to haul a wagonload of wheat, for example, very far, since the animals that were necessary to pull the wagon would quickly eat an amount of food equal to that which could be carried in the wagon itself. The solution to this problem was to move goods by sea. Scholars have estimated that the cost of shipping grain from one end of the Mediterranean to the other was cheaper than hauling the same amount of grain 75 miles overland. It was perhaps 40 times more expensive to transport goods by land rather than by sea, and while it was somewhat more costly to move goods along a river than over the open ocean, riverine transport was still many times more efficient than land transport.

Since Italian resources were not sufficient to feed Rome, they naturally looked to Roman-controlled areas that were closest and that had access to the sea. The first provinces that had surplus grain collected from them and transported to the city in large quantities were, logically enough, the nearby islands of Sicily and Sardinia. Once Rome had conquered the coast of North Africa, the surplus from this region was rounded up and routed toward the city of Rome as well. By the first century AD, Egypt and the coastal areas of Spain and Gaul had been added to this list. Despite its distance from Rome, Egypt in particular was an important source of grain, and the safe arrival of the Egyptian grain fleet off the coast of Italy was a major cause for celebration.

While necessary as the only practical way to transport enough food to Rome, this maritime traffic could also be problematic. Particularly during the winter, the Mediterranean Sea can produce violent storms that would have sunk their ships; thus, the prime sailing season was restricted to only three to four months during the summer. Most of the supplies for the city, then, had to reach Rome's ports during this narrow window of opportunity or else face greatly multiplied chances of being caught in a storm and sinking. Natural dangers were not the only threat to shipping, however. Piracy in the ancient Mediterranean was rampant, and despite sporadic attempts at suppression, pirates had nearly free rein to prey upon merchant ships. The Romans were aware of the precarious nature of the lifelines that kept the city fed. The Roman historian Tacitus commented, "Italy relies upon external supplies, and the life of the Roman people is daily at the uncertain mercies of sea and storm" (Tacitus, *Annals* 3.54). The scale of the food and the other supplies pouring into Rome demanded an appropriate infrastructure, both administrative and physical.

Rome is not located directly on the Mediterranean Sea but rather is about 22 kilometers inland on the Tiber River. The mouth of the Tiber lacked a natural harbor where ships could be safely unloaded. The smallest ships could have traveled upriver directly to Rome, but medium or large freighters had to be off-loaded somewhere else. During the republic, many ships (including the huge Egyptian grain freighters) docked at the good harbor at Puteoli on the Bay of Naples. From here, their cargoes had to be either shifted to smaller watercraft for their trip to Rome or else hauled overland. At the mouth of the Tiber was located the port city of Ostia. The harbor facilities at Ostia remained rudimentary through the republic, and larger ships that docked there simply had to ride offshore and have their cargoes transferred onto barges or small craft for the trip upriver. As Rome continued to grow and traffic increased, these harbor arrangements were clearly unacceptable, and in AD 42, the emperor Claudius tackled this problem and began to construct substantial harbor works at Ostia. Just north of the city, he excavated out of the coastline an artificial harbor known as Portus, although it was not a wholly successful project. Rome at last got a first-rate harbor when the emperor Trajan rebuilt Portus and added an inner harbor where ships could be completely safe.

At Rome, dock facilities seem to have been concentrated in the southern section of the city, particularly below the Aventine hill, in a region known as the Emporium district. Although much of these dock works was obliterated by the construction of the modern Tiber embankments, excavations have revealed evidence of long stretches of concrete quays and unloading platforms with ramps heading down into the water.

Ships tied up using large, stone mooring rings. Most ships seem to have been unloaded at Ostia or Portus and their cargoes either stored in warehouses there or else transferred to river barges that were hauled upstream to Rome. Such a barge was called a *codicarius* and was a specialized craft of about 70 tons made to be towed by gangs of either men or animals

Figure 12.4 Mosaic of a dockworker at Ostia loading *amphorae* (clay pots) onto a *codicarius* (river barge). The barges were pulled upriver to Rome by gangs of men marching along the riverbank.

walking along the bank. The actual course of the Tiber from Ostia to Rome is 32 kilometers, and it is thought that this trip took perhaps three days. One Roman poet makes reference to the rhythmic chants of these men as they hauled their barges upriver (Martial, *Epigrams* 4.64). Once the *codicarii* reached Rome, they would have been unloaded and the cargo stored in warehouses until it was needed. Particularly during the short sailing season, when several dozen ships might be arriving each day, Rome's harbor areas must have been the scene of truly frenzied activity. Simply loading and unloading the ships at the various points along this route would have required tens of thousands of laborers toiling long hours, hauling heavy sacks of grain or amphorae of liquids. A minimum estimate of the number of ships required to carry a year's worth of grain, wine, and olive oil for Rome suggests that a fleet of nearly 1,700 ships would have been necessary.

In addition to ships and docks, this system required storage space, and warehouses of truly gigantic proportions sprang up at Ostia, Portus, and Rome. Such a warehouse, known as a *horrea*, in its most typical form consisted of an open courtyard surrounded on all four sides by small storage rooms. These structures were often of massive construction, with thick walls, few external openings, elaborate lock systems on the doorways, and sometimes even multiple stories. Some *horrea* were specially designed to store grain, with raised internal floors to help increase ventilation, decrease vermin, and keep the grain cool and free of moisture. One warehouse at Rome, known as the Horrea Galbana, contained three internal courtyards surrounded by over 140 individual storage rooms covering an area of around 20,000 square meters. This monstrous structure may have had multiple stories as well.

An interesting feature of these *horrea* is that the doorways were quite narrow, and this, together with the use of stairways rather than ramps to get to the upper floors, indicates that the goods were transported by individual men carrying sacks or containers rather than by wagons or animals. This labor-intensive arrangement suggests that many of the inhabitants of Rome who were supported by the food supply system may actually have also found employment within it. The fourth-century *Regionary Catalog* lists over 300 *horrea* in the city of Rome.

The degree of direct involvement of the state in shipping supplies to Rome is a matter of scholarly debate. Most of the actual merchants and shipowners doing the transporting seem to have been private businessmen. At the very least, the Roman state offered incentives to make sure that enough supplies were being transported to the city. An example of this is a law passed by the emperor Claudius that stated that anyone owning a ship that could carry at least 10,000 *modii* of grain who used that ship for at least six years to bring grain to the city would be granted certain privileges, including Roman citizenship if the owner was a noncitizen.

Augustus created the administrative post of *praefectus annonae*, an official charged with general oversight of the grain supply. Over the next century, assorted subsidiary administrative posts were added to oversee very specific aspects of the supply system at Rome, at its ports, and even in key provinces such as Spain, Africa, and Egypt. The *praefectus annonae* was a high-ranking post, as suggested by the fact that the salary for his assistant was 100,000 sesterces per year. The prefect and his staff had their headquarters at the Porticus Minucius, which may have been one of the central distribution points of the grain dole. Keeping track of the rolls of eligible recipients would have been a major bureaucratic challenge. Those who were eligible seem to have been given tickets called *tesserae*, which they had to show to collect their ration.

When one factors in all the other items brought to Rome in large quantities, such as timber; stone; wild animals; luxury goods; oil for use in heating, cooking, and in the baths; and all the other things consumed by the city, it becomes apparent that there was a huge shipping and transportation industry serving Rome's needs. At Rome and Ostia, numerous guilds of merchants and workers developed.

Perhaps the most impressive expression of the scale of Rome's supply system is one of the hills of modern Rome, Monte Testaccio. Thirty-five

Figure 12.5 Monte Testaccio. This artificial hill is composed entirely of the remnants of millions of broken Spanish olive-oil containers.

meters high and several hundred meters long, it is not a natural feature at all but is in fact an artificial mountain composed entirely of the shattered remains of 50 million North African and Spanish olive-oil containers broken or discarded in the course of transporting olive oil around the dockyards of Rome.

13

Ostia: An Industrial Port City

HISTORY OF OSTIA

Inextricably linked with the history of the city of Rome is the history of its port, Ostia (literally translated as "the mouth"), located 22 kilometers downstream where the Tiber River empties into the Mediterranean Sea. Since Rome depended on importing overseas food for its survival (but the river up to Rome was not navigable by large ships), there was a clear need for a port where goods could be unloaded, stored, and then transferred to small ships or barges for the journey upriver to Rome. Unfortunately, the mouth of the Tiber was ill suited for such a port. The region was unhealthy, characterized by swamps and low-lying areas that bred swarms of disease-carrying insects. Additionally, the Tiber was prone to silting, and there was no natural protected inlet or harbor where ships could dock and be safe from storms. These drawbacks caused the development of Ostia to lag behind the growth of Rome; however, the sheer scale of the imports necessary to support the capital eventually ensured that Ostia was forced to assume a major role as a port and also made it the focus of gigantic building projects intended to rectify its shortcomings.

According to Roman legend, the king Ancus Marcius first established a city near the mouth of the Tiber to facilitate the mining of salt beds. Whether or not this town was on the same site as Ostia, or even whether it existed at all, is impossible to tell. The first firmly historical Roman settlement at the mouth of the Tiber dates to the fourth century BC, when a military fort, a *castrum*, was established to guard the entrance of the river

Figure 13.1 Map of Ostia. (Reprinted from Frank Sear: *Roman Architecture*. Copyright 1982 by Frank Sear. Used by permission of the publisher, Cornell University Press.)

against sea raiders. This camp was fairly small and was laid out in a standard rectangular shape around the intersection of two main streets, the *cardo* and the *decumanus.* A wall protected the *castrum,* the total enclosed area of which was only about 2.4 hectares. A civilian settlement subsequently grew up alongside the *castrum,* centered to the west of it.

As the city of Rome grew in population and as it became necessary to import food supplies, Ostia was forced to play a role in this transportation system. By at least the time of the Second Punic War, grain from Sardinia was passing through Ostia on its way to Rome. Ships either would have had to be small enough to be able to travel upriver directly to Rome or else had to anchor just offshore or in the mouth of the river where their cargoes were transferred to smaller lighters and barges for the trip upriver. This was a dangerous anchorage, and there were not really facilities to accommodate large ships, so much of the grain supply was alternately routed to the port of Puteoli on the Bay of Naples to the south. Puteoli had a well-protected harbor where large ships could tie up to the quays directly; thus, many of the largest grain freighters, including the grain fleets from Alexandria, preferred to dock at Puteoli rather than at Ostia. While the harbor facilities at Puteoli were superior, using this port meant that the cargoes then had to be carried overland for the final stretch of their journey to Rome, a much more cumbersome and expensive process than water transport.

Despite these factors, much traffic came through Ostia and the city steadily grew. In the first century BC, a new set of walls was constructed, which enclosed some 65 hectares, clearly demonstrating how much the city had expanded since its foundation as a *castrum.* The old *castrum* had by now been completely absorbed by the city and had become its forum space. Apartment buildings sprouted up to house the population of dockworkers and shipbuilders, and numerous warehouses appeared scattered throughout the city to store the vast quantities of goods arriving from overseas. Under Augustus, a number of important Ostian landmarks were constructed, including the theatre and its surrounding piazza, which were erected by Augustus's friend and helper, Agrippa. Under Tiberius, a large Temple to Rome and Augustus was built, as well as public baths and an aqueduct. During the first century of the empire, a squad of *vigiles* (firefighters) was established at Ostia; also during this time, Ostia gained a more defined harbor area. Just inside the mouth of the river, a rectangular harbor approximately 100 meters deep and 160 meters wide was excavated from the riverbank. Along the east side of this harbor was a huge platform with a vaulted substructure that served as a ship shed. Centered on top of this structure was a large temple oriented toward the sea. Around the harbor were more *horrea,* or warehouses.

Beginning under the reign of Claudius, Ostia experienced a boom time that would last for the next 100 years. While the existing harbor facilitated the loading and unloading of ships, there was still no anchorage safe from storms, and more dock space was needed for the hundreds of freighters coming to Ostia. In AD 42, the emperor Claudius tackled this problem and began to excavate substantial harbor works at a site approximately four kilometers north of Ostia. He dug out of the coastline a huge artificial harbor some 1,000 meters in diameter that was connected to the river and to Ostia by canals. This harbor was enclosed by two long, artificial moles constructed of travertine blocks and concrete. Atop one of these was erected a lighthouse that used as its foundation the giant ship that had been built to transport the obelisk of Heliopolis from Egypt to Rome under the reign of Caligula. This ship, over 100 meters long, was filled with concrete and sunk to form the lighthouse's base. This new harbor, known as Portus, was at this point not regarded as a separate town but rather as an extension of Ostia; thus, both sites were administered by the existing bureaucracy at Ostia. Portus must have provided desperately needed docking space to alleviate the crowding at Ostia. However, despite all the effort and expense that went into its construction, the problem of safety from storms was not solved; in AD 62 a storm sunk over 200 ships within the new harbor. There also seems to have been an attempt to raise the ground level of the area, probably to render it safer from Tiber floods. After the devastation of the Great Fire of AD 64 at Rome, Nero ordered that all grain barges bringing wheat from Ostia to Rome load up with rubble for the return trip to Ostia, where the debris was to be used to fill in the swampy lowlands.

Rome at last got a first-rate harbor when the emperor Trajan rebuilt Portus and added an inner harbor where ships could be completely safe. This inner harbor was a giant hexagon 700 meters across, lined with well-made quays and mooring points. The modern airport that serves Rome was built partially over Portus, and the outline of Trajan's hexagon is still quite visible to tourists landing in a plane. In the second century AD, there was much construction at Ostia and Portus, with many large *insulae* (apartment buildings) and *horrea* being built or rebuilt, as well as new bath facilities and a Temple to Jupiter. This phase of building included the widespread use of solid brick as a construction material in addition to some brick-faced concrete.

By the third century AD, a decline in the population of Rome, coupled with problems with the river mouth silting up, caused the end of Ostia's growth. As the volume of maritime traffic declined and the facilities at Portus were sufficient to carry the reduced load, Ostia began to lose its bustling industrial nature. In the late third century AD, many commercial areas and buildings seem to have no longer been heavily used or were turned to alternate purposes. Interestingly, it is from this period that many of the large private homes or villas appear to date, suggesting that Ostia was being transformed from a predominantly commercial city into more of a seaside resort for wealthy vacationers from Rome. Under Constantine, Portus was administratively split off from Ostia and became its own city.

Figure 13.2 Model of Trajan's harbor. Its distinctive hexagonal shape is still visible today as a depression in the ground.

In the fourth century AD and following, Ostia rapidly dwindled. With its purpose as Rome's port gone, the unhealthy, swampy nature of the site once again became a dominant factor, and Ostia was essentially abandoned. At its height, Ostia's population may have been as high as 50,000, but by the early Middle Ages it had become a ghost town, and because of its malarial nature, the ancient city was never really resettled or built over. This has proven to be of great benefit to historians and archaeologists since ancient Ostia is now one of the best-preserved Roman sites. Because of its extensive rebuilding in the first and second centuries AD, followed by its rapid decline, Ostia is also our best guide to what imperial Rome would have looked like at its height, especially in terms of residential and commercial structures.

Although Ostia suffered the same looting for statues, mosaics, and other works of art as most ancient cities from the Renaissance to the present, because it was never built over, the ruins of the city's buildings remained relatively untouched from the Renaissance to the present. In the late nineteenth century, more systematic and scholarly excavations began to uncover some of these structures, and this work continued gradually until the 1930s. As part of Mussolini's attempt to link his own government with the achievements of ancient Rome, interest in the site intensified, and from 1938 to 1942, extensive digging was carried out, which uncovered large sections of the city. While these excavations more than doubled the exposed areas of the city, the speed with which they were undertaken meant that the records of the digging were spotty and that much potentially useful data was lost. The regions revealed by the 1938–42 excavations remained the known parts of the city and the focal point of Ostian studies throughout most of the rest of the twentieth century. In the last few years, a new survey project using various sophisticated technologies to analyze what lies beneath the unexcavated areas has been undertaken, and promises to add substantially to our understanding of the city. Preliminary results suggest that the currently excavated regions represent only about one third of the original total area of the city, and this project has already identified the remains of many previously unknown but important urban structures. For example, the number of known *horrea*, or warehouses, has more than doubled. Once the data from this survey have been analyzed, the history of Ostia may need to be revised to take into account this new information.

THE BUILDINGS OF OSTIA

Unlike Pompeii, which had a high ratio of private homes to apartment buildings, Ostia overwhelmingly housed its largely working-class population in the multistory apartment buildings known as *insulae*. Most of Ostia's surviving *insulae* date to the first and second century AD rebuilding of the city and are composed of either brick or brick-faced concrete. The brick on these buildings seems to have been left exposed rather than covered over with plaster, stucco, or stone.

A typical such building known as the House of Diana enjoyed a central location near the Forum of Ostia. This building covered an area of approximately 23 by 40 meters, with frontage on two streets. Most of the rooms opening onto these streets were used as shops or taverns, while the inner rooms were private dwellings. Since many of these inner rooms had no direct access to an external wall, they lacked windows. To provide light, there was a small open-air courtyard at the center of the building, which would have served as a central shaft bringing light and air to these rooms. The courtyard, which measured six by nine meters, included a basin of water fed from pipes. This was probably the water source for all the building's inhabitants, so those on the upper floors would have had to carry water up to their dwellings. Traces clearly show that this *insulae* was at least three stories high, but the thickness of the lower walls suggests that it might originally have carried four or perhaps even five stories. A number of stairways were situated throughout the structure, some leading directly from the street to the upper floors, others located within the building. The ground floor also featured a large latrine, which presumably served all the inhabitants of the *insulae*. On the sides facing the streets, there were continuous rows of balconies supported on vaults, although these may have been more decorative than functional. Late in the history of this building, two ground-floor rooms in the northeast corner were converted into a *mithraeum*, illustrating the popularity of such cults among the diverse populace of Ostia.

Some *insulae* show evidence of having catered to higher-income residents. The building known as the House of the Muses boasts a large, internal colonnaded courtyard, or peristyle, similar to those found in the luxurious houses of the wealthy. The walls of this *insulae* also were painted decoratively and there were elaborate mosaics on the floors, all further evidence that this was a lodging with high rents and an elite clientele. In addition to having large, well-built, and carefully planned *insulae*, such as the House of Diana and the House of the Muses, Ostia included numerous more haphazard apartment complexes. Some of these contained only a handful of rooms, while others were larger. There do not seem to have been strong distinctions between upper- and lower-class neighborhoods. Instead, class stratification occurred along the vertical axis, with ground- and first-floor apartments being generally more desirable and expensive than those on the upper floors.

Literary evidence from Rome stresses the negative aspects of life in an *insulae*, portraying these structures as dark, squalid, crowded, shabbily built, and prone to frequent collapse. The physical remains from Ostia offer a different picture on the whole with most *insulae* well made, commodious, and often including pleasant amenities. Naturally those buildings made of inferior materials were less likely to have survived the centuries so that remaining examples may to some extent represent a skewed sampling, but it does nevertheless seem that the average apartment in Ostia may well have provided a decent lodging to its inhabitants.

During the republic, Ostia had both *insulae* and *domus*, or private homes. These *domus* were similar to those of Pompeii in design. At the city's peak in the early empire, however, *insulae* were clearly the dominant form of housing, and the extensive rebuilding of the city during this period saw many of the earlier *domus* buried beneath new, imposing apartment blocks. In the late empire, however, there was a recrudescence of the *domus*'s popularity. These later houses do not follow as standard a design as the earlier ones but exhibit a richness of furnishings that often included elaborate fountains, a heated room, and an extensive use of marble both as a surface covering and in architectural details.

One of the most common building types in Ostia was the *horrea*, or warehouse. The large number and capacity of Ostia's warehouses clearly demonstrate the importance of Ostia in the supply system that kept Rome fed. As previously mentioned, much of the supplies that came into Ostia during the prime sailing season were probably stored there and then gradually sent upriver to Rome over the rest of the year. Most *horrea* were constructed according to one of two basic designs: a group of rooms clustered around an internal courtyard, or a double row of rooms placed back to back. The Horrea of Hortensius is an example of the former type, which

Figure 13.3 Wall painting of a grain freighter being loaded and the grain being measured by an official.

Figure 13.4 Storage facility for *dolia* at Ostia. These large pots would have contained liquid goods such as wine or olive oil.

Figure 13.5 Piazza of the Corporations mosaic in front of an office for wild-animal importers based in Africa.

features nearly 40 storage cubicles (averaging about 5 by 12 meters) located around a very large, central, open courtyard. It seems to have been one of the earlier large *horrea* built in the town but one that nonetheless remained in use throughout the active life of the city. Many *horrea* had specially constructed false floors, indicating that these were used to store grain, which has to be kept cool and dry to prevent the growth of harmful molds. The excavated regions of Ostia include at least 15 major warehouses, and thus far the recent survey project suggests the presence of an additional 25, many of which are located near the unexcavated harbor area. Another interesting type of specialized warehouse consists of four-walled enclosures in which large ceramic containers called *dolia* have been embedded in the earth. Such *dolia* would have been used to store liquid goods such as wine and olive oil, and many of the *dolia* have a capacity of more than 750 liters. It has been estimated that the largest such repository, containing over 100 *dolia* could therefore have stored over 75,000 liters of wine or olive oil.

The prominent Theater of Ostia was originally constructed by Agrippa during the reign of Augustus but was later rebuilt in the second century AD. One of the earliest known Roman theaters, it could accommodate about 3,000 spectators. Built at the same time as and adjoining the theater was one of Ostia's most distinctive structures, a very large, double-colonnaded portico enclosing a central space some 125 by 80 meters. Around the three

Figure 13.6 Piazza of the Corporations mosaic in front of the office for shippers based in Narbonensis.

sides of the portico were 61 small rooms, and on the ground in front of each of these rooms were black-and-white mosaics. This complex, which was rebuilt in the second century AD, is called the Piazza of the Corporations and is thought to be the site where many of the shipping companies had their offices. Each mosaic indicated what was imported by the particular shipping company housed in the room behind it. Many of the businesses were clearly involved in importing grain, and their mosaics show sheaves of grain or ships. Other commodities, such as jars of wine, are also depicted. There are a number of mosaics that show animals such as elephants and camels, and these are perhaps the offices of the companies that supplied the amphitheater at Rome with animals used in beast hunts. Importing wild animals from Africa was a big business, and the Romans had specialized animal-carrying ships to transport the huge quantities of such beasts demanded by the games. The largest number of offices were for businesses based in various cities in Africa. Having branch offices of so many companies involved in aspects of the transportation system all located in the same place must have been helpful both for customers who wished to shop around for the best deals and for the state administrators in charge of regulating trade.

THE PEOPLE OF OSTIA

The population of Ostia would have been unusually diverse in terms of ethnicity, language spoken, and geographic origin, due to the many people associated with long-distance maritime trade who passed through the town. Sailors and merchants from all over the Mediterranean would have ended up living and working in the city. There also would have existed a large force of seasonal workers who flocked to the city during the busy summer sailing season and then dispersed to other jobs the rest of the year.

The majority of the inhabitants of Ostia were probably employed in various industries related to shipping and transportation. They were dockworkers, sailors, warehouse laborers, shipbuilders, and merchants. In ancient Rome, people who shared the same profession tended to group together in organizations called collegia, which were somewhat similar to the guilds found in later times. With so many people concentrated in a few professions, the collegia of Ostia were particularly prominent in the social, economic, and political life of the city.

These associations also acted as political lobby groups that petitioned the government for laws favorable to their interests. In connection with this process, collegia often erected monuments to state officials in order to curry favor with them. For example, the collegia of *mensores frumentarii*, or "grain measurers," based at Portus put up a statue to one of the officials in charge of overseeing the grain supply upon which they praised him for having "such fairness of judgement that all who approached him with disputes found in him a father rather than a judge" (*CIL* 6.1759).

The collegia showed a remarkable degree of specialization of jobs. For instance, there were three main types of rowboats used in the harbor and river, and the operators of each of these had their own collegia. Even within these categories, there was further specialization based upon the jobs for which the different boats were used. *Lenunculi* seem to have been larger craft with multiple oarsmen, and there were a number of separate collegia of *lenuncularii*, or operators of this type of boat. The *lenuncularii tabularii auxiliari* met arriving ships and escorted them to their berths, the *lenuncularii pleromarii auxiliari* transferred cargo from ship to shore, and the *lenucularii traiectus Luculli* were ferrymen.

Some collegia dealt with the construction and maintenance of ships, among them the *fabri navales* (the shipbuilders), the *stuppatores* (the caulkers), and the *restiones* (the ropemakers). Others worked in and around the docks and warehouses, such as the *mensores frumentarii* (the grain measurers), the *saccarii* (porters of grain sacks), the *custodiarii* (warehouse guards), the *geruli* (stevedores), the *phalangarii* (porters of clay amphorae), the *saburrarii* (porters of sand used for ballast in ships), and the *urinatores* (divers who recovered goods that fell into the water). These are only a sample of the more than 50 attested collegia at Ostia, which, in addition to

Figure 13.7 Piazza of the Corporations mosaic in front of the office for *stuppatores* (ship caulkers) at Ostia.

the many associated with transportation and maritime professions, also included standard urban trades such as fullers, bakers, carpenters, and general construction workers. The associative phenomenon extended to groups of youths in the city who had their own guilds and even to the public slaves of Ostia, who were allowed to form an organization. Women, however, were excluded from membership in the collegia, although some enterprising women clearly owned property and even businesses, such as two women who are listed among the owners of a shop that manufactured lead pipes.

Some inscriptions record the entire membership of a collegia in a certain year. From these lists it is possible to tell that freeborn citizens and former slaves, or freedmen, mingled together as members. Many of the club officials were former slaves, and thus the collegia offered a form of social respectability and upward mobility. Some of the largest surviving membership rolls belonged to the guild of general construction workers, who numbered 350 in AD 198, and the shipbuilders of Portus, who boasted 353 members in the early third century AD. There are a few instances of individuals who belonged to more than one collegia, but this seems to have been unusual. Collegia were not only professional associations but also served as social clubs. The members often constructed guild headquarters where they could gather to socialize, and they also frequently incorporated a temple or shrine, so these associations played a central part in religious life as well. These centers of worship were dedicated to a very wide range of gods, including many Eastern ones, and illustrate the cosmopolitan nature of Ostia's populace and its links to the broader world. At least 15 of these headquarters/temples have been identified with some degree of certainty. They range in size from the most humble ones to large complexes with over a dozen rooms and elaborate facilities.

SEA TRAVEL

Since Ostia functioned as the maritime gateway to the rest of the world for Rome, it is perhaps appropriate to consider some of the characteristics of sea travel in the Roman Mediterranean.

Roman merchant ships were fairly small on the whole, although the craft that operated as part of the food-supply system for the city were probably among the largest. The average size of these freighters is difficult to guess, but a reasonable estimate might be around 250 tons. Roman merchant ships were typically of a broad-beamed design, with a single mast and large, square sails. Ancient sources refer to some grain freighters, particularly those of the Egyptian fleet, as being very large. The river craft that brought goods from Ostia and Portus would have been much smaller, perhaps about 70 tons.

The lack of any method of weather prediction rendered sea travel very hazardous. Most ships accordingly clung to the coast both so that they could quickly seek shelter and because there were no reliable means of navigating across the open sea. The tendency of ships to stay close to shore made them vulnerable to a different menace—pirates.

Just as bandits owned the countryside, for most of Roman history, pirates ruled the seas. The shore-hugging nature of ancient sailing made it easy for greedy or desperate men to watch for such ships and, when they were sighted, to dash out to sea and seize them. They often killed the crew

Figure 13.8 Roman merchant ship of typical design. Hundreds of such ships carrying goods would have plied the waters of the Mediterranean.

or sold them into slavery and stole the goods to be sold later. If the pirates captured a wealthy or important person, they would hold him or her for ransom. In some coastal areas of the Mediterranean, piracy was a way of life. The most infamous area was along the coast of Asia Minor in a region called Cilicia. Piracy was most rampant in periods when central authority was weakest. The Late Republic was one of the worst times; pirate gangs attained the power and size of small kingdoms.

No one was safe from them, as is illustrated by the fact that when Julius Caesar was young, he was captured by pirates who held him for ransom. However, he was insulted that his captors only asked for 20 talents of ransom when Caesar thought that he was worth at least 50. He told his captors that as a result of this offence, he would have them all crucified. As soon as his ransom was paid and he was released, he gathered together some ships and soldiers, tracked down the pirates, and—true to his word—had them all crucified. Eventually piracy became so severe that the Romans had to act. In 67 BC, a special law called the Lex Gabinia was passed, giving the general Pompey an extraordinary command. He was awarded absolute power over the entire Mediterranean Sea as well as along the coasts to a distance of 50 miles inland. He was given 20 legions and 270 ships, and he was ordered to solve the pirate problem. He divided the sea into 13 regions and set up blockades so that no one could pass from one region to another. He then began at one end of the Mediterranean and swept across it, capturing and destroying all the pirates' strongholds on the coasts while driving the fleets ahead of him. In only three months, Pompey succeeded in purging the Mediterranean of piracy. Piracy naturally came back, but after the establishment of Roman naval bases, it was never as much of a threat as it had been during the Late Republic.

Because it was much faster to go by sea than by land, most people traveling long distances went by ship. There were no passenger vessels, so if one wished to travel, one had to arrange passage on a merchant ship. Since most long-distance travel was concerned with the food supply of Rome, these large freighters were the ships that passengers would travel on. Because of the harshness and unpredictability of winter storms at sea, ships mainly sailed in the summer. A few traveled in the spring and fall, but very few would risk sailing in the winter, when storms were most frequent.

The motivation for such travelers was varied. People often undertook trips to famous temples in attempts to cure an illness. Large, international contests such as the Olympics attracted travelers. Finally, many people simply went on holidays. Rich Romans liked to spend the summer on the coast, and the Bay of Naples in particular was a kind of resort area for the rich. If you were a passenger on a merchant ship, you had to bring all your own equipment, including your bed, the food you would eat, the pots and pans to cook it in, and the servants to do the work. Travelers were advised to conceal their valuables in a pouch under their shirt, and women were told not to wear any jewelry that might attract robbers. Once they had disembarked, travelers staying in foreign places would lodge at inns. Documents called *itineraria* were available, which listed the locations and characteristics of different lodgings.

There were a fair number of people whom today we would call tourists. These tourists were mostly interested in the past and in seeing famous sights or monuments. The Seven Wonders of the Ancient World were tourist destinations, as were sights associated with mythological events and stories, particularly the Trojan War. Some tourists would go to see the graves of heroes while others would visit the houses where famous men had lived, such as the house of Socrates in Athens. Like today, art attracted tourists. The ancients did not have museums, but most temples were almost like museums in that they were stuffed with sculptures, paintings, and war trophies. Certain statues became very famous, such as the cult statue of Zeus and a famous, extremely lifelike sculpture of a bronze cow by Myron in Athens.

A milestone in ancient travel occurred in the second century AD, when a Greek named Pausanias wrote the first comprehensive guidebook to a country. He penned a book describing all the famous sites and monuments of Greece. His guidebook is organized by regions and cities, and for major places like Athens, he even offers directions for different walking tours that will take one to the notable places in the city.

The permanent population of Ostia would have witnessed a constant stream of people passing through their city. Opportunities for employment as laborers during the busy shipping season probably meant that there was an annual surge of temporary workers who would swell the town's population for a few months and then dissipate. Also, as it was the main gateway between Rome and the rest of the world, many travelers, both famous and humble, would have passed through Ostia. Among these was St. Augustine, who in his *Confessions* describes in detail a conversation between himself and his mother that took place while they were staying at an inn at Ostia resting up before undertaking a sea voyage (Augustine, *Confessions* 9.10.23). Augustine even includes the pleasant detail that their room had a window overlooking an internal courtyard with a garden, but his experience as a traveler, stopping briefly in Ostia, was one that would have been shared by many.

14

Pompeii: A Time Capsule of Roman Daily Life

HISTORY OF POMPEII

On the 24th of August, AD 79, the 17-year-old nephew of the eminent Roman politician Pliny the Elder observed an enormous tree-shaped cloud arising from Mount Vesuvius, which was located across the Bay of Naples from Pliny's villa. Determined to investigate the phenomenon, Pliny ordered a ship to be readied and invited his nephew to accompany him. Astonishingly, the teenager replied that he preferred to continue doing his homework rather than take a closer look at the exploding mountain. This day resulted in both personal tragedy and personal advancement for the young man. His beloved uncle died while observing the eruption; however, Pliny in his will posthumously adopted his nephew, thus ensuring his heir's fortune and career. In broader historical terms, the eruption of Vesuvius resulted in similarly mixed consequences. On the one hand, a number of Roman cities were completely destroyed, buried beneath volcanic ash and lava flow, and thousands of their inhabitants were killed. On the other hand, these buried cities, in particular Pompeii and nearby Herculaneum, became in essence time capsules that, when finally opened over 1,500 years later, would prove to be one of the most significant and unique sources of information about Roman culture and urban daily life.

The city of Pompeii is located just southeast of the base of Mount Vesuvius on the Bay of Naples. The city straddles a key intersection of roads where a main branch splits off heading inland from the coastal road; this

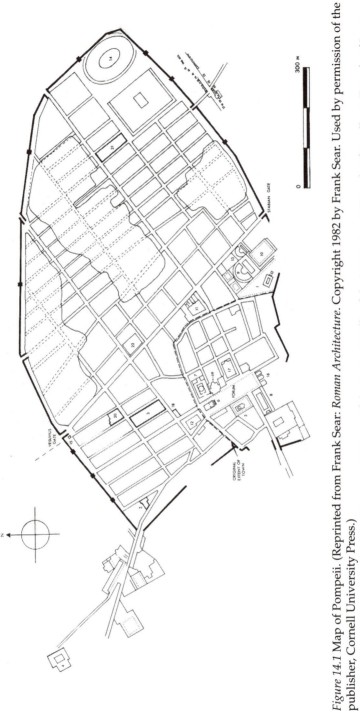

Figure 14.1 Map of Pompeii. (Reprinted from Frank Sear: *Roman Architecture.* Copyright 1982 by Frank Sear. Used by permission of the publisher, Cornell University Press.)

1. Triangular Forum; 2. House of the Surgeon; 3. House of the Faun; 4. Villa of the Mysteries; 5. Temple of Apollo; 6. Temple of Jupiter; 7. Meat and Fish Market; 8. Basilica; 9. Theater; 10. Quadriporticus; 11. Stabian Baths; 12. Forum Baths; 13. Small Theater; 14. Amphitheater; 15. Castellum Aquae; 16. Civic Offices; 17. Building of Eumachia; 18. Temple of Fortuna Augusta; 19. Temple of Vespasian; 20. House of the Vettii; 21. House of Loreius Tiburtinus; 22. Central Baths.

was certainly a factor in its growth and affluence. Archaeological evidence suggests that the city was founded in the sixth century BC and that it exhibited early Etruscan and Greek influences, but Pompeii probably only began to assume its final form when it became a settlement of the Samnites, an Oscan-speaking people.

By the third century BC, many of the main public spaces in Pompeii, such as the forum and street grid, had taken shape. The Samnites fell under Roman domination in 290 BC, but the city continued to evolve and prosper while retaining its distinctive Samnite identity. Thus, when the Social War broke out between Rome and its Italian allies in the early first century BC, Pompeii joined with the allies. Rome emerged victorious, and as part of his actions after the war, the Roman general Sulla settled several thousands of his veterans in Pompeii and refounded the city as a colony. The new Roman settlers spurred another wave of building activity in Pompeii, including the construction of an amphitheater and updated bath facilities. Within a generation or two, the old Samnite families began to show up again in urban administrative posts, and the blended populace advanced together in affluence, as revealed by the many fine private houses that dotted the city. This era of economic prosperity continued smoothly into the period of the Roman Empire.

A new phase in the city's life began in AD 62, when the volcanically active region produced a powerful earthquake that struck the city, causing widespread destruction. In general, the Pompeians quickly and energetically began to rebuild, but some wealthy families seem to have fled the unstable region, as evidenced by the conversion of some former elite homes to serve more industrial uses. Many of the wealthy inhabitants of this era seem to have been freedmen, a number of whom commemorated their rise in status and wealth through the construction of sumptuous homes and monuments. The city at this time probably had a population of 15,000–20,000 inhabitants and was one of the wealthy cities of the region of Campania. The Bay of Naples area in general was a favorite vacation spot for wealthy Romans, and many of the elites from Rome owned summer villas along the scenic landscape of the bay. The repairs from the earthquake of AD 62 were still incomplete, however, when an even more catastrophic event overtook the city and the region. In AD 79, Mount Vesuvius erupted with such fury that the entire city was engulfed and buried beneath a layer of pumice and volcanic ash more than four meters deep. Other cities, including the nearby seaside town of Herculaneum, were similarly destroyed and buried. This time there was nothing to rebuild; Pompeii was simply covered over by the eruption, and the entombed city would lie beneath its blanket of volcanic ash for the next 15 centuries.

The first trenches to the buried city were dug in the 1700s. Scholars of that time had a reasonable understanding of Roman history, but their conception of the Romans was heavily influenced by the existing evidence, which consisted primarily of literary texts and works of art. Such sources presented a view of Roman civilization that was skewed toward the experiences of the wealthy and powerful. These early excavators were also mainly interested in finding artworks to adorn the private collections of rich contemporaries. For the next hundred years, Pompeii and Herculaneum were plundered in a haphazard fashion. In this hunt for fine statuary, the unique evidence preserved at these cities remained largely underappreciated.

Eventually, however, the digging became more systematic and careful, and the excavators began to realize the unprecedented nature of the evidence that had been preserved by the eruption. Today, approximately two-thirds of Pompeii has been excavated in an archaeological park of over 60 hectares. Because of the damage that exposure to air and tourism traffic is causing to the unearthed sections, there is reluctance to uncover more of the city until means can be provided to properly preserve the finds. Much of our current understanding of Roman culture and civilization, and in particular our knowledge about the lives of ordinary citizens and nonelites, stems from these special types of data recovered from Pompeii and Herculaneum. The volcanic flows that destroyed the two cities paradoxically also preserved otherwise ephemeral objects, some of which have survived nowhere else in the Roman world: wooden furniture, wall paintings, graffiti, household tools, papyri, and even the bodies of the ancient inhabitants. Collectively, this highly perishable evidence of everyday life has done much to help us understand Roman civilization as a real, living culture.

PUBLIC BUILDINGS

The well-preserved buildings of Pompeii and Herculaneum present textbook examples of a variety of standard Roman building techniques and types. Builders made extensive use of local stones, especially Sarno travertine and Nocera tufa, and in the oldest buildings the walls are sometimes made solely of carefully laid courses of blocks of these stones. Later, mortars and cements were employed, and walls could also be made with a stone or brick facing enclosing a rubble core. The stone blocks were often arrayed in a variety of geometric arrangements. For example, in a technique known as *opus reticulatum,* diamond-shaped blocks are arranged to form an attractive net pattern. Terra-cotta roof tiles covered the structures, and clay was also used to form other architectural elements such as drain spouts. Finally, in important public buildings or fancy private dwellings, the walls might be adorned with facings of imported colored marbles and decorative stones.

Just as it offers a range of typical building techniques, Pompeii (which has been more completely excavated than Herculaneum) also illustrates the standard assortment of public buildings that a self-respecting Roman town of any size would strive to possess. One way for provincial towns to

Figure 14.2 Forum of Pompeii with Mount Vesuvius in the background.

enhance their status was to attempt to emulate (admittedly on a reduced scale) the magnificent public buildings that were found in the capital city, Rome. The three main categories of such public buildings were structures related to government and commerce, religion, and entertainment, and the Pompeians eventually acquired an impressive assortment representing all three areas.

The focal point for the governmental and commercial buildings was the Civil Forum, a large, rectangular, open plaza at the east end of town. Around this space were the principal civic buildings: the basilica, an imposing two-story set of rectangular, roofed colonnades that housed judicial affairs and was used for business and financial transactions; the *curia*, the assembly hall of the town magistrates; the *tabularium*, or records office; the *macellum*, which was the public marketplace and included special drains probably used to remove waste from the fish and meat stalls; and the *comitium*, an open structure perhaps used for elections or court trials.

Some significant religious buildings also clustered around the forum, including two temples to important gods: the Temple of Jupiter, which dominated the north side of the Forum, and the even larger Temple of Apollo. Rebuilt several times, the Temple of Apollo is one of the oldest structures in the city, dating back to the sixth century BC. It was the center of worship for centuries until the arrival of the Roman colonists led to the construction of the Temple of Jupiter. The Temple of Jupiter seems to have been self-consciously rebuilt to emulate the design of the great Temple of Jupiter on the Capitoline hill in Rome. Emperor worship is reflected in a small temple to the posthumously deified emperor Augustus, which later was likely converted into a temple to the emperor Vespasian. Reflecting the diversity of worship typical of the Roman Empire, Pompeii also had a large temple dedicated to the cult of the Egyptian goddess Isis, along with dozens of smaller neighborhood shrines to an assortment of other gods.

Figure 14.3 Amphitheater at Pompeii. This is the earliest known stone amphitheater in Italy.

Finally, Pompeii boasted a full set of buildings devoted to entertaining the populace. Pompeii's amphitheater, the site of gladiatorial combats, is the oldest known stone amphitheater and could seat 20,000 spectators. The semicircular theater accommodated 5,000 people and would have hosted comic plays, Atellan farces (a type of comic theatrical entertainment), and pantomime shows. The yet smaller odeon, resembling a roofed-over theater, would have been the setting for various theatrical performances. The intensity of emotions that could be aroused by entertainments is exemplified by the famous riot of AD 59, which broke out among the audience at the amphitheater when the citizens of Pompeii began fighting with spectators from the nearby rival town of Nuceria. In the ensuing riot, a number of people were killed and injured, and the incident resulted in an imperial ban on gladiator games at Pompeii for 10 years.

Another central focus of Roman urban social life was the public baths. While the colossal bathing complexes of Rome are justifiably famous, the more modest baths of Pompeii and Herculaneum present a much more typical image of life in a Roman town. The well-preserved nature of the bath establishments in these towns has greatly aided archaeologists and historians in understanding the construction and operation of these specialized buildings. A full-fledged Roman bath contained a sequence of separate bathing rooms with pools of cold, warm, and hot water as well as areas for exercise, massages, relaxing, and dressing. The logistics of how this was achieved was revealed at Pompeii, where the furnace rooms sur-

Figure 14.4 Stabian Baths at Pompeii.

vive, showing how hot- and warm-water tanks were heated. In addition, some of the rooms themselves were heated by resting on double floors separated by piles of bricks (known as a hypocaust system), through which hot air from the furnace was circulated. The largest bath complex at Pompeii, the Stabian baths, covered an area of over 8,000 square feet and included separate rooms for male and female bathers. However, the city also boasted a number of smaller bathing establishments.

Pompeii, like many Roman towns, was laid out on a general grid pattern, with streets intersecting at more or less regular intervals and at right angles to one another. The streets around the forum are somewhat less gridlike, although several major thoroughfares run straight from one side of the city to the other. While there is a concentration of public buildings near the forum in the southwest corner of the city, Pompeii is a typical Roman city in that residential and commercial areas are intermingled rather than being zoned into separate regions. Indeed, it is extremely common for the same building to contain a mixture of businesses and private dwellings, with shops lining the street front and apartments or a house behind them. The theater and odeon are located together near one city gate, and the amphitheater is at one extreme corner of the city near another gate. Businesses such as inns, bars, bakeries, and fullers were scattered throughout the city, although they tended to cluster along the major through streets. About the only type of business that seems to have been concentrated in one place was the brothels, most of which were tightly packed into several blocks just east of the Forum area.

Another important structural feature of these streets was the public fountains that were commonly found at intersections. If plotted onto a map of Pompeii, the city's fountains are nicely spaced out at nearly regular intervals so that most neighborhoods had ready access to water. Thus, the majority of Pompeii's inhabitants lived within 90 meters of a public fountain. The local fountain was undoubtedly an important site of social interaction, as residents of a neighborhood regularly encountered one another while fetching water. Originally the water was supplied by wells and cisterns, but at the same time that the fountain system was regularized in the early first century AD, an aqueduct was constructed to supply the city with water.

The main streets were covered with flagstones and had high, raised sidewalks adjoining them. At major intersections, a series of stepping-stones was often placed across the street so that pedestrians could traverse from one side to the other without venturing down into the street itself. This practice may reveal something about Roman sanitation, since it was common practice for Romans to dispose of their sewage by dumping their chamber pots onto the roadway. The streets themselves bear the marks of heavy traffic, and the stones of some roads are heavily rutted with grooves made by the passing of countless cart and wagon wheels.

PRIVATE HOMES

In terms of design, decoration, and social functioning, our knowledge of the Roman aristocratic house, or *domus*, is derived mainly through the study of the houses of Pompeii and Herculaneum. These houses were not the dwellings of average Romans but rather of the elite. Pompeii is famous for having a very large number of lavish private homes and in this respect may not be typical of most Roman cities. Its location on the Bay of Naples may have made Pompeii the chosen dwelling place of a disproportionate number of wealthy Romans. Certainly the percentage of private homes as opposed to apartments was much higher at Pompeii than it was at Rome or Ostia. In addition to the large number of private dwellings found at Pompeii, their size and richness of decor illustrate that these were the mansions of the very wealthy and cannot be taken as indicative of an ordinary Roman's domestic experience.

The standard house design revolved around an open courtyard (the atrium), connected by a passageway to the street entrance. The atrium was typically surrounded by rooms, including a dining room *(triclinium)*, small bedrooms *(cubicula)*, and a kind of multipurpose reception hall *(tablinum)*. Behind these might be the kitchen, slave or servant quarters, and additional *cubicula*. More elaborate houses featured a second courtyard lined with columns (a peristyle), sometimes enclosing a garden.

The most obvious and famous feature of these houses is the lavish decoration of the walls and floors. Much of the expense and effort that in a modern home might be spent on furniture and decorative objects the Romans directed toward ornamenting the structure itself. All four walls of many rooms were plastered over and then completely covered with elaborate wall paintings, while the floors were coated with intricate mosaics. The styles of wall paintings and mosaics have already been described earlier in the chapter on housing, but it is worth noting here that had it not been for the unique way in which the volcanic eruption preserved these delicate decorations at Pompeii and Herculaneum, our understanding of Roman interior decor would be far less complete. Many of the wall paintings have been removed and can now be seen in the archaeological museum in modern Naples, but numerous others remain in their original settings on the walls of Pompeii.

Not only did the floors and walls that made up Roman houses survive at Pompeii and Herculaneum, but much of the contents of these rooms was also preserved. By current standards, Roman houses would have appeared surprisingly empty. A great deal of the basic furniture was made of bronze. Romans could choose from an assortment of bronze chairs, stools, and sofas with varying numbers of legs to sit upon. Bronze chests and boxes are common finds, ranging from small jewelry cases with delicate designs to sturdy strongboxes to harbor the family wealth, some of which were found with their coin hoards intact—a further indication of the rapidity of the disaster. Several types of low, bronze braziers testify to attempts to provide heat to cold rooms in the winter. Marble was also employed for benches and tables, some of the more elegant examples of which feature elaborately carved legs and supports. In addition to furniture, smaller household objects that have been uncovered include a full set of pots and pans, eating utensils, wood and wax tablets to write on, and the ubiquitous olive oil–burning clay lamps that brought light to dark interiors.

In reconstructing home furnishings, the small seaside town of Herculaneum has proven to be a particularly fruitful site because, unlike Pompeii, which was buried in volcanic ash, Herculaneum was engulfed by hot volcanic mud. This substance eventually hardened to a rocklike consistency that, while it made excavation difficult, also preserved the wood in a carbonized state. This fortunate fluke of preservation has supplied information about a number of objects that would otherwise have remained mysterious to us. Herculaneum has yielded the remains of wooden chairs, cupboards, bed frames (within which a mattress would have been suspended), and folding wooden partitions that could have been used to subdivide rooms and that suggest how the inhabitants of crammed Roman apartments might have provided a modicum of privacy for themselves. Our image of Roman windows has been augmented by the discovery of wooden shutters, some solid and others exhibiting an intricate latticework pattern. Excavators even found the remnants of a small, wooden crib with raised sides to restrain the baby.

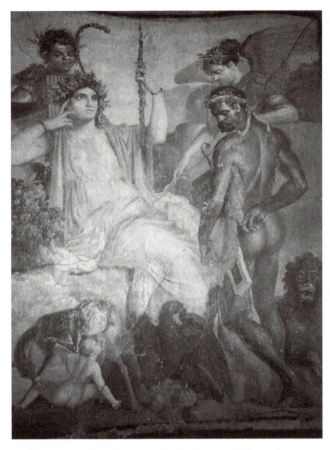

Figure 14.5 Wall painting from Pompeii depicting mythological scene.

Herculaneum's unique carbonized timber also informs our understanding of Roman construction techniques. One type of wall consisted of wooden frames filled with rubble, and the remains of wooden roof beams and trusses suggest how Roman roofs were built. Roof timbers seem to have often projected out into the street, providing shady overhangs or support for balconies and upper-story additions built hanging over the street. Also of interest are several wooden staircases and door frames.

Roman houses were oriented inward; external windows were small in size and few in number so that the courtyards brought both light and air into the house. Particularly inviting are the houses with substantial gardens either enclosed within the peristyle or attached at the back. The most elaborate gardens at Pompeii were adorned with sculptures, shaded by trees and vine-covered trellises, scented with flowers and herbs, enlivened by streams or pools of water, and cultivated to supply the household with fruits and vegetables.

ECONOMY

The preservation of entire neighborhoods allows the reconstruction of daily life in the lively streets of Pompeii and Herculaneum. One focus of urban life was the many small inns *(cauponae)* and bars *(popinae)* that lined the streets. At Pompeii, a city of perhaps up to 20,000 inhabitants, over 120 *popinae* and at least 30 *cauponae* have been identified. These were usually small establishments with a counter from which drinks and food were served. Often, these counters had round holes in them into which pots or amphorae could be placed; some also had space beneath for hearths to heat the comestibles. Graffiti occasionally records the names of both proud innkeepers: "Inn of Hyginius Firmus" is painted beside the door of one establishment (Mau 392), and lonely guests: "Vibius Restitutus slept here alone with his heart filled with longing for his Urbana" (*CIL* 4.2146). The large overall number and small average size of the *popinae* suggest that most of them had the character of neighborhood bars where locals gathered to drink, eat, and gossip. Another activity that seems to have been popular in these locations was gambling. While frowned upon in upper-class literature, dicing and other games of chance were clearly popular pastimes. One bar had a painting on the wall depicting patrons gambling, and a lucky winner left a graffito testifying, "At Nuceria, I won at dice 855 sesterces without cheating" (Mau 487).

Vesuvius entombed evidence of another vice as well: prostitution. Pompeii had a number of brothels, the largest of which featured a half-dozen cubicles along a central hallway on the ground floor alone. The walls of these rooms were covered with suggestive and obscene paintings along with matching graffiti.

Our conception of typical Roman daily economic life is enhanced by the many more legitimate shops and businesses that were also found along the thoroughfares of these cities. The business establishments of bakers, fullers, potters, shoemakers, metalworkers, and other craftsmen have all been identified. The region around Pompeii was renowned for its olives and grapes and the production of olive oil and wine would have been major components of the Pompeian economy. Pliny the Elder specifically praised the wine produced from the grapes that grew in the volcanic soil on the slopes of Vesuvius, and the olives of this region were similarly well regarded. Pompeii had a small port on the Sarno River, and from here, fresh fish were delivered to the city for sale in its markets. The production of *garum,* the popular fermented fish sauce, may also have been a significant local industry. Finally, the uneven slopes of Vesuvius nurtured herds of sheep, and the production of wool also seems to have been a factor in the Pompeian economy.

The bakeries of Pompeii have been particularly well studied and offer a glimpse into the daily economy of the city. Approximately 30 bakeries have been excavated, and the majority did not just bake bread, but

Figure 14.6 Relief of grain being milled. The grain was poured between the hourglass-shaped stone and the cone-shaped stone on which it rested. The top stone was rotated by the horse, causing the grain to be ground between them.

milled flour as well, as evidenced by the presence of sometimes up to five large flour mills. Each mill consisted of a conical bottom stone several feet high that was capped by an hourglass-shaped upper stone. The grain was poured between the two stones, and then the upper stone was rotated by either animal or human power, grinding the grain between them. Typical bakeries additionally contained rooms for kneading dough, the ovens to bake it in, and a shop on the street to sell the newly baked loaves. We even know what some of the ancient bread produced in these bakeries looked like because, when the eruption of Vesuvius overtook the bakery of Modestus in Pompeii, 81 loaves of bread had just been placed in the oven, and their form was preserved. These loaves are circular in shape with an impressed pattern that conveniently subdivides each loaf into eight wedges.

DAILY LIFE

The rapid and unusual way in which the cities of Pompeii and Herculaneum were destroyed has offered opportunities for archaeologists to retrieve unparalleled types of evidence. The most evocative example is that when an unfortunate inhabitant of Pompeii was overwhelmed and died, the pumice and ash quickly hardened around the corpse, and once it had decayed, an exact impression of the body remained inside the resulting cavity. In the mid-1800s, excavator Giuseppe Fiorelli realized that by pouring plaster into these spaces prior to removing the ash, casts of the bodies could be made. These casts so perfectly recreate the original appearance of the bodies that clothing, hair, and even the expressions on faces can be clearly discerned. Often the position of the bodies vividly tells the story of their unsuccessful struggle to survive the catastrophe. Some perished while vainly trying to wait out the disaster, such as the nearly three dozen people who hid in the basement of a house together with a stock of food including a goat, or the man and his young daughter in the House of Menander who desperately sought protection by piling cushions around themselves. Others were struck down by collapsing buildings as they tried to flee the city, like the refugees from the Temple of Isis who seem to have been caught in the street, along with the precious temple treasures they carried. Even pets failed to escape, like the dog in the House of Vesonius Primus, which was secured by a chain in the atrium, and thus was trapped by the rising ash and died, its contorted form illustrating its death throes.

Just outside Herculaneum, diggers uncovered an especially sumptuous villa that initially yielded nearly 100 fine statues, among them an excellent collection of bronze portrait busts. This house then produced an even rarer treasure. A small interior room was found to be lined with the carbonized remains of wooden shelves, on which were hundreds of charred papyrus rolls. This was the first complete ancient library to be discovered and remains a rarity since the overwhelming majority of surviving papyrus texts have come from Egypt, where they were protected from decay by the arid climate. Subsequent excavation of the so-called House of the Papyri had to be abandoned due to the presence of toxic fumes, but once again the eruption of Vesuvius had preserved a unique source of information about ancient Rome.

One additional special kind of evidence deserves mention here, which, perhaps more than any other, allows historians to recapture a sense of the culture, values, and personalities of the Pompeians. The whitewashed exterior walls of buildings in Pompeii were covered with thousands of painted or scratched graffiti, and more were found on interior walls, including (or perhaps especially) those of latrines, inns, and brothels. These graffiti provide invaluable testimony about countless factual details of everyday life that would otherwise have been lost. Our knowledge about the ancient economy is enhanced, for example, by graffiti in inns that record the prices for various foods and services and by others that identify the occupations and trades of the writers.

One of these occupations seems to have been that of professional graffiti writer, who was hired to advertise events and businesses or to scrawl political slogans and exhortations to elect a particular candidate. Aemilius

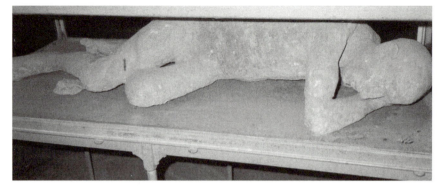

Figure 14.7 Cast of a victim of the volcanic eruption at Pompeii.

Celer was one such painter who left several signed graffiti, including the following announcement for some gladiator games: "Twenty pairs of gladiators sponsored by Decimus Lucretius Satrius Valens, priest of Nero Caesar, and ten pairs of gladiators sponsored by his son, Decimus Lucretius Valens, will fight on April 8, 9, 10, 11, and 12. A wild animal hunt will additionally be offered. The awnings will be employed. Aemilius Celer, alone in the moonlight, wrote this" (*CIL* 4.3884).

Celer even marked his own home with the simple inscription, "Aemilius Celer lives here" (*CIL* 4.3794). This industrious painter also took an interest in local politics, as evidenced by the following testimonial: "The neighbors of Lucius Statius Receptus urge you to elect him *duovir* with judicial power. He is deserving of the office. Aemilius Celer, his neighbor, wrote this. If you deliberately deface this sign, may you fall seriously ill" (*CIL* 4.3775).

The many graffiti related to political campaigns provide a glimpse into the workings of Roman politics at the civic level. Hopeful politicians might appeal to special-interest groups who in turn would endorse candidates, as demonstrated by the following graffiti: "As a group, the worshipers of Isis demand the election of Gnaeus Helvius Sabinus as aedile" (*CIL* 4.787), and "The chicken vendors request that you elect Epidius and Suettius as *duovirs*" (*CIL* 4.6426). Other inscriptions urge the members of certain professions to vote for a candidate: "Innkeepers, make Sallustius Capito aedile" (*CIL* 4.336). Some testify to a person's qualities or promises, such as a number of graffiti that describe candidates as "honest men" or one that claims that, if elected, "he will act as the guard dog of the treasury" (Mau 477).

As today, much of the graffiti represents the spontaneous comments of individuals. There are numerous variations on the timeless statement, "so-and-so was here," such as "Sabinus was here" (Mau 483) and "Publius Comicius Restitutus stood here with his brother" (*CIL* 4.1321). Others record the minutiae of household events: "On October 17 Puteolana [a dog?] had a litter of three males and two females" (Mau 487); reflect the work of bored individuals amusing themselves for a few moments by scratching inanities on a convenient wall: "On April 19 I baked bread" (*CIL* 4.8972); or consist of the musings of street philosophers: "When you are dead, you are nothing" (*CIL* 4.5279). One vast subcategory of graffiti tells of success or failure at love: "Portumnus loves Amphianda," "Serena hates Isidore" (*CIL* 4.3117), "Thyas, don't give your love to Fortunatus" (*CIL* 4.4498), "I have screwed many girls here" (*CIL* 4.2175), "May I always be as potent with women as I was here."

Graffiti even allowed children a voice, judging by the many graffiti inscribed at child's eye level. Often consisting of quotes from Virgil and including even the occasional complaint about cruel teachers, these seem to have been written by students practicing their lessons.

The graffiti of Pompeii offer rare insights into the lives of ordinary people and help compensate for the bias of the literary sources toward the rich and powerful. Through graffiti, we can learn about the attitudes, fears, and aspirations of the average Roman, who is able to speak to us directly via his or her impromptu scribblings.

The finds unearthed at Pompeii and Herculaneum have advanced our knowledge of Roman civilization beyond its previous narrow focus on high art to encompass the entire range of human experience. In particular, our current understanding of Roman urban daily life rests very heavily on the evidence buried by the eruption of Vesuvius and on the unique way that the volcanic ash and mud preserved materials that would not normally have survived. Just as important is the fact that all this material was recovered together, in context with one another, not as a series of random finds divorced from their original setting. It is impossible, for example, to properly evaluate an individual wall painting without knowing the other paintings that surrounded it; the architectural structure and furnishings of the room that contained it; and even the size, decoration, and ownership of the villa within which it was located. Because all these things were interred together, literally frozen in a moment of time, such artworks can be assessed in their own original and particularly Roman context, rather than in the artificial modern setting of a museum. Finally, Pompeii and Herculaneum offer information about a full cross section of society, representing the complete range of living conditions from rich to poor and free to slave. While the violent and terrifying eruption of Vesuvius was a tragedy for those individual Romans who lost their homes and lives, it was also a milestone for Roman civilization as a whole because it preserved for future civilizations a more complete knowledge and understanding of Roman life and culture.

15

Conclusion: Three Visions of Roman Urbanism: Rome, Ostia, and Pompeii

"Rome is the emporium of the world. Here all things converge: trade, shipping, agriculture, metallurgy, all the arts and crafts that have ever existed, all things whether man-made or grown from the earth. If it is not found at Rome, it does not exist." Thus spoke the Greek orator, Aelius Aristides, of the city of Rome at the height of its power in the second century AD. At this time, Rome truly was the focal point of a huge empire. It was not only the political capital, but the center of culture and the economy as well. The resources from the entire empire were marshaled together and redirected to Rome in order to feed its gigantic population, to construct the lavish buildings that adorned its hills and valleys, and to provide ever more exotic and extravagant entertainments for its inhabitants. All lesser cities aspired to be like Rome, and local elites poured out their own capital to transform their towns into smaller-scale marble imitations of the capital, replete with baths, amphitheaters, and aqueducts. The Roman Empire encompassed an enormous diversity of geographies, ethnicities, and languages, but what gave the empire its overall identity was its cities. These were the nodes from which administration disseminated, and the Romans were remarkably successful at instilling Roman culture in these key points. Roman civilization was an urban culture, and one whose presence was instantly recognizable through its architecture. Rome itself was the model, but the hundreds of other cities were the ones that gave the empire cohesion. Whether these were new foundations established by the Romans or preexisting cities that were taken over by them, once incorporated into the empire, they all sprouted the telltale structures that identified them as part of the empire.

The three cities studied in this book demonstrate the uniformity that characterized Roman cities as well as some of the range of their differences. In their development, all show the importance of geography. Rome and Pompeii grew up at crucial communication crossroads, while Ostia owed its very existence to the need for a port to serve the capital city. In this respect, Ostia almost has to be considered as a satellite of Rome rather than as a separate city, and its fortunes waxed and waned with those of Rome. Ostia's initial purpose was to guard the route of communication between Rome and the sea. It expanded most dramatically when it served as Rome's primary port, and it not only declined, but was actually abandoned when Rome no longer needed its services. While this close association with Rome makes Ostia unique, in other respects its history is typical of many Roman cities. Like innumerable cities, it began as a Roman military outpost that eventually expanded into a civilian town. Like thousands of other such foundations, its street grid reflects this origin and focuses around a forum that is itself surrounded by the principal political and religious structures of the city. As the city grew, it acquired the standard Roman urban amenities, including baths and a theater as well as homes, apartment buildings, taverns, and shops. Pompeii, on the other hand, existed as a prosperous city long before it fell under Roman dominion. Its history reflects a fusion of Roman and indigenous traditions, but as soon as the city acquired a substantial population of Roman citizens, its transformation into a thoroughly Roman city was ensured, and it too acquired all the architectural trappings of Roman culture.

These three cities also illustrate some pronounced variations on the basic Roman city. Ostia was perhaps one of the most thoroughly industrial Roman cities due to its special purpose as a key transportation waypoint for much of the vast quantities of supplies destined for Rome. It was a port city, and its economic life focused on maritime transportation. It possessed a physical economic infrastructure of warehouses and docks far out of proportion to its actual populace. A dense concentration of shippers, merchants, and middlemen were based there, and it was also the seat of an extensive administrative structure to oversee all this economic activity. With its many associations of tradesmen and laborers it was a solidly working-class city. This working population lived predominantly in modest yet well-built apartments; the number of lavish individual homes was relatively low, at least during the prime of the city as an active port. Pompeii, by contrast, had an economy based on local agriculture whose important products were olives, wine, and wool, all of which were grown or nurtured on the slopes of Vesuvius. It was also located in a prime resort area, and as a result the city boasted many luxurious mansions and probably a relatively large population of wealthy families. Despite the dramatic differences between Ostia and Pompeii in terms of their economy, history, and purpose, they are in many respects more similar than disparate. What gives them their similarity is what bound together all cities across the empire: a uniformity of Roman culture and architecture that was derived from the capital city.

Ancient Rome boasted gold-encrusted temples, stadiums holding hundreds of thousands of cheering spectators, fabulous palaces, extensive aqueduct and sewer systems, and sumptuous bath complexes, all built so soundly that much of it still stands today. On the other hand, the city was the site of bloody gladiatorial contests and spectacles and was haunted by all the ills of a modern big city, including poverty, crime, injustice, disease, and overcrowding. This book has not focused exclusively on one aspect or the other because both visions of Roman urban life are true. Roman architectural wonders should not be admired without considering their cost, and the glories of Roman civilization have to be balanced against the experiences of the many who did not share in them, or who suffered to provide them. Above all, this book has tried to give a balanced sense of what it would have been like to be an average inhabitant of an ancient Roman city. It has attempted to offer a glimpse of the rituals, buildings, and people that collectively would have shaped and formed that person's life and experiences.

Appendix I
A Brief Guide to Understanding Roman Names

What family you belonged to mattered greatly in Roman society. At certain periods in Roman history, it could even determine your legal rights. Thus it is no surprise that Roman names were not randomly chosen, but instead were meant to reveal a great deal about a person and his family. Most Roman men possessed a tripartite name. The three components were the *praenomen, nomen,* and *cognomen.*

The *praenomen,* equivalent to a modern first name and chosen by the parents shortly after a son's birth, was limited to only about 16 possibilities: Appius, Aulus, Decimus, Gaius, Gnaeus, Lucius, Manius, Marcus, Numerius, Publius, Quintus, Servius, Sextus, Spurius, Tiberius, and Titus.

The second name was the *nomen.* This was the name of a person's *gens,* or family. It was the most important section of one's name because it told who one's ancestors were. The *nomen* also determined whether one was a patrician or a plebeian.

The third name was the *cognomen.* It was a personal name that identified the particular branch of a family. These names were often, but not always, hereditary. They frequently referred to a physical characteristic or an action of some famous member of the family. One famous *cognomen* was Ahenobarbus, meaning "red beard." Others included Strabo "cross-eyed," Verrucosus "warty," and Clodius "gimpy." Gaius Julius Caesar's *cognomen* in Latin means "hairy," which was ironic since Caesar himself was balding.

When it came to naming women, the only thing that the Romans viewed as important about them was their clan or family. Therefore, all daughters were named by simply giving them the female form of the *nomen*. The daughter of Gaius Julius Caesar, for example, would have been named Julia. What happened if he had a second daughter? The Roman solution was to call the older daughter Julia Maior (meaning "Julia the elder") and the younger one Julia Menor (meaning "Julia the younger"). If a man had even more daughters, he simply began to assign them numbers, starting with Julia Tertia ("Julia the third") and so on. In reality, many women probably used nicknames to avoid confusion.

Slaves also got only one name, which was chosen for them by their owner. Sometimes these names seem to have been given with a touch of irony, since one popular slave name was Felix, meaning "Lucky." When a male slave was freed, he took the *praenomen* and *nomen* of his ex-master, then added his slave name as *cognomen*. For example, the famous orator Marcus Tullius Cicero had a slave named Tiro who acted as his personal secretary. Eventually Cicero freed his faithful servant, who then went by the name Marcus Tullius Tiro. Thus, even when freed, slaves could not fully escape their former masters.

Appendix II

A Brief Guide to Roman Timekeeping and the Calendar

For an economy to function efficiently, a society needs to develop basic methods of timekeeping and noting the passage of time. For the Romans, each day was divided into two periods: the time when it was light outside, and the time when it was dark. Each of these periods was then subdivided into hours. Superficially, this sounds a lot like our modern system of 24 hours in a day. However, there was one rather significant difference: Roman hours were not of a fixed length because they were simply equal to the amount of light or darkness on a given day divided by twelve. Since the amount of daylight varies greatly from day to day over the course of the year—with perhaps as many as 15 hours of daylight in the summer and only 8 or 9 in the winter—a Roman hour in the summer might be equivalent to a modern hour and a half, and, similarly, in the winter, a Roman hour might be only 40 of our minutes long. When telling time, the Romans referred to the hour after sunrise as the "first hour of the day," the next as the "second hour of the day," and so on up to the 12th hour. The 12 nighttime hours worked in the same way except that the starting point was sunset. Thus, you would have the first or second hour after sunset and so on. The length of an hour changed from day to day, so meetings could only be set very approximately. If, for example, someone said, "Meet me at the fifth hour," you simply had to make your best guess when that might be.

To indicate a given year, the usual method was to refer to the names of the two consuls elected for that year. Thus, for example, to specify the year 59 BC, the Romans would have said "in the consulship of Caesar and Bibulus" since those two men were the consuls for that year. In practice, this meant that one had to carry around a mental list of all the pairs of consuls in Roman history in order to tell dates—an impressive feat of memorization and obviously a somewhat awkward procedure. To get around this, the Romans sometimes used an alternate numbering system for the years. In this scheme, they dated things from the foundation of the city of Rome, which in our numbering system was 753 BC. Thus, a Roman might say, "such and such happened in the 480th year since the city was founded." The Latin phrase for "from the foundation of the city" is *ab urbe condita.* When the historian Livy wrote his account of the entire history of Rome, he titled this work *Ab Urbe Condita,* suggesting that he was going to tell everything that had happened since the city was founded.

Like us, the Romans divided the year into 12 months. During the republic, they only had 355 days in a year. Since, as we know, there are really 365 and one-quarter days in an astronomical year, after a few years, the calendar began to get severely out of line with the natural seasons. If left uncorrected for long enough, this could have had disastrous consequences for farmers, since it might have led to their planting crops at the wrong time of year. The solution that the Romans came up with was that every so often the priests declared an intercalary month. This was a month without a name inserted between two existing months in order to bring the months back into line with the natural seasons. Since there was no set time table for inserting intercalary months, in times of crisis when the priestly colleges were not meeting regularly, the calendar could get way out of line. The most obvious example of this occurred in the Late Republic during the civil wars between Julius Caesar and his rivals. By the time Caesar emerged as sole ruler of the Roman world, the calendar was off by a full six months, and Caesar had to insert six intercalary months all at once. Therefore, in the late 40s BC, there was one extra-long year that was, in reality, one-and-a-half years long.

To make sure that this did not happen again, Caesar undertook a major reform of the Roman calendar. He added 10 days to the calendar, making a year 365 days long. Like our own months, each of the Roman months had between 28 and 31 days. To take care of the extra quarter of a day, Caesar instituted the leap year, so that every four years there would be one extra day added. This reformed calendar, known as the Julian Calendar, is pretty much the same one that we are using today.

The modern names of the months are all derived from the Roman ones. The Roman names were Januarius, Februarius, Martius, Aprilis, Maius, Junius, Julius, Augustus, September, October, November, and December. The names of January through June refer to Roman gods; for example, January is named after the Roman god Janus. The months of July and August were named by the Romans to honor Julius Caesar and the emperor Augustus. (Originally, July was *Quinctilus,* "the fifth," and August was

Sextilus, "the sixth.") The names for September through December are derived from numbers, with September meaning "the seventh," up to December, "the tenth." The reason December was called the 10th month rather than the 12th one is that the Romans began each year on March 1 rather than on January 1.

To indicate a day within a month, the Romans did not say, as we would, "on the 17th." Instead, they picked three days of each month, which they gave special names, and then indicated all other days by their relationship to these three. The first day of each month was known as the kalends of the month. The day of the month on which the moon was full was called the ides, which usually fell on what we would call the 13th or the 15th of the month. Finally, the nones was the day nine days before the ides. Because the Romans used an inclusive numbering system, the nones fell on what we would call the 5th or the 7th. One of the more famous dates in Roman history, for example, was the Ides of March, the day on which Julius Caesar was assassinated. According to our calendar, this would be March 15. For all days that were not one of these three, the Romans would designate it by the number of days before the next of the special days. Thus, for example, if the Romans wanted to indicate March 13, they would say, "three days before the ides of March."

A lot is known about Roman calendars because the Romans were very fond of putting calendars on the sides of their public buildings or temples, either actually carved into the stone or else painted on it. The letters were painted in red on a white background. These calendars listed not just the dates, but also almost always commented about important days as well. Such a calendar is known as a *fasti*. All *fasti* consisted of 12 vertical columns, one for each month. Each month column was further subdivided. First came the name of the day. Next was a column of the letters A through H, repeating. This was to keep track of when market day came. For the Romans, every 8th day was market day, called *nundinae*. This cycle of days was the equivalent of our week. Thus, whereas we have a 7-day week because of Christianity, the pre-Christian Romans had an 8-day week. In a third column was an abbreviation that gave further information about what type of day it was. There were many of these types of days, but four were particularly important. The first type was symbolized by the capital letter *F*. This stood for *dies fasti,* of which there were 42 each year. These were the only days on which it was valid to institute a legal action. Days labeled *N* stood for *dies nefasti,* of which there were 58 per year. On these days, it was forbidden to conduct any legal business. The third type was marked with a *C* for *dies comitiales,* of which there were 195 per year. These were the only days on which the *Comitia,* the voting assembly, could meet. Finally, there were days marked *NP,* meaning *dies nefasti publici.* These were public holidays when no business should be conducted, and everyone had the day off to celebrate. There was no set number of holidays.

The Romans believed that certain days were luckier than others. Odd-numbered days were thought to be luckier than even ones, and thus all holidays began on odd-numbered days. The days after the kalends, the ides, and the nones were called "black days" and were thought to be particularly unlucky. Superstitious people tried to do as little as possible on these days and certainly would never begin any new endeavor on such a "black day."

Appendix III
A Brief Guide to Roman Clothing and Appearance

The Romans referred to themselves as the "people of the toga," and even today, the toga is closely identified with the Romans. It was not an every-day garment, however, and was worn by citizens primarily on formal occasions. The toga was the mark of a citizen, and it was illegal for nonci-tizens to dress in it. A toga was made of heavy, bleached wool; when unrolled, it was a large, D-shaped piece of fabric approximately six meters long and two and a half meters wide. This was wrapped around the wearer and over his arms in a complex fashion, with much of the excess fabric draped upon the left shoulder. The toga developed over time from the republic to the empire, gradually becoming a bit larger and with the method of folding growing more ornate. By the early empire, the pre-scribed method of folding a toga included the creation of features known as the *sinus* and *umbo,* which could sometimes serve as pockets or be pulled over the head like a hood. Beneath the toga, a belted tunic was worn.

Togas reflected the general Roman preoccupation with rank and status. The basic white toga of the citizen was called the *toga virilis* (toga of man-hood). If you were a magistrate, you were entitled to wear a special toga with a purple stripe on it known as the *toga praetexta* (bordered toga). The width of the stripe further indicated your wealth and status, since sena-tors sported wide purple stripes called the *latus clavus* (broad stripe) whereas equestrians had to make do with thinner stripes known as the *clavus angustus* (narrow stripe). Interestingly, male children of citizens wore miniature *toga praetextas* complete with the purple stripe. Another

Figure Appendix III.1 Statue of the emperor Titus dressed in a typical toga of the early imperial period.

type of specialized toga was the *toga candida* (white toga), an extra-white toga that was only worn by candidates running for political office. It is from this term that our modern term *candidate* is derived. Finally, it is thought that victorious generals celebrating a triumph may have been allowed to wear an all-purple toga.

Figure Appendix III.2 Roman woman with Flavian hairstyle. (Drawing by Alicia Aldrete, Phaeton Group, Scientific Graphic Services Division.)

While it was a distinctively Roman garment, the toga was by no means the only item of clothing available to the Romans. In casual everyday life, a short-sleeved tunic extending to the knees was the standard item of clothing for Roman men and was widely worn by children and slaves as well. The tunics of equestrians and senators also carried the purple stripes, and when they put on their togas, these tunics were worn underneath the toga. If it was raining or cold, the Romans used a large cloak called a *lacerna*, which could be thrown over the tunic or toga. Another variety of cloak, the *paenula*, may have been a more close-fitting and waterproofed variant.

Roman women were expected to dress modestly and to be largely covered up by their clothes. As a first layer, they wore a longer version of the tunic that reached down to their ankles and had longer sleeves, but the stereotypical garb of the adult Roman woman was the *stola*, a full-length dress with multiple folds. Women's clothes were often dyed bright colors and were made of a variety of materials. A related garment derived from the Greeks was the *peplos,* which was similar to a tunic but had an extra fold of cloth over the upper half of the body. When going out in public, aristocratic women donned an additional covering called the *palla,* a large, rectangular piece of cloth that could be wrapped around the body in a variety of ways.

What sort of undergarments the Romans wore is uncertain. They may well have worn nothing. In art, gladiators and athletes are sometimes shown wearing a kind of loincloth, and this may have been a variant of a standard undergarment.

Romans did not wear trousers or pants and in fact regarded the wearing of such with great disdain, as the mark of a barbarian. This attitude caused considerable discomfort to Roman troops posted to the frigid northern provinces, and eventually these soldiers gave in to reality and began wearing leather pants. For footwear, there was a wide range of leather boots and sandals to choose from. The most famous Roman footwear was the *caligae,* the hobnailed boots issued to Roman soldiers.

While ordinary Roman women probably had little time or money to spend on personal ornamentation, wealthy Roman women devoted considerable effort to decorating themselves with elaborate hairstyles and thick makeup. Rich women probably had several slaves whose full-time job it was to arrange their mistress's hair. These hairstylists achieved their effects through the use of curling irons, mousse-like stiffening agents, and various combs, pins, and fasteners. Roman sculptures record the various hairstyles that were popular in different periods. A famous bust of a Flavian woman depicts her with an enormous fan of curls, probably affixed to a wood or wire underframe, piled up on top of her head. In the second century AD, a more severe hairstyle seems to have dominated, with hair gathered into a tight bun or pulled back in plaits.

Women also commonly dyed their hair, and dying the hair red using henna seems to have been particularly popular. Experimenting with dyes was not without its risks, however. Ovid mentions an account of a dye job gone wrong, which resulted in a woman losing her hair (Ovid, *Love Affairs* 1.14.1–46). Since few Italians naturally have blond hair, blond wigs were very fashionable. The most common source for blond wigs was German prisoners of war, and the hair of many Germans ultimately ended up on the heads of Roman women.

Roman women wore a considerable amount of makeup. They started off with various foundations, and every woman had her own secret recipe that she would use. One that survives calls for a mixture of eggs, barley, ground antler, honey, lead, flowers, wheat, and crushed beans. To make the face whiter, they applied powdered chalk or a lead-based white substance. Black pigments would be used around the eyes, and red was applied to the lips and cheeks. Women could choose from an assortment of powerful perfumes, often made by some combination of flowers or herbs in an olive-oil base.

Finally, wealthy Roman women wore large quantities of jewelry in the form of rings, pins, necklaces, and earrings. Often these earrings were very large and heavy and dangled from the ears in a succession of levels. Such jewelry was fashioned from gold and studded with precious stones.

Roman men of the middle republic to the early empire were usually clean shaven. In the second century AD, emperors such as Hadrian and Marcus Aurelius adopted beards, and this fashion seems to have trickled down to the average Roman man. Roman men also wore rings, although sporting too many or excessively ostentatious ones was frowned upon.

Both sexes made use of a variety of metal clasps to hold their clothing together and to close their cloaks. These ranged from simple functional bronze fasteners to highly decorated and bejeweled brooches.

Appendix IV
A Brief Guide to Roman Construction Techniques

The Romans were master builders who, while they only developed a few new building technologies, used those that were already available to their fullest potential and produced many structures that have remained standing for thousands of years.

In the early stages of Roman history, buildings would have been simple constructs of timber, mud, thatch, and stones. A number of deposits of good clay located in or near Rome were exploited for making mud bricks. The clay was combined with a tempering agent such as grass or straw and then formed into bricks, which were exposed to the sun to dry. The ideal drying time for such bricks was as long as several years, but many were probably used sooner than that. Although such bricks were vulnerable to water, they were nonetheless one of the standard components of republican buildings. The same clay was also shaped into tiles, then fired in an oven to render them waterproof, and thus were employed as a common roofing material.

It was not until around the last century of the republic that the Romans seem to have begun firing the bricks used in construction. These bricks were formed by packing wooden molds with a mixture of clay, sand, and water and then either placing them in a kiln to harden or firing a whole stack of bricks. Bricks most commonly resembled low, flat squares or rectangles and seem to have been made in a number of standard sizes. The manufacturers frequently stamped bricks with their names or other information. Particularly during the high empire, these stamps sometimes included a wide range of data useful to archaeologists and historians such

Figure Appendix IV.1 View of ruins in Ostia showing brick-faced construction technique.

as the name of the landowner where the clay was gathered, the name of the manufacturer, the site of manufacture, the distributor, the current consuls, and even the construction project for which they were intended.

One of the truly brilliant innovations of the Romans was their development of a useable form of concrete. Lime mortars had been used from at least the third century BC, but by the time of Augustus, a highly flexible type of concrete had been discovered. Roman mortar was created by mixing lime with aggregates and water. The lime had to be properly burned, and the proportions of different materials had to be accurate or else the end result would not set properly and would be prone to cracking.

When one thinks of Roman monumental public architecture, one often envisions structures of shining marble, but this was usually only the exterior surface. The structural core of these buildings was usually composed of much more humble materials such as rubble fill, brick, and concrete. Typically, a core of concrete and aggregates would be poured, and then the surface would be dressed in one of several possible ways. When faced with an irregular outer layer of small stones, the style was called *opus incertum;* with square stones, it was called *opus reticulatum;* and with brick, it was known as *opus testaceum.* Concrete could also be poured in a variety of forms using wooden molds, so this opened up new possibilities of architecture since structures could be made in many shapes, including ones with curves and irregularities. The Romans even invented a special type of concrete using pozzolana, a volcanic stone, that would harden under water. This was used to build gigantic harbors and breakwaters to protect the ships. The concrete revolution was a very important part of Roman architecture since buildings would have a core of concrete, which was then covered up by a layer of marble or brick depending on how fancy or expensive a building it was.

While the exteriors of major public buildings such as temples or theaters were covered with sheets of fine decorative stone such as marble, the floors, columns, carvings, and other ornamental elements were also fashioned out of such materials. These decorative stones were imported at an enormous expense from quarries all around the Mediterranean. Some of the main varieties of stone imported included fine, white marble from mines in Carrara in Italy, Mount Pentelikon near Athens in Greece, and the island of Paros in the Aegean. Green *cippollino* arrived from Carystos in Greece, and yellow- and purple-veined *pavonazzetto* from the Docimion quarries in Asia Minor. From Egypt came hard purple and green porphyry that had been hauled across the desert, as was grey granite from the Egyptian mines at Mons Claudianus.

A second Roman innovation was widespread use of the vault. A series of stones was cut so that, when put together, they created a curved arch. This form was self-supporting since the stones' own weight held them together. Architects soon realized that if they put two vaults together meeting at right angles, they would create a roof that could span huge rooms without the need for columns.

There was a wide variation in the quality of Roman buildings. The *insulae,* or high-rise apartment buildings, in which the majority of the inhabitants of Rome lived, were often poorly made, using inferior materials, shoddy workmanship, and insufficient structural supports. The predictable result was that they often crumbled or collapsed. The Romans also tended to make widespread use of plaster as a final layer over walls, and this finishing technique was sometimes exploited to cover up poor-quality construction. Even in the houses of the wealthy at Pompeii, a layer of plaster often conceals a myriad of flaws. On the other hand, most of the monumental public buildings erected by the Romans seem to have been made with great solidity that rendered them immune to disasters such as floods as well as to centuries of plundering and neglect. The continued existence today of such monuments as the Pantheon is an impressive testimony to the soundness and longevity of high-quality Roman construction and engineering.

Appendix V

The History of the City of Rome from Antiquity to Today

The postclassical histories of Ostia and Pompeii have already been described in the chapters on those cities; in each case, the active life of the city was cut short in antiquity, preserving its ruins. The history of Rome after the Roman Empire, however, is a very different story and is one that deserves at least a brief retelling. Rome has been continuously occupied from antiquity to the present, and the city has been repeatedly rebuilt so that today it consists of innumerable layers, some of which overlap and others of which are superimposed on top of one another. To a large extent, the history of the ancient ruins of Rome from antiquity to now is a survey of destruction, decay, and intermittent attempts to recover or restore monuments.

The beginnings of Rome's decline within the Roman Empire might be ascribed to the actions of the emperor Constantine, who founded a new, second capital city for the empire at Constantinople in the East in the early 300s AD. From this point on, Rome would at best serve only as the capital of the western half of the Roman Empire, and even this role would soon be lost. At the time of Constantine, Rome was still a huge and prosperous city, with a population of probably around three-quarters of a million. In the fifth century AD, the strength of the western empire declined in the face of multiple waves of barbarian invaders. Partly in response to these threats, the later emperors of this century shifted their court from Rome to the northern Italian city of Ravenna. Ravenna was surrounded by swamps, with a sea on one side, which made it a more easily defensible city with a ready escape route.

In AD 410, Rome was captured by foreign invaders for the first time in 1,000 years when the Visigoths (Germanic barbarians), under their king Alaric, sacked the city. In AD 455, another barbarian group, the Vandals, occupied Rome. During the same period, the city was repeatedly menaced by the Huns. All these depredations caused the population to plummet, and by the sixth century AD, the great Roman buildings were being abandoned, and much of the city began to resemble a ghost town of ruins.

In the Middle Ages, the only thing that saved Rome from complete obscurity was the splendor of its ruins and the presence of the pope. Although the city had lost its political role as capital of an empire, it had a new identity as the seat of the Catholic Church. Many of the Roman structures that have survived to the present only did so because they were co-opted by the popes and turned into Christian churches. Some of the most notable examples of this are the Pantheon and the Curia (the senate house).

Other Roman buildings were not so fortunate, however, and suffered plundering and destruction. As early as the sixth century AD, Roman structures began to be used as quarries from which builders stripped marble, bricks, iron, and other construction materials. The destruction of Rome's buildings proceeded with apparently no concern for the great works of art and architecture that were being irreparably damaged or even destroyed. Beginning in the eighth century AD and continuing for several hundred years, limekilns were set up in the Roman Forum itself, and their operators tore down marble buildings and flung the marble into the fires to be burned, producing lime. The lime fires consumed not only the marble walls, floors, columns, and decoration of buildings, but even priceless marble sculptures. The population continued to decline, reaching a nadir in perhaps the tenth or eleventh century. One author suggests that war, plague, and relocation at one point reduced the populace of the once-great city to a mere 500 people.

With the rise of the pilgrimage movement, there was somewhat of a revival of interest in the city, and religious pilgrims began to travel to Rome to visit famous places associated with the lives of the apostles and the early saints. This led in the twelfth century to the appearance of what were, in essence, tourist travel guides describing for visitors famous pagan and Christian sites and buildings, even suggesting recommended routes for walks through the ruins of the city. One of the most famous of these guides is the *Mirabilia Urbis Romae*, or "The Marvels of Rome." The information contained in these books often included misidentifications of ancient monuments and fanciful legends about buildings, but these were probably not that much worse than some of the stories that modern tour guides tell visitors to the city.

The Renaissance era, with its intense interest in classical antiquity, perhaps marked the beginning of a more rigid systematic study of the ancient city. Renaissance scholars and humanists scoured monasteries in order to rediscover lost works of Greek and Roman authors and began rudimentary archaeological excavations in their quest to uncover examples of ancient sculpture and art. One sensational discovery at this time occurred when diggers broke through the roof of the by-then completely buried Golden House of Nero. The well-preserved frescoes, mosaics, and artifacts that emerged heavily influenced Renaissance artists and architects.

While these early scholars were rediscovering and preserving artifacts of ancient Rome, other forces were continuing to promote the destruction of the ancient ruins. One especially significant example of this was the gigantic construction project undertaken by the popes to erect the enormous basilica of St. Peter in the Vatican. Much of this church was built using materials recycled (or plundered) from Roman ruins. In 1540, the pope condemned the Roman Forum and the surrounding area and issued permits to contractors that allowed them to demolish the Roman buildings in order to supply materials for his church. Wealthy Renaissance families competed with one another to see who could amass the largest collections of ancient statues, and there was a healthy trade in antiquities, prompting many profit seekers to dig about in the ruins, hoping to unearth a well-preserved work of art that they could sell.

As the classical styles uncovered by Renaissance scholars gradually spread throughout Europe, Rome became a standard destination for artists in training to visit in order to copy the ancient works of art. In the seventeenth, eighteenth, and nineteenth centuries, not only did artists continue to come to Rome to view the antiquities, but the city also became an obligatory stop on the "Grand Tour" undertaken by wealthy and aristocratic members of European society as a kind of finishing touch to their education. Poets such as Keats and Shelley and philosophers such as Goethe lived in Rome for extended periods to soak up the remnants of Roman culture.

Unfortunately, the city was again plundered by foreign invaders when the French sacked Rome in 1798 and made off with much of the accumulated collections of art. These were taken back to Paris, where they eventually formed part of the core collections of the Louvre. The French depredations sparked a new movement of concern for attempting to protect Rome's remaining cultural heritage, and in the nineteenth century there was once again a recrudescence of classical scholarship. This was the era of the great nineteenth-century historians and archaeologists who classified ancient texts, inscriptions, and works of art.

This movement also saw the foundation of national academies based in Rome and dedicated to the study of its antiquities. Among these were the German Archaeological Institute and the French School at Rome, which were eventually joined by the British School at Rome and the American Academy at Rome. All of these institutions are still present and active today.

In the mid-nineteenth century, Italy achieved independence and unification, and in 1870 Rome was declared the capital of Italy. This sparked a number of major construction projects, including the Tiber embankments, which finally protected the city from floods. In 1870, the population of Rome was still a modest quarter of a million people, and the inhabited portion of the city made up only a relatively small proportion of the area enclosed within the old Aurelian Walls. The renewed pride in Italy's present fostered interest in the city's past, and notable Italian archaeologists such as Rodolfo Lanciani systematically surveyed the ruins of the city and oversaw ambitious excavations.

As the seat of government of a unified Italy, the city became known as Roma Capitale, and the desire to commemorate its new status led to some unfortunate projects, most notably the construction of an enormous and ugly monument to King Victor Emmanuel II. Like some sort of hideous wedding cake run amok, it is an enormous, multilayered, marble monument built in a mishmash of conflicting architectural styles, including pseudoclassical, Greco-Roman, Etruscan, Italic, Renaissance, and Baroque. It was erected at the heart of the city, beginning atop the east side of the Capitoline hill and cascading down toward the Roman Forum. Sadly, its construction obliterated much of the hill and its ancient monuments.

The rise of fascism and Mussolini in the 1930s prompted yet another round of both interest in ancient Rome and destruction of its monuments. Mussolini had grandiose dreams of founding a new Roman empire and self-consciously imitated Roman symbols and imagery to promote himself and his political agenda. Because of this, he was intensely interested in uncovering the remains of the ancient city and therefore initiated a number of major excavations.

Unfortunately, Mussolini was very impatient and not interested in minor artifacts; in his zeal to get at hoped-for monuments, many sites were literally bulldozed and thus destroyed. One of the most famous examples of Mussolini's methods stemmed from his desire to have a grand, straight boulevard stretching out from the heart of the city on which he could stage parades. This led to the construction in 1932 of a major road, known as the Via Dei Fori Imperiali, beginning at the Victor Emmanuel Monument and stretching off to the east. This road plowed right through parts of the Roman Forum and especially the Imperial Fora, burying and forever obliterating much of them. Recent excavations have begun the attempted reclamation of some of this historically significant area.

In the latter twentieth century, the population of Rome exploded. Today, it is a city of several million people and has become a major tourist site. The density of people living there and visiting the ruins has created its own problems, most notably related to air pollution. The fumes created by factories, cars, and other aspects of modern life not only have coated the surviving ancient monuments with a black layer of grime, but, even worse, have produced acid rain, which is rapidly eating away at and dissolving exposed ancient stones and sculptures. The often-shaky state of the Italian economy has made initiatives to protect and preserve these monuments controversial.

Despite this long history of destruction, the monuments built by the ancient Romans, such as the Colosseum, Trajan's Column, the Baths of Caracalla, and the Pantheon, are still impressive today, and their solid construction will hopefully ensure that they remain standing for some time to come.

Bibliography

PRIMARY SOURCES

The first three books listed here are collections of primary sources. The rest are all works by ancient authors identified by their common modern titles. All the ancient authors listed here are available in numerous accessible translations.

Lewis, N., and M. Reinhold. *Roman Civilization.* 3rd ed. 2 vols. New York: Columbia University Press, 1990.
Shelton, Jo-Ann. *As the Romans Did: A Sourcebook in Roman Social History.* 2nd ed. New York: Oxford University Press, 1998.
Sherk, Robert, ed. *The Roman Empire: Augustus to Hadrian.* Cambridge: Cambridge University Press, 1988.
Aelian. *On Animals.*
Ammianus Marcellinus. *History of the Later Roman Empire.*
Appian. *Roman History.*
Apuleius. *The Golden Ass (The Metamorphosis).*
Augustine. *Confessions.*
Augustus. *Res Gestae.*
Aulus Gellius. *Attic Nights.*
Caesar. *The Gallic Wars; The Civil Wars.*
Cassiodorus. *Variae.*
Cassius Dio. *Roman History.*
Cato the Elder. *On Agriculture.*
Catullus. *Poems.*
Celsus. *On Medicine.*

Cicero. *Letters; Speeches; Philosophical Works; On Oratory.*
Columella. *On Farming.*
Dionysius of Halicarnassus. *Roman Antiquities.*
Frontinus. *About the Waters of the City of Rome.*
Horace. *Odes; Epodes; Satires; Art of Poetry.*
Josephus. *Antiquities; The Jewish War.*
Justinian. *Digest of Roman Law.*
Juvenal. *Satires.*
Livy. *History of Rome.*
Martial. *Epigrams.*
Orosius. *Against the Pagans.*
Ovid. *The Art of Love; The Metamorphoses; Love Affairs.*
Petronius. *The Satyricon.*
Plautus. *Curculio; Amphitryon.*
Pliny the Elder. *Natural History.*
Pliny the Younger. *Letters.*
Plutarch. *Parallel Lives of Famous Greeks and Romans.*
Polybius. *History of Rome.*
Quintilian. *Institutes on Oratory.*
Sallust. *The War Against Jugurtha; The Conspiracy of Catiline.*
Seneca. *Moral Epistles.*
Suetonius. *The Twelve Caesars.*
Tacitus. *The Annals; The Histories; Agricola; Germania.*
Valerius Maximus. *Memorable Deeds and Sayings.*
Varro. *On the Latin Language; On Agriculture.*
Virgil. *The Aeneid; Georgics; Eclogues.*
Vitruvius. *On Architecture.*

SECONDARY SOURCES

The bibliography of modern secondary sources is organized by chapter. The works recommended for chapter 2 include the most essential general books on ancient Rome and Roman urban life, and their content is relevant to almost any of the other chapters. Readers curious about ancient Rome are advised to begin with these works and then to explore specific topics through the bibliography listed for other chapters.

Chapter 2: History of Ancient Rome

Adkins, L., and R. Adkins. *Handbook to Life in Ancient Rome.* New York: Facts on File, 1994.
Claridge, Amanda. *Rome: An Oxford Archaeological Guide.* New York: Oxford University Press, 1998.
Connolly, Peter, and Hazel Dodge. *The Ancient City: Life in Classical Athens and Rome.* New York: Oxford University Press, 1998.
Coulston, J., and H. Dodge, eds. *Ancient Rome: The Archaeology of the Eternal City.* Oxford: Oxford University School of Archaeology, 2000.
Dupont, Florence. *Daily Life in Ancient Rome.* Cambridge, MA: Blackwell, 1992.

Lanciani, Rodolfo. *The Ruins and Excavations of Ancient Rome.* New York: Bell Publishing, 1967.

Potter, D. S., and D. J. Mattingly, eds. *Life, Death, and Entertainment in the Roman Empire.* Ann Arbor: University of Michigan Press, 1999.

Richardson, L. *A New Topographical Dictionary of Ancient Rome.* Baltimore: The Johns Hopkins University Press, 1992.

Stambaugh, J. E. *The Ancient Roman City.* Baltimore: The Johns Hopkins University Press, 1988.

Steinby, Eva Margareta. *Lexicon Topographicum Urbis Romae.* 6 Vols. Rome: Edizioni Quasar, 1993–99.

Ward, A. M., F. M. Heichelheim, and C. A. Yeo. *A History of the Roman People.* 3rd ed. Upper Saddle River, NJ: Prentice Hall, 1999.

Chapter 3: Infrastructure of Ancient Rome

Aicher, P. J. *Guide to the Aqueducts of Ancient Rome.* Chicago: Chicago University Press, 1995.

Bruun, C. *The Water Supply of Ancient Rome: A Study of Roman Imperial Administration.* Commentationes Humanarum Litterarum 93. Helsinki, 1991.

Chevallier, Raymond. *Roman Roads.* Rev. ed. London: Batsford, 1989.

Hodge, A. Trevor. *Roman Aqueducts and Water Supply.* 2nd ed. London: Duckworth, 2002.

Laurence, Ray. *The Roads of Roman Italy.* New York: Routledge, 1999.

Chapter 4: Government of Ancient Rome

Abbott, F. F. *A History and Description of Roman Political Institutions.* 3rd ed. New York: Biblio and Tannen, 1963.

Lintott, Andrew. *Imperium Romanum: Politics and Administration.* New York: Routledge, 1993.

Nicolet, Claude. *The World of the Citizen in Republican Rome.* Berkeley: University of California Press, 1980.

Robinson, O. F. *Ancient Rome: City Planning and Administration.* New York: Routledge, 1992.

Sherwin-White, A. N. *The Roman Citizenship.* 2nd ed. New York: Oxford University Press, 1973.

Talbert, Richard. *The Senate of Imperial Rome.* Princeton: Princeton University Press, 1984.

Chapter 5: The People of Ancient Rome

Bonner, S. F. *Education in Ancient Rome.* Berkeley: University of California Press, 1977.

Bradley, K. R. *Discovering the Roman Family.* New York: Oxford University Press, 1991.

———. *Slavery and Society at Rome.* Cambridge: Cambridge University Press, 1994.

———. *Slaves and Masters in the Roman Empire: A Study in Social Control.* New York: Oxford University Press, 1987.

Cantarella, E. *Pandora's Daughters: The Role and Status of Women in Greek and Roman Antiquity.* Trans. M. Fant. Baltimore: The Johns Hopkins University Press, 1987.

Dixon, S. *The Roman Family.* Baltimore: The Johns Hopkins University Press, 1992.
Eyben, E. *Restless Youth in Ancient Rome.* Trans. Patrick Daly. New York: Routledge, 1993.
Fantham, Elaine, Helene Peet Foley, Natalie Boymel Kampen, Sarah B. Pomeroy, and H. Alan Shapiro. *Women in the Classical World.* New York: Oxford University Press, 1994.
Finley, M. I. *Ancient Slavery and Modern Ideology.* London: Chatto and Windus, 1980.
Hopkins, K. *Conquerors and Slaves.* New York: Cambridge University Press, 1978.
Lefkowitz, Mary, and Maureen Fant. *Women's Life in Greece and Rome.* Baltimore: The Johns Hopkins University Press, 1982.
Rich, John, and Graham Shipley, eds. *War and Society in the Roman World.* New York: Routledge, 1993.
Treggiari, S. *Roman Marriage.* Oxford: Clarendon Press, 1991.
Watson, G. R. *The Roman Soldier.* Ithaca, NY: Cornell University Press, 1969.
Webster, G. *The Roman Imperial Army of the First and Second Centuries.* 3rd ed. Totowa, NJ: Barnes & Noble Books, 1985.
Wiedemann, T. *Adults and Children in the Roman Empire.* New Haven, CT: Yale University Press, 1989.

Chapter 6: Living and Dying in Ancient Rome

Champlin, Edward. *Final Judgments: Duty and Emotion in Roman Wills.* Berkeley: University of California Press, 1991.
Clarke, John. *The Houses of Roman Italy.* Berkeley: University of California Press, 1991.
Grmek, M. D. *Diseases in the Ancient World.* Trans. M. Muellner and L. Muellner. Baltimore: The Johns Hopkins University Press, 1989.
Hopkins, Keith. *Death and Renewal.* Cambridge: Cambridge University Press, 1983.
Jackson, R. *Doctors and Diseases in the Roman Empire.* London: British Museum Publications, 1988.
Toynbee, J.M.C. *Death and Burial in the Roman World.* Baltimore: The Johns Hopkins University Press, 1971.
Wallace-Hadrill, A. *Houses and Society in Pompeii and Herculaneum.* Princeton: Princeton University Press, 1994.

Chapter 7: Dangers of Life in Ancient Rome

Aldrete, Gregory S. *Floods in Ancient Rome.* Forthcoming.
Crook, J. A. *Law and Life of Rome.* Ithaca, NY: Cornell University Press, 1967.
Grmek, M. D. *Diseases in the Ancient World.* Trans. M. Muellner and L. Muellner. Baltimore: The Johns Hopkins University Press, 1989.
Jackson, R. *Doctors and Diseases in the Roman Empire.* London: British Museum Publications, 1988.
Nicholas, Barry. *An Introduction to Roman Law.* Oxford: Oxford University Press, 1962.
Nippel, Wilfried. *Public Order in Ancient Rome.* New York: Cambridge University Press, 1995.
Reynolds, P.K.B. *The Vigiles of Imperial Rome.* Chicago: Ares Publishers, 1996.

Scobie, Alex. "Slums, Sanitation and Mortality in the Roman World." *Klio* 68 (1986): 399–433.

Chapter 8: Pleasures of Life in Ancient Rome

Balsdon, J.P.V.D. *Life and Leisure in Ancient Rome.* New York: McGraw Hill, 1969.
Fagan, Garrett. *Bathing in Public in the Roman World.* Ann Arbor: University of Michigan Press, 1999.
Hallett, J., and M. Skinner, eds. *Roman Sexualities.* Princeton: Princeton University Press, 1997.
Horsfall, Nicholas. *The Culture of the Roman Plebs.* London: Duckworth, 2003.
Toner, J. P. *Leisure and Ancient Rome.* Cambridge: Polity Press, 1995.
Yegül, Fikret. *Baths and Bathing in Classical Antiquity.* Cambridge, MA: The MIT Press, 1992.

Chapter 9: Entertainment in Ancient Rome

Beacham, Richard. *The Roman Theatre and Its Audience.* Cambridge, MA: Harvard University Press, 1992.
———. *Spectacle Entertainments of Early Imperial Rome.* New Haven, CT: Yale University Press, 1999.
Bomgardner, D. L. *The Story of the Roman Amphitheatre.* New York: Routledge, 2000.
Cameron, Alan. *Circus Factions.* Oxford: Clarendon Press, 1976.
Coleman, K. M. "Fatal Charades: Roman Executions Staged as Mythological Enactments." *Journal of Roman Studies* 80 (1990): 44–73.
Csapo, Eric, and William J. Slater. *The Context of Ancient Drama.* Ann Arbor: University of Michigan Press, 1995.
Köhne, E., and Cornelia Ewigleben, eds. *Gladiators and Caesars.* Berkeley: University of California Press, 2000.
Kyle, Donald. *Spectacles of Death in Ancient Rome.* New York: Routledge, 1998.
Scullard, H. H. *Festivals and Ceremonies of the Roman Republic.* Ithaca, NY: Cornell University Press, 1981.
Slater, William J., ed. *Roman Theater and Society.* Ann Arbor: University of Michigan Press, 1996.
Wiedemann, Thomas. *Emperors and Gladiators.* New York: Routledge, 1992.

Chapter 10: Religion in Ancient Rome

Adkins, Lesley, and Roy Adkins. *Dictionary of Roman Religion.* New York: Facts on File, 1996.
Beard, Mary, and John North, eds. *Pagan Priests.* Ithaca, NY: Cornell University Press, 1990.
Betz, Hans Dieter. *The Greek Magical Papyri in Translation.* Chicago: University of Chicago Press, 1986.
Ferguson, J. *The Religions of the Roman Empire.* Ithaca, NY: Cornell University Press, 1971.
Luck, Georg. *Arcana Mundi: Magic and the Occult in the Greek and Roman Worlds.* Baltimore: The Johns Hopkins University Press, 1985.

MacMullen, Ramsay. *Paganism in the Roman Empire.* New Haven, CT: Yale University Press, 1981.

Ogilvie, R. M. *The Romans and Their Gods in the Age of Augustus.* London: Chatto and Windus, 1969.

Turcan, Robert. *The Cults of the Roman Empire.* Oxford: Blackwell, 1996.

Chapter 11: The Emperors and Ancient Rome

Boatwright, Mary Taliaferro. *Hadrian and the City of Rome.* Princeton: Princeton University Press, 1987.

Boëthius, Axel. *The Golden House of Nero.* Ann Arbor: University of Michigan Press, 1960.

Bourne, F. C. *The Public Works of the Julio-Claudians and Flavians.* Princeton: Princeton University Press, 1946.

Favro, Diane. *The Urban Image of Augustan Rome.* New York: Cambridge University Press, 1996.

Packer, J. E. *The Forum of Trajan.* Berkeley: University of California Press, 1997.

Zanker, Paul. *The Power of Images in the Age of Augustus.* Ann Arbor: University of Michigan Press, 1988.

Chapter 12: The Economy and Ancient Rome

Charlesworth, M. P. *Trade-Routes and Commerce of the Roman Empire.* 2nd ed. Chicago: Ares Publishers, 1974.

Crawford, M. *Coinage and Money under the Roman Republic.* Berkeley: University of California Press, 1954.

D'Arms, J. *Commerce and Social Standing in Ancient Rome.* Cambridge, MA: Harvard University Press, 1981.

Duncan-Jones, R. *The Economy of the Roman Empire: Quantitative Studies.* 2nd ed. New York: Cambridge University Press, 1982.

———. *Money and Government in the Roman Empire.* Cambridge: Cambridge University Press, 1994.

———. *Structure and Scale in the Roman Economy.* New York: Cambridge University Press, 1990.

Finley, Moses. *The Ancient Economy.* 2nd ed. Berkeley: University of California Press, 1973.

Garnsey, P., ed. *Non-Slave Labour in the Greco-Roman World.* Cambridge: Cambridge Philological Society, 1980.

Garnsey, P., K. Hopkins, and C. R. Whittaker, eds. *Trade in the Ancient Economy.* Berkeley: University of California Press, 1983.

Greene, Kevin. *The Archaeology of the Roman Economy.* Berkeley: University of California Press, 1986.

Howgego, Christopher. *Ancient History from Coins.* New York: Routledge, 1995.

Loane, H. J. *Industry and Commerce of the City of Rome, 50 B.C.–200 A.D.* Baltimore: The Johns Hopkins University Press, 1938.

White, K. D. *Roman Farming.* Ithaca, NY: Cornell University Press, 1970.

Chapter 13: Ostia: An Industrial Port City

Casson, Lionel. *Ships and Seamanship in the Ancient World.* Princeton: Princeton University Press, 1971.

Hermansen, Gustav. *Ostia: Aspects of Roman City Life.* Edmonton: University of Alberta Press, 1982.

Martin, A., et al. "The Urbanistic Project on the Previously Unexcavated Areas of Ostia." *Memoirs of the American Academy in Rome* 47 (2002): 259–304.

Meiggs, Russell. *Roman Ostia.* 2nd ed. Oxford: Oxford University Press, 1973.

Ormerod, H. A. *Piracy in the Ancient World.* New York: Dorset Press, 1987.

Packer, James. *The Insulae of Imperial Ostia.* Rome: American Academy in Rome, 1971.

Rickman, Geoffrey. *Roman Granaries and Store Buildings.* New York: Cambridge University Press, 1971.

Chapter 14: Pompeii: A Time Capsule of Roman Daily Life

Amery, Colin, and Brian Curran. *The Lost World of Pompeii.* Los Angeles: Getty Publications, 2002.

Clarke, John R. *The Houses of Roman Italy, 100 B.C.–A.D. 250: Ritual, Space, and Decoration.* Berkeley: University of California Press, 1991.

Etienne, Robert. *Pompeii: The Day a City Died.* Trans. Caroline Palmer. New York: Harry Abrams, 1992.

Franklin, James, Jr. *Pompeii: The Electoral Programmata, Campaigns and Politics, A.D. 71–79.* Papers and Monographs of the American Academy in Rome. Vol. 28. Rome: American Academy, 1980.

Jashemski, Wilhelmina. *The Gardens of Pompeii, Herculaneum, and the Villas Destroyed by Vesuvius.* New York: Caratzas Brothers, 1979.

Jongman, Willem. *The Economy and Society of Pompeii.* Amsterdam: J. C. Gieben, 1991.

Kraus, Theodore. *Pompeii and Herculaneum: The Living Cities of the Dead.* Trans. Robert Wolf. New York: Harry Abrams, 1975.

Laurence, Ray. *Roman Pompeii: Space and Society.* New York: Routledge, 1994.

Mau, August. *Pompeii: Its Life and Art.* New York: The Macmillan Company, 1899.

Nappo, Salvatore. *Pompeii: A Guide to the Ancient City.* New York: Barnes and Noble, 1998.

Richardson, L., Jr. *Pompeii: An Architectural History.* Baltimore: The Johns Hopkins University Press, 1988.

Wallace-Hadrill, Andrew. *Houses and Society in Pompeii and Herculaneum.* Princeton: Princeton University Press, 1994.

Zanker, Paul. *Pompeii: Public and Private Life.* Trans. Deborah Lucas Schneider. Cambridge, MA: Harvard University Press, 1998.

Appendix II: A Brief Guide to Roman Timekeeping and the Calendar

Bickerman, E. J. *Chronology of the Ancient World.* London: Thames and Hudson, 1980.

Scullard, H. H. *Festivals and Ceremonies of the Roman Republic.* Ithaca, NY: Cornell University Press, 1981.

Appendix III: A Brief Guide to Roman Clothing and Appearance

Houston, M. G. *Ancient Greek, Roman, and Byzantine Costume and Decoration.* 2nd ed. London: A. and C. Black, 1947.

Sebesta, Judith L., and L. Bonfante, eds. *The World of Roman Costume.* Madison: University of Wisconsin Press, 1994.

Appendix IV: A Brief Guide to Roman Construction Techniques

Adam, Jean-Pierre. *Roman Buildings: Materials and Techniques.* Trans. Anthony
        Mathews. Bloomington: Indiana University Press, 1994.
Sear, Frank. *Roman Architecture.* Ithaca, NY: Cornell University Press, 1982.
Ward-Perkins, J. B. *Roman Architecture.* New York: Harry Abrams, 1977.

Appendix V: The History of the City of Rome from Antiquity to Today

Bondanella, Peter. *The Eternal City: Roman Images in the Modern World.* Chapel Hill:
        University of North Carolina Press, 1987.
Krautheimer, Richard. *Rome: Profile of a City, 312–1308.* Princeton: Princeton Uni-
        versity Press, 1980.
Moatti, Claude. *The Search for Ancient Rome.* New York: Harry N. Abrams, 1993.

Index

About the Author

GREGORY S. ALDRETE is Associate Professor of History and Humanistic Studies at the University of Wisconsin, Green Bay. He is the author of *Gestures and Acclamations in Ancient Rome* (1999), and editor of *The Ancient World* volume in *The Greenwood Encyclopedia of Daily Life* (Greenwood, 2004).